Practical Node.js

Building Real-World Scalable Web Apps

Azat Mardan

Apress·

Practical Node.js: Building Real-World Scalable Web Apps

ISBN-13 (pbk): 978-1-4302-6595-5

ISBN-13 (electronic): 978-1-4302-6596-2

Publisher: Heinz Weinheimer
Lead Editor: Ben Renow-Clarke
Technical Reviewer: Peter Elst
Editorial Board: Steve Anglin, Mark Beckner, Ewan Buckingham, Gary Cornell, Louise Corrigan, Jim DeWolf, Jonathan Gennick, Jonathan Hassell, Robert Hutchinson, Michelle Lowman, James Markham, Matthew Moodie, Jeff Olson, Jeffrey Pepper, Douglas Pundick, Ben Renow-Clarke, Dominic Shakeshaft, Gwenan Spearing, Matt Wade, Steve Weiss
Coordinating Editor: Christine Ricketts
Copy Editor: Cat Ohala
Compositor: SPi Global
Indexer: SPi Global
Artist: SPi Global
Cover Designer: Anna Ishchenko

Distributed to the book trade worldwide by Springer Science+Business Media New York, 233 Spring Street, 6th Floor, New York, NY 10013. Phone 1-800-SPRINGER, fax (201) 348-4505, e-mail orders-ny@springer-sbm.com, or visit www.springeronline.com. Apress Media, LLC is a California LLC and the sole member (owner) is Springer Science + Business Media Finance Inc (SSBM Finance Inc). SSBM Finance Inc is a Delaware corporation.

For information on translations, please e-mail rights@apress.com, or visit www.apress.com.

Apress and friends of ED books may be purchased in bulk for academic, corporate, or promotional use. eBook versions and licenses are also available for most titles. For more information, reference our Special Bulk Sales–eBook Licensing web page at www.apress.com/bulk-sales.

Any source code or other supplementary material referenced by the author in this text is available to readers at www.apress.com. For detailed information about how to locate your book's source code, go to www.apress.com/source-code/.

To Vladimir Nabokov and The Defense

Contents at a Glance

Contents at a Glance

Contents

About the Author

Azat Mardan has more than a dozen years of experience in web, mobile, and software engineering. With a Bachelor's degree in informatics and a Master of Science degree in information systems technology, Azat possesses deep academic knowledge as well as extensive practical experience.

Currently, Azat works as a team lead/senior software engineer at DocuSign, where his team rebuilds 50 million user products (DocuSign web app) using the technical cutting-edge stack of Node.js, Express.js, Backbone.js, CoffeeScript, Jade, Stylus, and Redis.

Previously Azat worked as a senior software engineer at Storify.com (acquired in 2013), National Center for Biotechnology Information, Federal Deposit Insurance Corporation, Lockheed Martin, and others. He taught programming classes at Marakana (acquired in 2013), pariSOMA, General Assembly San Francisco, and Hack Reactor to much acclaim. In his spare time, Azat writes about technology on his blog webapplog.com. He is also the author of four other books on JavaScript and Node.js, including Amazon's #1 Best Seller in the Client Server category: *Rapid Prototyping with JS: Agile JavaScript Development*.

Azat is the creator of open-source Node.js projects: ExpressWorks, mongoui, HackHall, and NodeFramework.com, as well as a contributor to Express, OAuth, jade-browser, and other Node Package Manager modules.

About the Technical Reviewer

Peter Elst is a web standards enthusiast with a multimedia and application development background. He works as a web solutions engineer in creative innovation at Google.

With well more than a decade of experience, Elst is a regular technical reviewer; has co-authored a number of books, including *HTML5 Solutions: Essential Techniques for HTML5 Developers*; and is a well-respected speaker at many industry events. You can find out more about his latest interests and ongoing projects on his personal blog peterclst.com.

Acknowledgments

I convey my gratitude to all the wonderful people I have encountered during my software engineering career. These people supported, mentored, and trusted me with new challenges, helped me to find mistakes, and pushed my limits.

Of course, this book wouldn't be possible without the assistance, research, and championing done by my Apress editors. I especially thank Ben Renow-Clarke, Christine Ricketts, James Markham, Cat Ohala, and Peter Elst.

Also, many thanks and appreciation go to the readers who kindly provided feedback to the alpha version of *Practical Node.js*, my webapplog.com (http://webapplog.com) blog posts, and my prior books (http://webapplog.com/books).

Introduction

There are more and more books and online resources being published that cover Node.js basics (e.g., how-to's of Hello World and simple apps). For the most part, these tutorials rely on core modules only or maybe one or two Node Package Manager (NPM) packages. This "sandbox" approach of tutorials is easy and doesn't require many dependencies, but it can't be further from the actual Node.js stack. This is especially true with Node.js, the core of which—by design—is kept lean and minimal. At the same time, the vast "userland" (i.e., NPM) provides an ecosystem of packages/modules to serve specific granular purposes. Therefore, there is a need to show effectively how Node.js is used in the industry and to have it all in one place—the all-encompassing *practical* resource that can be used as a learning tool, a code cookbook, and a reference.

What This Book Is

Practical Node.js: Building Real-World Scalable Web Apps is a hands-on manual for developing production-ready web applications and services by leveraging the rich ecosystem of Node.js packages. This is important because real applications require many components, such as security, deployment, code organization, database drivers, template engines, and more. This is why we include extensive 12-chapter coverage of third-party services, command-line tools, NPM modules, frameworks, and libraries.

Just to give you some idea, *Practical Node.js* is a one-stop place for getting started with Express.js 4, Hapi.js, DerbyJS, Mongoskin, Mongoose, Everyauth, Mocha, Jade, Socket.IO, TravisCI, Heroku, Amazon Web Services (AWS), and many others. Most of these items are vital for any serious project.

In addition, we create a few projects by building, step by step, from a straightforward concept to a more complicated application. These projects can also serve as a boilerplate for jump-starting your own development efforts. Also, the examples show industry best practices to help you avoid costly mistakes.

Last but not least, many topics and chapters serve as a reference to which you can always return later when you're faced with a challenging problem.

Practical Node.js aims to save you time and make you a more productive Node.js programmer!

What You'll Learn

Practical Node.js takes you from an overview of JavaScript and Node.js basics, installing all the necessary modules to writing and deploying web applications, and everything in-between. We cover libraries including, but not limited to, Express.js 4 and Hapi.js frameworks, Mongoskin and the Mongoose object-relational mapping (ORM) library for the MongoDB database, Jade and Handlebars template engines, OAuth and Everyauth libraries for OAuth integrations, the Mocha testing framework and Expect test-driven development/behavior-driven development language, and the Socket.IO and DerbyJS libraries for WebSocket real-time communication.

In the deployment chapters (10 and 11), the book covers how to use Git and deploy to Heroku, as well as examples of how to deploy to AWS, daemonize apps, and use Nginx, Varnish Cache, Upstart, init.d, and the forever module.

The hands-on approach of this book walks you through iterating on the Blog project in addition to many other smaller examples. You'll build database scripts, representational state transfer (RESTful) application programming interfaces (APIs), tests, and full-stack apps all from scratch. You'll also discover how to write your own Node.js modules and publish them on NPM.

Practical Node.js will show you how to do the following:

- Build web apps with Express.js 4, MongoDB, and the Jade template engine

- Use various features of Jade and Handlebars

- Manipulate data from the MongoDB console

- Use the Mongoskin and Mongoose ORM libraries for MongoDB

- Build REST API servers with Express.js 4 and Hapi.js

- Test Node.js web services with Mocha, Expect, and TravisCI

- Use token and session-based authentication

- Implement a third-party (Twitter) OAuth strategy with Everyauth

- Build WebSocket apps using Socket.IO and DerbyJS libraries

- Prepare code for production with Redis, Node.js domains, and the cluster library using tips and best practices

- Deploy apps to Heroku using Git

- Install necessary Node.js components on an AWS instance

- Configure Nginx, Upstart, Varnish, and other tools on an AWS instance

- Write your own Node.js module and publish it on NPM

You already know what Node.js is; now, learn what you can do with it and how far you can take it.

What This Book Is Not

Although the entire first chapter is dedicated to installations and a few important differences between Node.js and browser JavaScript, we didn't want to dilute the core message of making production-ready apps, or make *Practical Node.js* even larger and more convoluted. Therefore, the **book is not a beginner's guide** and there is no extensive immersion into the inner workings of the Node.js platform and its core modules.

We also can't guarantee that each component and topic are explained to the extent you need, because the nature of your project might be very specific. Most chapters in the book help you to get started with the stack. There is simply no realistic way to fit so many topics in one book and cover them comprehensively.

Another caveat of this book (or virtually any other programming book) is that the versions of the packages we use will eventually become obsolete. Often, this isn't an issue because, in this book, versions are stated and locked explicitly. So no matter what, the **examples will continue to work with our versions**.

Even if you decide to use the latest versions, in many cases this still might not be an issue, because essentials remain the same. However, if you go this off-path route, once in a while you might be faced with a breaking change introduced by the latest versions.

Who Can Benefit from This Book

Practical Node.js is an intermediate- to advanced-level book on programming with Node.js. Consequently, to get the most out of it, you need to have prior programming experience and some exposure to Node.js. We assume readers' prior knowledge of computer science, programming concepts, web development, Node.js core modules, and the inner workings of HTTP and the Internet.

However, depending on your programming level and ability to learn, you can fill in any knowledge gaps very quickly by visiting links to official online documentations and reading external resources referenced in this book. Also, if you have a strong programming background in some other programming language, it would be relatively easy for you to start Node.js development with *Practical Node.js*.

As mentioned earlier, *Practical Node.js* is written for **intermediate and advanced software engineers**. For this reason, there are three categories of programmers who can benefit from it the most:

1. Generalist or full-stack developers including development operation (DevOps) and quality assurance (QA) automation engineers

2. Experienced front-end web developers with a strong background and understanding of browser JavaScript

3. Skilled back-end software engineers coming from other languages such as Java, PHP, and Ruby, who don't mind doing some extra work get up to speed with the JavaScript language

Source Code

Learning is more effective when we apply our knowledge right away. For this reason, virtually every chapter in *Practical Node.js* ends with a hands-on exercise. For your convenience, and because we believe in open source and transparency, all the book's examples are available publicly (i.e., free of charge) for exploration and execution on GitHub at https://github.com/azat-co/practicalnode.

Errata and Contacts

If you spot any mistakes or typos (and I'm sure you will), please open an issue or, even better, fix it and make a pull request to the GitHub repository of the book's examples at https://github.com/azat-co/practicalnode. For all other updates and contact information, the canonical home of *Practical Node.js* on the Internet is http://practicalnodebook.com.

Notation

This book follows a few formatting conventions. Code is in monospace font—for example, var book = {name: 'Practical Node.js'};. If the code begins with $, this code is meant to be executed in the terminal/command line. However, if the code line starts with >, the code is meant for the virtual environment (a.k.a., console—either for Node.js or MongoDB). If the Node.js module name is in code font, this is the NPM name and you can use it with NPM and the require() method, such as superagent.

Why You Should Read This Book

Practical Node.js was designed to be one stop for going from Hello World examples to building apps in a professional manner. You get a taste of the most widely used Node.js libraries in one place, along with best practices and recommendations based on years of building and running Node.js apps in production. The libraries covered in *Practical Node.js* greatly enhance the quality of code and make you more productive. Also, although the material in this book is not groundbreaking, the convenience of the format saves hours of frustration researching the Internet. Therefore, *Practical Node.js* is here to help you to jump-start your Node.js development!.

■ ■ ■

CHAPTER 1

Setting up Node.js and Other Essentials

As with many technologies, it's vital to have the proper foundation set up first, before moving on to solving more complex problems. In this chapter, we cover the following:

- Node.js and (NPM) Node Package Manager installation
- Node.js script launches
- Node.js syntax and basics
- Node.js integrated development environments (IDEs) and code editors
- Awareness of file changes
- Node.js program debugging

Installing Node.js and NPM

Although your operating system (OS) might have Node.js installed on it already, you should update to at least 0.10.x. In the following subsection, we examine a few different approaches to installing Node.js:

- *One-click installers*: probably the easiest and fastest way to get started with the platform
- *Installing with HomeBrew or MacPorts*: straightforward installation for Max OS X users
- *Installing from a tar file*: an alternative installation from an archive file
- *Installing without sudo*: the best way to avoid needing sudo (admin rights) when using the node and npm commands
- *Installing from a Git repo*: an option for advanced developers who need the latest version and/or contribute to the project
- *Multiversion setup with Nave*: a must-have for developers contributing to projects that use different Node.js versions
- *Multiversion setup with Node Version Manager* (*NVM*): alternative to Nave (see previous entry)

One-Click Installers

First, let's go to http://nodejs.org and download a one-click installer for your OS (Figure 1-1) by clicking on the Install button. Don't choose binaries or source code unless you know what to do with them or your OS is not present there (i.e., not Windows or Mac).

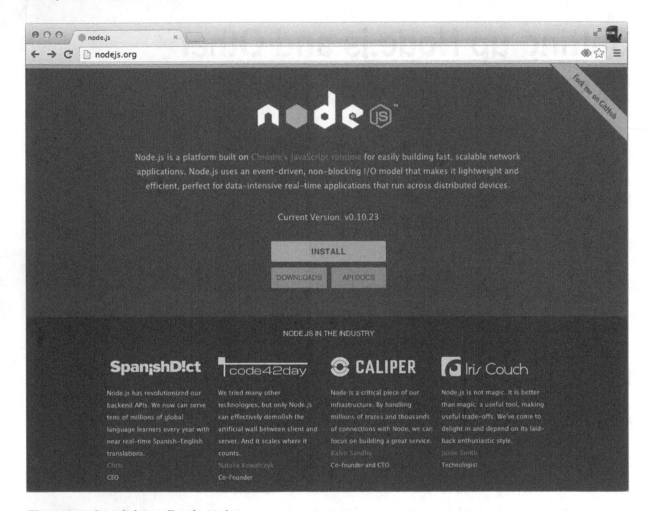

Figure 1-1. *One-click installers for Node.js*

The installers come with NPM (Node Package Manager)— an important tool for managing dependencies. If there's no installer for your OS (page http://nodejs.org/download/), you can get the source code and compile it yourself (Figure 1-2).

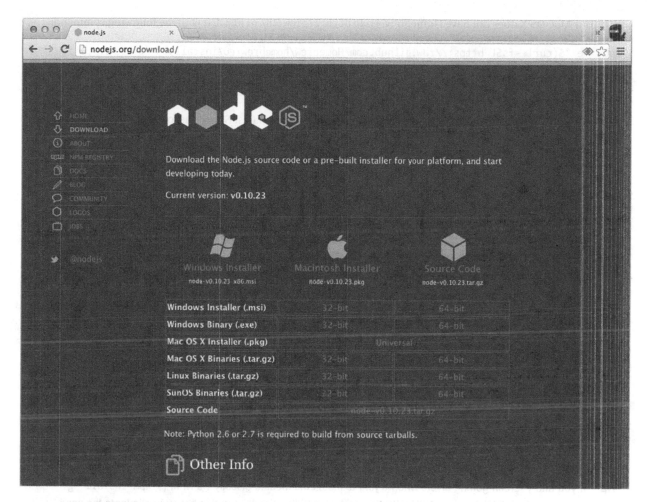

Figure 1-2. *Multiple options for downloading*

■ **Note**   For older Mac OS X machines, you can pick 32-bit versions.

Installing with HomeBrew or MacPorts

If you already have HomeBrew (brew) installed, run the following in a straightforward manner:

```
$ brew install node
$ brew install npm
```

Similarly, for MacPorts, run

```
$ sudo port install nodejs
```

If your Mac OS X does not have HomeBrew, go to `http://brew.sh/` or install it with the following command:

```
$ ruby -e "$(curl -fsSL https://raw.github.com/Homebrew/homebrew/go/install)"
```

Installing from a Tar File

To install from a tar file (which is type of archive), set up a folder for the latest Node.js as follows:

```
$ echo 'export PATH=$HOME/local/bin:$PATH' >> ~/.bashrc
$ . ~/.bashrc
$ mkdir ~/local
$ mkdir ~/node-latest-install
$ cd ~/node-latest-install
```

■ **Note** Advanced users who choose to make their own Node.js builds need to have certain compilers installed first. For more information, refer to the official documentation (`https://github.com/joyent/node/wiki/Installation`).

Download the tar file with CURL and unpack it:

```
$ curl http://nodejs.org/dist/node-latest.tar.gz | tar xz --strip-components=1
$ ./configure --prefix=~/local
```

Build Node.js and install it:

```
$ make install
$ curl https://npmjs.org/install.sh | sh
```

■ **Tip** If you find yourself getting errors when trying to install the module globally via NPM (`$ npm install -g <packagename>`), reinstall Node.js and NPM with the "Installing Without sudo" solution below to eliminate the need to use sudo with the installation command. For more solutions for advanced users, there's a Gist from Isaac Z. Schlueter: `https://gist.github.com/isaacs/579814`.

Installing Without sudo

Sometimes, depending on your configuration, NPM asks users for sudo— root user permissions. To avoid using sudo, advanced developers can use the following::

```
$ sudo mkdir -p /usr/local/{share/man,bin,lib/node,include/node}
$ sudo chown -R $USER /usr/local/{share/man,bin,lib/node,include/node}
```

■ **Note** Please be sure you are comfortable with the functionality of the chown command before you run it.

Then, proceed with a normal installation:

```
$ mkdir node-install
$ curl http://nodejs.org/dist/node-v0.4.3.tar.gz | tar -xzf - -C node-install
$ cd node-install/*
$ ./configure
$ make install
$ curl https://npmjs.org/install.sh | sh
```

Installing from a Git Repo

If you want to use the latest core Node.js code, and maybe even contribute to the Node.js and NPM projects, it's possible to build the installation from the cloned Git repo. (This step requires Git. To install it, go to http://git-scm.com/ and click Download.) For basic Git commands, refer to Chapter 11, where we explore deployment; otherwise, do the following:

1. Make the folders and add the path:

   ```
   $ mkdir ~/local
   $ echo 'export PATH=$HOME/local/bin:$PATH' >> ~/.bashrc
   $ . ~/.bashrc
   ```

To clone the original Node.js repo from Joyent (alternatively, you can fork it and clone your own repository), do the following:

```
$ git clone git://github.com/joyent/node.git
$ cd node
$ ./configure --prefix=~/local
```

2. Make the build:

   ```
   $ make install
   $ cd ..
   ```

3. Repeat for NPM:

   ```
   $ git clone git://github.com/isaacs/npm.git
   $ cd npm
   $ make install
   ```

For a more cutting-edge NPM version, use

```
$ make link
```

Multiversion Setup with Nave

If you plan to run multiple versions of Node.js, use Nave (https://github.com/isaacs/nave), which is a virtual environment for Node.js. First, make a folder:

```
mkdir ~/.nave
cd ~/.nave
```

Then, download Nave and set the link to the PATH-ed folder:

```
$ wget http://github.com/isaacs/nave/raw/master/nave.sh
$ sudo ln -s $PWD/nave.sh /usr/local/bin/nave
```

An example of switching to Node.js version 0.4.8 with Nave in a virtual environment is as follows:

```
$ nave use 0.4.8
```

To use NPM in this particular virtual environment, use

```
$ curl https://npmjs.org/install.sh | sh
```

It is now possible to install something via NPM:

```
$ npm install express
```

Last, exit the virtual environment with

```
exit
```

More approaches to install Node.js and NPM are in gist (https://gist.github.com/isaacs/579814).

Multiversion Setup with NVM

Another option to Nave is NVM—Node Version Manager (GitHub, https://github.com/creationix/nvm). Install NVM as follows:

```
$ curl https://raw.github.com/creationix/nvm/master/install.sh | sh
```

or

```
$ wget -qO- https://raw.github.com/creationix/nvm/master/install.sh | sh
```

Then, harness NVM's install:

```
$ nvm install 0.10
```

To switch to the 0.10 version, apply the use command. For example:

```
$ nvm use 0.10
```

Alternative Multiversion Systems

Alternatives to Nave and NVM include the following:

- neco (https://github.com/kuno/neco)
- n (https://github.com/visionmedia/n)

Checking the Installation

To test your installation, run the following commands in your Terminal app (command line cmd.exe in Windows):

```
$ node -v
$ npm -v
```

You should see the latest versions of Node.js and NPM that you just downloaded and installed, as shown in Figure 1-3.

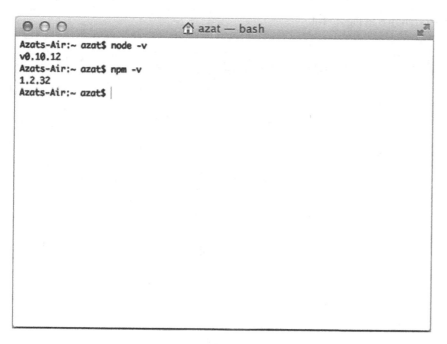

Figure 1-3. *Checking Node.js and NPM installations*

That's it! You now have Node.js and NPM installed, and you should be ready to dig deeper into using the platform. The simplest way to run Node.js is through its virtual environment, which is often called *read–eval–print-loop,* or REPL.

Node.js Console (REPL)

Like most platforms/languages (e.g., Java, Python, Ruby, and PHP), Node.js comes with a virtual environment: REPL. Using this shell program, we can execute pretty much any Node.js/JavaScript code. It's even possible to include modules and work with the file system! Other REPL use cases involve controlling nodecopters (http://nodecopter.com/) and debugging remote servers (more about this in Chapter 10). To start the console, run the following command in your terminal:

```
$ node
```

The prompt should change from $ to > (or something else, depending on your shell). From this prompt, we can run any JavaScript/Node.js (akin to the Chrome Developer Tools console) we want. For example:

```
> 1+1
> "Hello"+" "+"World"
> a=1;b=2;a+b
> 17+29/2*7
> f = function(x) {return x*2}
> f(b)
```

The result of the previous snippet is shown in Figure 1-4.

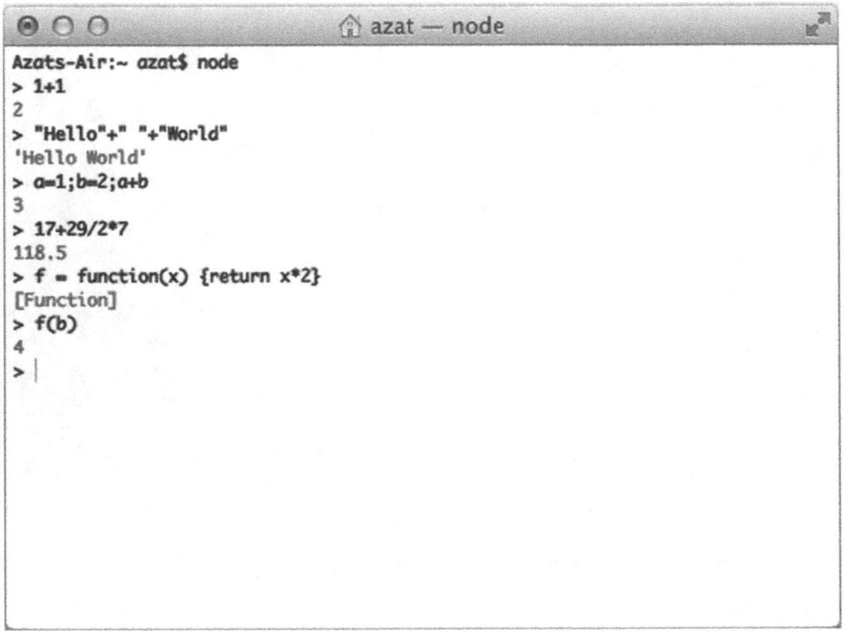

Figure 1-4. *Executing JavaScript in Node.js REPL*

There are slight deviations in ECMAScript implementations in Node.js and browsers such as the Chrome Developer Tools console. For example, {}+{} is '[object Object][object Object]' in Node.js REPL, whereas the same code is NaN in the Chrome console because of the automatic semicolon insertion (ASI) feature. However, for the most part, Node.js REPL and the Chrome/Firefox consoles are similar.

Launching Node.js Scripts

To start a Node.js script from a file, simply run $ node filename—for example, $ node program.js. If all we need is a quick set of statements, there's a -e option that allows us to run inline JavaScript/Node.js—for example, $ node -e "console.log(new Date());".

If the Node.js program uses environmental variables, it's possible to set them right before the node command. For example:

```
$ NODE_ENV=production API_KEY=442CC1FE-4333-46CE-80EE-6705A1896832 node server.js
```

Preparing your code for production is discussed later in Chapter 10.

Node.js Basics and Syntax

Node.js was built on top of the Google Chrome V8 engine and its ECMAScript, which means most of the Node.js syntax is similar to front-end JavaScript (another implementation of ECMAScript), including objects, functions, and methods. In this section, we look at some of the most important aspects; let's call them *Node.js/JavaScript fundamentals*:

- Loose typing
- Buffer—Node.js super data type
- Object literal notation
- Functions
- Arrays
- Prototypal nature
- Conventions

Loose Typing

Automatic typecasting works well most of the time. It's a great feature that saves a lot of time and mental energy! There are only a few types of primitives:

- String
- Number (both integer and real)
- Boolean
- Undefined
- Null
- RegExp

Everything else is an object (i.e., mutable keyed collections, read Stackoverflow on "What does immutable mean?"[1] if in doubt).

Also, in JavaScript, there are String, Number, and Boolean objects that contain helpers for the primitives, as follows:

```
'a' === new String('a') //false
```

but

---

[1]http://stackoverflow.com/questions/3200211/what-does-immutable-mean

```
'a' === new String('a').toString() //true
```

or

```
'a' == new String('a') //true
```

By the way, == performs automatic typecasting whereas === does not.

Buffer—Node.js Super Data Type

Buffer is a Node.js addition to four primitives (boolean, string, number, and RegExp) and all-encompassing objects (array and functions are also objects) in front-end JavaScript. Think of buffers as extremely efficient data stores. In fact, Node.js tries to use buffers any time it can, such as when reading from file systems and when receiving packets over the network.

Object Literal Notation

Object notation is super readable and compact:

```
var obj = {
    color: "green",
    type: "suv",
    owner: {
        ...
    }
}
```

Remember, functions are objects:

```
var obj = function () {
    this.color: "green",
    this.type: "suv",
    this.owner: {
        ...
    }
}
```

Functions

In Node.js (as well as in JavaScript), functions are *first-class citizens*, and we treat them as variables, because they are objects! Yes, functions can even have properties/attributes. First, let's learn how to define a function.

Define/Create a Function

The three most common ways to define/create a function are to use a named expression, an anonymous expression assigned to a variable, or both. The following is an example of a named expression:

```
function f () {
    console.log('Hi');
    return true;
}
```

An anonymous function expression assigned to a variable looks as follows (note that it must precede the invocation, because the function is not hoisted, unlike the previous example):

```
var f = function () {
    console.log('Hi');
    return true;
}
```

The following is an example of both approaches:

```
var f = function f () {
  console.log('Hi');
  return true;
}
```

A function with a property (remember, functions are just objects that can be invoked/initialized) is as follows:

```
var f = function () {console.log('Boo');}
f.boo = 1;
f(); //outputs Boo
console.log(f.boo); //outputs 1
```

■ **Note** The return keyword is optional. When it is omitted, the function returns undefined on invocation.

Pass Functions as Parameters

JavaScript treats functions like any other objects, so we can pass them to other functions as parameters (usually, callbacks in Node.js):

```
var convertNum = function (num) {
 return num + 10;
}

var processNum = function (num, fn) {
    return fn(num);
}

processNum(10, convertNum);
```

Function Invocation vs. Expression

The function definition is as follows:

```
function f () {};
```

On the other hand, the function invocation looks like

```
f();
```

Expression, because it resolves to some value (which could be a number, string, object, or boolean), is as follows:

```
function f() {return false;}
f();
```

A statement looks like

```
function f(a) {console.log(a);}
```

Arrays

Arrays are also objects that have some special methods inherited from the `Array.prototype`[2] global object. Nevertheless, JavaScript arrays are *not* real arrays; instead, they are objects with unique integer (usually 0 based) keys.

```
var arr = [];
var arr2 = [1, "Hi", {a:2}, function () {console.log('boo');}];
var arr3 = new Array();
var arr4 = new Array(1,"Hi", {a:2}, function () {console.log('boo');});
```

Prototypal Nature

There are *no classes* in JavaScript because objects inherit directly from other objects, which is called *prototypal inheritance*. There are a few types of inheritance patterns in JavaScript:

- Classical
- Pseudoclassical
- Functional

This is an example of the functional inheritance pattern:

```
var user = function (ops) {
  return { firstName: ops.name || 'John'
         , lastName: ops.name || 'Doe'
         , email: ops.email || 'test@test.com'
         , name: function() { return this.firstName + this.lastName}
         }
}

var agency = function(ops) {
  ops = ops || {}
  var agency = user(ops)
  agency.customers = ops.customers || 0
  agency.isAgency = true
  return agency
}
```

---

[2]https://developer.mozilla.org/en-US/docs/Web/JavaScript/Reference/Global_Objects/Array/prototype

Conventions

It's important to follow the most common language conventions. Some of them are listed here:

- Semicolons
- camelCase
- Naming
- Commas
- Indentations
- Whitespace

These JavaScript/Node.js conventions (with semicolons being an exception) are stylistic and highly preferential. They don't impact the execution; however, it's strongly suggested that you follow one style consistently, especially if you are a developer working in teams and/or on open-source projects. Some open-source projects might not accept pull requests if they contain semicolons (e.g., NPM) or if they don't use comma-first style (e.g., request).

Semicolons

The use of semicolons is optional, except for two cases:

1. In for loop construction: `for (var i=0; i++; i<n)`
2. When a new line starts with parentheses, such as when using an immediately invoked function expression (IIFE): `;(function(){...}())`

camelCase

camelCase is the main naming pattern in JavaScript, except for class names, which are CapitalCamelCase. An example follows:

```
var MainView = Backbone.View.extend({...})
var mainView = new MainView()
```

Naming

_ and $ are perfectly legitimate characters for literals (jQuery and Underscore libraries use them a lot). Private methods and attributes start with _ (and it does nothing by itself!).

Commas

An example of a comma-first approach is as follows:

```
var obj = { firstName: "John"
          , lastName: "Smith"
          , email: "johnsmith@gmail.com"
          }
```

Indentation

Indentation is usually done using either a tab, or four- or two-space indentation, with supporting camps split almost religiously between the two options.

Whitespace

Usually, there is a space before and after the =, +, {, and } symbols. There is no space on invocation (e.g., `arr.push(1);`), but there's a space when we define an anonymous function: `function () {}`.

Node.js Globals and Reserved Keywords

Despite being modeled after one standard, Node.js and browser JavaScript differ when it comes to globals. This was done intentionally because when `var` is omitted, browser JavaScript leaks variables infamously to the global space, thus polluting it. This has been dubbed as one of the bad parts of JavaScript in the canonical book *JavaScript: The Good Parts* by Douglas Crockford (2008 O'Reilly).

As you might know, in browser JavaScript we have a `window` object. However, in Node.js, it is absent (obviously we don't deal with a browser window), but developers are provided with new objects/keywords:

- `process`
- `global`
- `module.exports` and `exports`

So, let's take a look at the main differences between Node.js and JavaScript.

Node.js Process Information

Each Node.js script that runs is, in essence, a process. For example, `ps aux | grep 'node'` outputs all Node.js programs running on a machine. Conveniently, developers can access useful process information in code with the `process` object (e.g., `node -e "console.log(process.pid)"`), as shown in Figure 1-5.

```
 ○ ○ ○              1. azat.mardanov@DSA002579: ~/code (zsh)
    (node)     ..xpressjsgui..    (bash)       (node)      ~/code (zsh)
  ⌘  code  $ node -e "console.log(process.pid)"
  41270
  ⌘  code  $ node -e "console.log(process.cwd())"
  /Users/azat.mardanov/code
  ⌘  code  $ node -e "console.log(process.pid)"
  41280
  ⌘  code  $ node -e "console.log(process.pid)"
  41284
  ⌘  code  $ |
```

Figure 1-5. *Node.js process examples using* pid *(process ID) and* cwd *(current working directory)*

Accessing Global Scope in Node.js

As you know, browser JavaScript, by default, puts everything into its global scope. On the other hand, Node.js was designed to behave differently, with everything being local by default. In case we need to access globals, there is a global object. And, when we need to export something, we should do so explicitly.

In a sense, the window object from front-end/browser JavaScript metamorphosed into a combination of global and process objects. Needless to say, the document object, which represents the DOM (Document Object Model) of the web page, is nonexistent in Node.js.

Exporting and Importing Modules

Another *bad part* in browser JavaScript is that there is no way to include modules. Scripts are supposed to be linked together using a different language (HTML), but dependency management is lacking. CommonJS (http://www.commonjs.org/) and RequireJS (http://requirejs.org/) solve this problem with the AJAX-y approach. Node.js borrowed many things from the CommonJS concept.

To export an object in Node.js, use exports.name = object;. An example follows:

```
var messages = {
  find: function(req, res, next) {
  ...
  },
  add: function(req, res, next) {
  ...
  },
  format: 'title | date | author'
}
exports.messages = messages;
```

While in the file where we import the aforementioned script (assuming the path and the file name is route/messages.js), write the following:

```
var messages = require('./routes/messages.js');
```

However, sometimes it's more fitting to invoke a constructor, such as when we attach properties to the Express.js app (which is explained in detail in *Express.js FUNdamentals: An Essential Overview of Express.js [2013]*, http://webapplog.com/express-js-fundamentals/). In this case, module.exports is needed:

```
module.exports = function(app) {
  app.set('port', process.env.PORT || 3000);
  app.set('views', __dirname + '/views');
  app.set('view engine', 'jade');
  return app;
}
```

In the file that includes the previous sample module, write

```
...
var app = express();
var config = require('./config/index.js');
app = config(app);
...
```

The more succinct code is var = express(); require('./config/index.js')(app);.

The most common mistake when including modules is creating a wrong path to the file. For core Node.js modules, use the name without any path—for example, require('name'). The same goes for modules in the node_modules folder (more on this when we examine NPM later in the chapter).

For all other files (i.e., not modules), use . with or without a file extension. An example follows:

```
var keys = require('./keys.js'),
  messages = require('./routes/messages.js');
```

In addition, for including files, it's possible to use longer statements with __dirname and path.join()—for example, require(path.join(__dirname, ,'routes', 'messages'));. This is a recommended approach, because path.join() will produce a path with valid slashes (forward or backward depending on your OS).

If require() points to a folder, Node.js attempts to read the index.js file in that folder.

__dirname vs. process.cwd

__dirname is an absolute path to the file in which the global variable is called, whereas process.cwd is an absolute path to the process that runs the script. The latter might not be the same as the former if we started the program from a different folder, such as $ node ./code/program.js.

Browser Application Programming Interface Helpers

There are myriad helper functions in Node.js from the browser JavaScript application programming interface (API). The most useful come from String, Array, and Math objects. To make you aware of their existence, or to remind you, here is a list of the most common functions and their meanings:

- **Array**

  - some() and every(): assertions for array items

  - join() and concat(): convertion to a string

  - pop(), push(), shift(), and unshift(): working with stacks and queues

  - map(): model mapping for array items

  - filter(): querying array items

  - sort(): ordering items

  - reduce(), reduceRight(): computing

  - slice(): copying

  - splice(): removing

  - indexOf(): lookups of finding the value in the array

  - reverse(): reversing the order

  - The in operator: iteration over array items

- **Math**

  - random(): random real number less than one

- **String**

  - substr() and substring(): extracting substrings

  - length: length of the string

  - indexOf(): index of finding the value in the string

  - split(): converting the string to an array

In addition, we have setInterval(), setTimeout(), forEach(), and console methods in Node.js. For the complete list of methods and examples, visit the following sites:

- *String* (https://developer.mozilla.org/en-US/docs/Web/JavaScript/Reference/Global_Objects/String)

- *Array* (https://developer.mozilla.org/en-US/docs/Web/JavaScript/Reference/Global_Objects/Array)

- *Math* (https://developer.mozilla.org/en-US/docs/Web/JavaScript/Reference/Global_Objects/Math)

Node.js Core Modules

Unlike other programming technologies, Node.js doesn't come with a heavy standard library. The core modules of node.js are a bare minimum, and the rest can be cherry-picked via the NPM registry. The main core modules, classes, methods, and events include the following:

- `http` (http://nodejs.org/api/http.html#http_http)
- `util` (http://nodejs.org/api/util.html)
- `querystring` (http://nodejs.org/api/querystring.html)
- `url` (http://nodejs.org/api/url.html)
- `fs` (http://nodejs.org/api/fs.html)

http (http://nodejs.org/api/http.html)

`http` is the main module responsible for the Node.js HTTP server. The main methods are as follows:

- `http.createServer()`: returns a new web server object
- `http.listen()`: begins accepting connections on the specified port and hostname
- `http.createClient()`: is a client and makes requests to other servers
- `http.ServerRequest()`: passes incoming requests to request handlers
  - **data**: emitted when a part of the message body is received
  - **end**: emitted exactly once for each request
  - `request.method()`: the request method as a string
  - `request.url()`: request URL string
- `http.ServerResponse()`: creates this object internally by an HTTP server — not by the user— and is used as an output of request handlers
  - `response.writeHead()`: sends a response header to the request
  - `response.write()`: sends a response body
  - `response.end()`: sends and ends a response body

util (http://nodejs.org/api/util.html)

The util module provides utilities for debugging. One method is as follows:

- `util.inspect()`: returns a string representation of an object, which is useful for debugging

querystring (http://nodejs.org/api/querystring.html)

The querystring module provides utilities for dealing with query strings. Some of the methods include the following:

- `querystring.stringify()`: serializes an object to a query string
- `querystring.parse()`: deserializes a query string to an object

url (http://nodejs.org/api/url.html)

The url module has utilities for URL resolution and parsing. One method is as follows:

- parse(): takes a URL string and returns an object

fs (http://nodejs.org/api/fs.html)

fs handles file system operations such as reading to and writing from files. There are synchronous and asynchronous methods in the library. Some of the methods include the following:

- fs.readFile(): reads files asynchronously
- fs.writeFile(): writes data to files asynchronously

There is no need to install or download core modules. To include them in your application, all you need is to use the following syntax:

```
var http = require('http');
```

A list of noncore modules is found at the following locations:

- npmjs.org (https://npmjs.org): for the NPM registry
- GitHub hosted list (https://github.com/joyent/node/wiki/Modules): for Node.js modules maintained by Joyent
- nodetoolbox.com (http://nodetoolbox.com/): for a registry based on stats
- Nipster (http://eirikb.github.com/nipster/): for NPM search tools for Node.js
- Node tracking (http://nodejsmodules.org): for a registry based on GitHub stats

If you want to know how to code your own modules, take a look at the article "Your First Node.js Module[3]."

Handy Node.js Utilities

Although the core of the Node.js platform was, intentionally, kept small, it has some essential utilities, including the following:

- *Crypto*(http://nodejs.org/api/crypto.html): has randomizer, MD5, HMAC-SHA1, and other algorithms
- *Path*(http://nodejs.org/api/path.html): handles system paths
- *String decoder*(http://nodejs.org/api/string_decoder.html): decodes to and from buffer and string types

The method we use throughout is path.join and it concatenates the path using an appropriate folder separator (/ or \\).

---

[3]http://cnnr.me/blog/2012/05/27/your-first-node-dot-js-module/

Reading to and Writing from the File System in Node.js

Reading from files is done via the core fs module (http://nodejs.org/api/fs.html). There are two sets of reading methods: async and sync. In most cases, developers should use async methods, such as fs.readFile:

```
var fs = require('fs');
var path = require('path');
fs.readFile(path.join(__dirname, '/data/customers.csv'), {encoding: 'utf-8'}, function (err, data) {
  if (err) throw err;
  console.log(data);
});
```

To write to the file, execute the following:

```
var fs = require('fs');
fs.writeFile('message.txt', 'Hello World!', function (err) {
  if (err) throw err;
  console.log('Writing is done.');
});
```

Streaming Data in Node.js

Streaming data is a phrase that means an application processes the data while it's still receiving it. This feature is useful for extra large datasets such as video or database migrations.

Here's a basic example of using streams that output the binary file content back:

```
var fs = require('fs');
fs.createReadStream('./data/customers.csv').pipe(process.stdout);
```

By default, Node.js uses buffers for streams. For more immersive instruction, take a look at stream-adventure (http://npmjs.org/stream-adventure) and Stream Handbook (https://github.com/substack/stream-handbook).

Installing Node.js Modules with NPM

NPM comes with the Node.js platform and allows for seamless Node.js package management. The way npm install works is similar to Git in the way it traverses the working tree to find a current project (https://npmjs.org/doc/files/npm-folders.html). For starters, keep in mind that we need either the package.json file or the node_modules folder to install modules locally with $ npm install name. For example, $ npm install superagent; in the program. js write: var superagent = require('superagent');.

The best thing about NPM is that it keeps all the dependencies local, so if module A uses module B v1.3, and module C uses module B v2.0 (with breaking changes compared with v1.3), both A and C will have their own localized copies of different versions of B. This proves to be a more superior strategy than that of Ruby and other platforms that use global installations by default.

The best practice is *not to include* a node_modules folder in the Git repository when the project is a module that is supposed to be used in other applications. However, it's recommended *to include* node_modules for deployable applications to prevent breakage caused by unfortunate dependency updates.

■ **Note**   The NPM creator likes to call it npm (lowercase, http://npmjs.org/doc/misc/npm-faq.html).

Taming Callbacks in Node.js

Callbacks (https://github.com/maxogden/art-of-node) are able to make Node.js code asynchronous, yet programmers unfamiliar with JavaScript, who work with Java or PHP, might be surprised when they see Node.js code described on Callback Hell (http://callbackhell.com/):

```
fs.readdir(source, function(err, files) {
  if (err) {
    console.log('Error finding files: ' + err)
  } else {
    files.forEach(function(filename, fileIndex) {
      console.log(filename)
      gm(source + filename).size(function(err, values) {
        if (err) {
          console.log('Error identifying file size: ' + err)
        } else {
          console.log(filename + ' : ' + values)
          aspect = (values.width / values.height)
          widths.forEach(function(width, widthIndex) {
            height = Math.round(width / aspect)
            console.log('resizing ' + filename + 'to ' + height + 'x' + height)
            this.resize(width, height).write(destination + 'w' + width + '_' + filename, function(err) {
              if (err) console.log('Error writing file: ' + err)
            })
          }.bind(this))
        }
      })
    })
  }
})
```

There's nothing to be afraid of here as long as two-space indentation is used. ;-) However, callback code can be rewritten with the use of event emitters or promises, or by using the async library.

Hello World Server with HTTP Node.js Module

Although, Node.js can be used for a wide variety of tasks, it's used primarily for building web applications. Node.js thrives in the network as a result of its asynchronous nature and built-in modules such as net and http.

Here's a quintessential Hello World example in which we create a server object, define the request handler (function with req and res arguments), pass some data back to the recipient, and start up the whole thing (hello.js):

```
var http = require('http');
http.createServer(function (req, res) {
  res.writeHead(200, {'Content-Type': 'text/plain'});
  res.end('Hello World\n');
}).listen(1337, '127.0.0.1');
console.log('Server running at http://127.0.0.1:1337/');
```

Let's break it down a bit (if you know this already, skip to the next section). The following loads the core http module for the server (more on the modules later):

```
var http = require('http');
```

This snippet below creates a server with a callback function which contains the response handler code:

```
var server = http.createServer(function (req, res) {
```

To set the right header and status code, use the following:

```
res.writeHead(200, {'Content-Type': 'text/plain'});
```

To output Hello World with the line end symbol, use

```
res.end('Hello World\n');
});
```

The req and res arguments have all the information about a given HTTP request and response correspondingly. In addition, req and res can be used as streams (see previous section).

To make the server accept requests, use the following:

```
... listen(1337, '127.0.0.1');
```

From the folder in which you have server.js, launch in your terminal the following command:

```
$ node server.js
```

Open localhost:1337 or 127.0.0.1:1337 or any other address you see in the terminal as a result of the console.log() function and you should see Hello World in a browser. To shut down the server, press Control + c (on Mac OS X).

■ **Note**   The name of the main file could be different from server.js (e.g., index.js or app.js). In case you need to launch the app.js file, just use $ node app.js.

Debugging Node.js Programs

Modern-day software developers, especially those who use compiled languages such as Java, get accustomed to rich tool sets for debugging purposes. Back in the day, before JavaScript and AJAX apps were starting to gain momentum (~2005–2007), the only way to debug was to put a bunch of alert() statements everywhere. Now, there are amazing environments such as Chrome Developer Tools and Firefox Firebug! Also, because Node.js has a lot of things in common with the browser JavaScript environment, we have plenty of options for debugging in Node.js, including the following:

- *Core Node.js Debugger*: a nongraphic user interface (non-GUI) minimalistic tool that works everywhere
- *Node Inspector*: port of Google Chrome Developer Tools
- WebStorm and other IDEs (covered in the next section)

Core Node.js Debugger

The best debugger is console.log(), because it doesn't break/interrupt the flow, and it is fast and informative. However, to use it, we first need to know where to put it. Sometimes, we just don't know where to put the logs! Other times, we need to see the call stack and orient ourselves in the async code a bit more. To do this, put debugger statements in your code and use $ node debug program.js to start the debugging process (http://nodejs.org/api/debugger.html).

For example, the Hello World from the previous section can be enhanced with debugger in two places: when an instance is created and when a request is made (hello-debug.js):

```
var http = require('http');
debugger;
http.createServer(function (req, res) {
  res.writeHead(200, {'Content-Type': 'text/plain'});
  debugger;
  res.end('Hello World\n');
}).listen(1337, '127.0.0.1');
console.log('Server running at http://127.0.0.1:1337/');
```

Now, if we run the previous snippet (hello-debug.js), just like we did earlier ($ node hello-debug.js), nothing changes, because we need to use $ node debug hello-debug.js. And only then, the execution halts at the first line, and then again on the next debugger statement if we use the cont command.

The main node debug commands are as follows:

- next, n: step to the next statement

- cont, c: continue until the next debugger/break point

- step, s: step inside the function call

- out, o: step outside the function call

- watch(expression): watch the expression

The full list of commands is available through the help command or on the official web site (http://nodejs.org/api/debugger.html).

So, in our example (hello-debug.js), after we start the debugger client and execute cont or c twice (first for the first line and second for our debugger on the second line), the server will be up and running. After that, we can open the browser at (http://localhost:1337/) or execute $ curl "(http://localhost:1337/)" in the Terminal/Command line, and the debugger client stops inside the request handler (line 5). Now we can use repl and console. log(req) to inspect the HTTP response object dynamically.

Debugging with Node Inspector

The built-in Node.js debugger client is extensive, but it's not intuitive because of the lack of a GUI. Therefore, for a more developer-friendly interface than the core Node.js debugger provides, node-inspector (https://github.com/node-inspector/node-inspector) comes to the rescue!

To download and install Node Inspector, we use our beloved NPM in the global mode (-g or --global):

```
$ npm install -g node-inspector
```

Then, we start Node Inspector with the following (Figure 1-6):

```
$ node-inspector
```

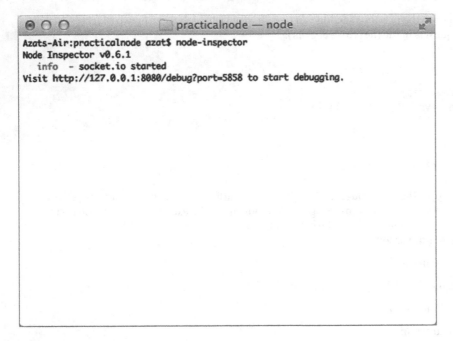

```
⊖ ○ ○                  practicalnode — node
Azats-Air:practicalnode azat$ node-inspector
Node Inspector v0.6.1
   info  - socket.io started
Visit http://127.0.0.1:8080/debug?port=5858 to start debugging.
```

Figure 1-6. *Running the Node Inspector tool*

Now start the program in a new terminal window/tab/session with --debug or --debug-brk flags (not just debug; Figure 1-7). For example:

```
$ node --debug-brk hello-debug.js
```

or

```
$ node --debug hello-debug.js
```

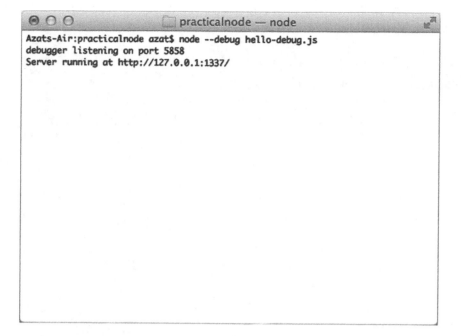

Figure 1-7. *Running node server in --debug mode*

Open http://127.0.0.1:8080/debug?port=5858 or http://localhost:8080/debug?port=5858 in Chrome (it must be Chrome and not another browser because Node Inspector uses the Web Developer Tools interface). You should be able to see the program halted at a break point. Clicking the blue play button resumes the execution, as shown in Figure 1-8.

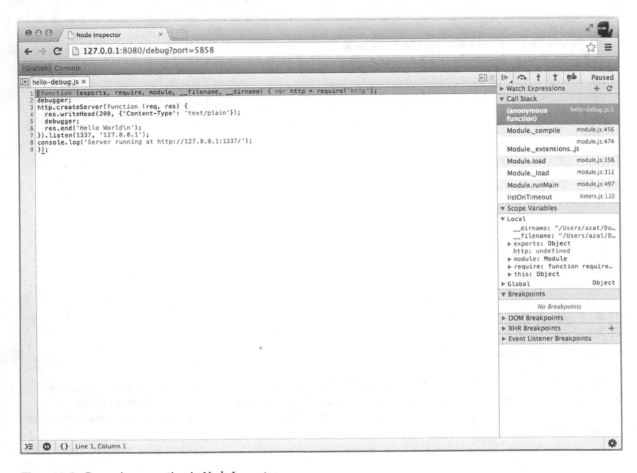

Figure 1-8. *Resuming execution in Node Inspector*

If we let the server run and open `http://localhost:1337/` in a new browser tab, this action pauses the execution on the second break point, which is inside the request handler. From here, we can use Node Inspector's right GUI and add a `res` watcher (Figure 1-9), which is way better than the terminal window output!

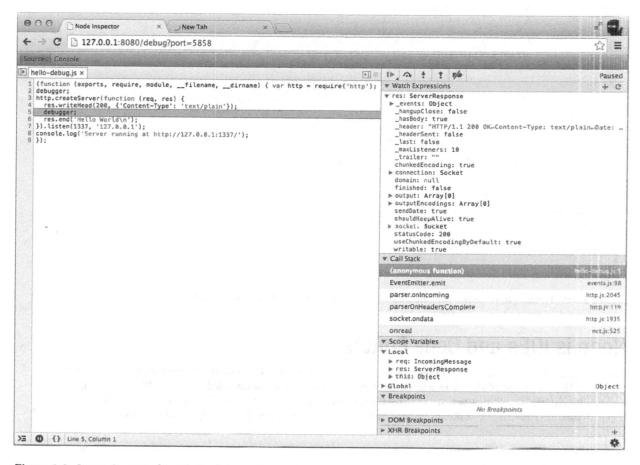

Figure 1-9. *Inspecting* `res` *object in Node Inspector*

In addition, we can follow the call stack, explore scope variables, and execute any Node.js command in the console tab (Figure 1-10)!

Figure 1-10. *Writing to response (i.e., the* res *object) from the Node Inspector console*

Node.js IDEs and Code Editors

One of the best things about Node.js is that you don't need to compile the code, because it's loaded into memory and interpreted by the platform! Therefore, a lightweight text editor is highly recommended, such as Sublime Text (Figure 1-11), vs. a full-blown IDE. However, if you are already familiar and comfortable with the IDE of your choice, such as Eclipse (http://www.eclipse.org/), NetBeans (http://netbeans.org/), or Aptana (http://aptana.com/), feel free to stick with it.

Figure 1-11. *Sublime Text code editor home page*

The following is a list of the most popular text editors and IDEs used in web development:

- *TextMate* (http://macromates.com/): Mac OS X version only, free 30-day trial for v1.5, dubbed *The Missing Editor for Mac OS X*

- *Sublime Text* (http://www.sublimetext.com/): Mac OS X and Windows versions are available, an even better alternative to TextMate, with an unlimited evaluation period

- *Coda* (http://panic.com/coda/): an all-in-one editor with an FTP browser and preview, has support for development with an iPad

- *Aptana Studio* (http://aptana.com/): a full-size IDE with a built-in terminal and many other tools

- *Notepad* ++ (http://notepad-plus-plus.org/): a free, Windows-only lightweight text editor with the support of many languages

- *WebStorm IDE* (http://www.jetbrains.com/webstorm/): a feature-rich IDE that allows for Node.js debugging, developed by JetBrains and marketed as "the smartest JavaScript IDE" (Figure 1-12)

Figure 1-12. *WebStorm IDE home page*

For most developers, a simple code editor such as Sublime Text 2, TextMate, or Emacs is good enough. However, for programmers who are used to working in IDEs, there's WebStorm by JetBrains (http://www.jetbrains.com/webstorm). For an example of the WebStorm work space, see Figure 1-13.

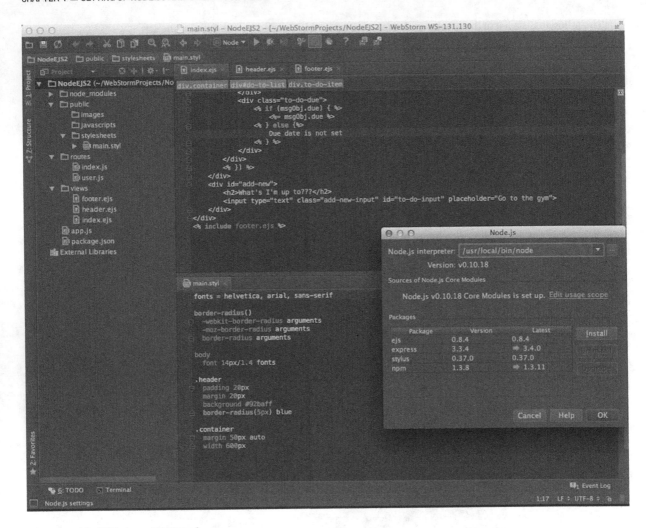

Figure 1-13. *Webstorm IDE work space*

Watching for File Changes

If you are familiar with watching for file changes or it's not an issue for you, feel free to skip this section.

Node.js applications are stored in memory, and if we make changes to the source code, we need to restart the process (i.e., node). We do this manually by killing the process and starting a new one (Control + c on Macs and Ctrl + c on Windows). However, it's faster for development if this constant sequence of restarts is automated. There are brilliant tools that leverage the watch method from the core Node.js fs module and restart servers when we save changes from an editor:

- forever (http://npmjs.org/forever) (GitHub, http://github.com/nodejitsu/forever) usually used in production (we examine this topic in Chapter 11)

- node-dev (https://npmjs.org/package/node-dev) (GitHub, https://github.com/fgnass/node-dev)

- nodemon (https://npmjs.org/package/nodemon) (GitHub, https://github.com/remy/nodemon)

- supervisor (https://npmjs.org/package/supervisor) (GitHub, https://github.com/isaacs/node-supervisor)

- up (https://npmjs.org/package/up) (GitHub, https://github.com/LearnBoost/up), now a deprecated module

Any one of these tools is as easy to use as installing globally with $ npm install -g node-dev, then running the Node.js script with $ node-dev program.js. Just replace node-dev with another module name.☺

For a comparison between these tools, refer to Comparison: Tools to Automate Restarting Node.js Server After Code Changes (http://strongloop.com/strongblog/comparison-tools-to-automate-restarting-node-js-server-after-code-changes-forever-nodemon-nodesupervisor-nodedev/).

■ **Tip** It's good to know that Express.js reloads a template file for every new request by default. So, no server restart is necessary. However, we can cache templates by enabling the view cache setting. For more Express.js setting, take a look at Pro Express.js 4 [2014, Apress].

Summary

In this chapter, we explored Installing Node.js and NPM, and launching Node.js scripts from the command line. We also looked at the essential concepts of Node.js syntax and the platform. Last, lists of Node.js IDEs and libraries for development were provided.

In the next chapter, we dive deep into using the most popular Node.js framework for creating web apps.

■ ■ ■

CHAPTER 2

Using Express.js 4 to Create Node.js Web Apps

It's only logical that, by using frameworks, software engineers become more productive and can achieve results faster. Often, the results are of a better quality because the frameworks are used and maintained by many other developers and contributors. Even if developers build everything from scratch, they end up with *their own framework* in the end. It's just a very customized one!

Node.js is a relatively young platform when it comes to frameworks (unlike Ruby or Java), but there's already a leader that has become a de facto standard used in the majority of Node.js projects: Express.js.

Express.js is an amazing framework for Node.js projects, and it's used in the majority of web apps, which is why this second chapter is dedicated to getting started with this framework.

In this chapter we cover the following topics, which serve as an introduction to Express.js:

- What Express.js is
- How Express.js works
- Express.js Installation
- Express.js scaffolding (command-line tool)
- The Blog Project overview
- Express.js 4 Hello World example

What Is Express.js?

Express.js is a web framework based on the core Node.js http module and Connect (http://www.senchalabs.org/connect/) components. The components are called *middleware* and they are the cornerstones of the framework philosophy *configuration over convention*. In other words, Express.js systems are highly configurable, which allows developers to pick freely whatever libraries they need for a particular project. For these reasons, the Express.js framework leads to flexibility and high customization in the development of web applications.

If you write serious apps using only core Node.js modules (refer to the following snippet for an example), you most likely find yourself reinventing the wheel by writing the same code continually for similar tasks, such as the following:

- Parsing of HTTP request bodies
- Parsing of cookies
- Managing sessions

- Organizing routes with a chain of `if` conditions based on URL paths and HTTP methods of the requests

- Determining proper response headers based on data types

To illustrate my point, here is an example of a two-route representational state transfer: `http://en.wikipedia.org/wiki/Representational_state_transfer`.

(REST) API server, i.e., we have only two end points and they are also called *routes*. In this application, we use only core Node.js modules for server functions. A single "userland"/external native MongoDB driver module is used for persistence. This example is taken from beginner-friendly Rapid Prototyping with JS (`http://rpjs.co/`): Agile JavaScript Development by Azat Mardan [2013]:

```javascript
var http = require('http');
var util = require('util');
var querystring = require('querystring');
var mongo = require('mongodb');

var host = process.env.MONGOHQ_URL ||
  'mongodb://@127.0.0.1:27017';
//MONGOHQ_URL=mongodb://user:pass@server.mongohq.com/db_name
mongo.Db.connect(host, function(error, client) {
  if (error) throw error;
  var collection = new mongo.Collection(
      client,
    'test_collection'
  );
  var app = http.createServer(
    function (request, response) {
      if (
        request.method === 'GET' &&
        request.url === '/messages/list.json'
      ) {
        collection.find().toArray(function(error, results) {
          response.writeHead(
            200,
            {'Content-Type': 'text/plain'}
          );
          console.dir(results);
        response.end(JSON.stringify(results));
        });
      };
      if (
        request.method === "POST" &&
        request.url === "/messages/create.json"
      ) {
        request.on('data', function(data) {
          collection.insert(
            querystring.parse(data.toString('utf-8')),
            {safe: true},
            function(error, obj) {
              if (error) throw error;
              response.end(JSON.stringify(obj));
            }
```

```
      );
    });
  };
});
var port = process.env.PORT || 5000;
app.listen(port);
})
```

As you can see, developers have to do a lot of manual work themselves, such as interpreting HTTP methods and URLs into routes, and parsing input and output data.

Express.js solves these and many other problems as abstraction and code organization. The framework provides a model-view-controller-like (MVC-like) structure for your web apps with a clear separation of concerns (views, routes, models).

For the models (M in MVC), we need to use Mongoose (`http://mongoosejs.com/`) or Sequelize (`http://sequelizejs.com/`) libraries in *addition* to Express.js—more on this later in the book in Chapter 7. In this chapter we'll cover the basics of Express.js. Built on top this framework, Express.js applications can vary from bare-bones, back-end-only REST APIs to full-blown, highly scalable, full-stack with jade-browser (`https://npmjs.org/package/jade-browser`) and Socket.IO (`http://socket.io/`), real-time web apps. To give some analogies to developers who are familiar with Ruby—Express.js is often seen as Sinatra, which has a very different approach to the Ruby on Rails framework. Express.js and Sinatra promote the configurability while Ruby on Rails *convention over configuration*.

Although Express.js is the most starred library on NPM (as of May 2014), and the most mature and used Node.js framework, the playing field is still relatively level with many different frameworks, and new ones are released every month. Some of them, such as Meteor (`http://meteor.com/`) and DerbyJS (`http://derbyjs.com/`), show an interesting trend in attempts to merge front-end and back-end code bases. For a handpicked list of Node.js frameworks, refer to the Node Framework (`http://nodeframework.com/`) resource.

When evaluating a Node.js framework for your project, use these easy steps to guide you:

- Build a sample app which is usually provided by the creators of frameworks on GitHub or official web sites. See how the app feels in terms of styles and patterns.

- Consider the type of application you're building: prototype, production app, minimum viable product (MVP), small scale, large scale, and so on.

- Consider the libraries already familiar to you and determine whether you can or plan to reuse them, and whether your framework plays nicely with them. Provide out-of-the-box solutions: template engines, database object-relational mapping (`http://en.wikipedia.org/wiki/Object-relational_mapping`) libraries (ORMs) / drivers, cascading style sheets (`http://en.wikipedia.org/wiki/Cascading_Style_Sheets`) (CSS) frameworks.

- Consider the nature of your application: REST API (with a separate front-end client), a traditional web app, or a traditional web app with REST API end points (such as Blog).

- Consider whether you need the support of reactive templates with WebSocket from the get-go. (the Meteor framework, anyone?)

- Evaluate the number of stars and follows on NPM and GitHub to judge the popularity of the framework. More popular typically means more blog posts, books, screencasts, tutorials, and programmers exist; less popular means this is a newer framework, a niche/custom choice, or a poor choice. With newer frameworks, there is a greater chance that contributing back to them will be valued, so pick your comfortable spot.

- Evaluate NPM, GitHub pages, and a framework's website for the presence of good API documentation with examples or open issues/bugs. If there are more than a few hundred, depending on popularity, this may not be a good sign. Also, determine the date of the last commit on the GitHub repository. Anything older than six months is not a good sign.

How Express.js Works

Express.js usually has an entry point—aka, a main file. Most of the time, this is the file that we start with the node command; or export as a module, in some cases. And in this file, we do the following:

1. Include third-party dependencies as well as our own modules, such as controllers, utilities, helpers, and models

2. Configure Express.js app settings such as template engine and its file extensions

3. Connect to databases such as MongoDB, Redis, or MySQL (optional)

4. Define middleware such as error handlers, static files folder, cookies, and other parsers

5. Define routes

6. Start the app

7. Export the app as a module (optional)

When the Express.js app is running, it's listening to requests. Each incoming request is processed according to a defined chain of middleware and routes, starting from top to bottom. This aspect is important in controlling the execution flow. For example, routes/middleware that are higher in the file have precedence over the lower definitions.

Because we can have multiple middleware functions processing each HTTP request, some of the functions are in the middle (hence the name *middleware*). Here are some examples of middleware purposes:

1. Parse cookie information and put it in req object for following middleware/routes

2. Parse parameters from the URL and put it in req object for following middleware/routes

3. Get the information from the database based on the value of the parameter if the user is authorized (cookie/session) and put it in req object for following middleware/routes

4. Authorize users/requests, or not.

5. Display the data and end the response

Express.js Installation

The Express.js package comes in two flavors:

1. express-generator: a global NPM package that provides the command-line tool for rapid app creation (scaffolding)

2. express: a local package module in your Node.js app's node_modules folder

Express.js Version

Before we proceed with installations, let's check the Express.js versions. We'll use an exact version 4.1.2 to avoid confusion resulting from potential future changes to the Express.js skeleton-generating mechanism and the module API.

For the Express.js Generator, which is a separate module, we'll use version 4.0.0, which is compatible with Express.js 4.x. If you have a version other than 4.0.0 ($ express -V to check), you can uninstall it using $ sudo npm uninstall -g express-generator. Or $ sudo npm uninstall -g express for Express.js 2.x and 3.x. Before, version 4.x, Express.js Generator was a part of the Express.js module itself. After you've uninstalled the older versions, install the proper version with the next section's commands.

Express.js Generator

To install the Express.js Generator as global package, run $ npm install -g express-generator@4.0.0 from anywhere on your computer. This downloads and links the $ express terminal command to the proper path, so that later we can access its command-line interface (CLI) for the creation of new apps.

■ **Note**   For Max OS X and Linux users, if there is an error installing globally, most likely your system requires root/ administrator rights to write to the folder. In this case, $ sudo npm install -g express-generator@4.0.0 might be needed. Refer to Chapter 1 for more information on changing NPM ownership.

Of course, we can be more vague and tell NPM to install the latest version of express-generator: $ npm install -g express-generator. But in this case your results might be inconsistent with the book's examples.

The Figure 2-1 shows us results of running the aforementioned command. Please notice the path in Figure 2-1: /usr/local/lib/node_modules/express-generator. This is where, on Max OS X / Linux systems, NPM puts global modules by default. We verify the availability of Express.js CLI by running $ express -V.

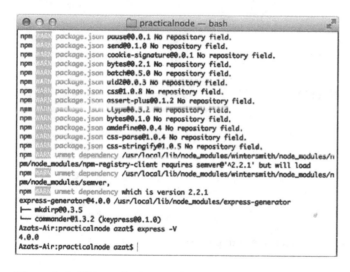

Figure 2-1. *The result of running NPM with* -g *and* $ express -V

Local Express.js

For the local Express.js 4.1.2 module installation, let's create a new folder express-cli somewhere on your computer: $ mkdir express-cli. This will be our project folder for the chapter. Now we can open it with $ cd express-cli. When we are inside the project folder, we can create package.json manually in a text editor or with the $ npm init terminal command (Figure 2-2).

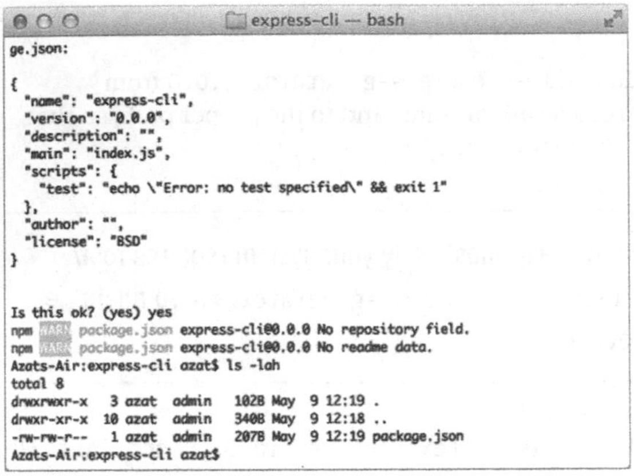

```
ge.json:

{
  "name": "express-cli",
  "version": "0.0.0",
  "description": "",
  "main": "index.js",
  "scripts": {
    "test": "echo \"Error: no test specified\" && exit 1"
  },
  "author": "",
  "license": "BSD"
}


Is this ok? (yes) yes
npm WARN package.json express-cli@0.0.0 No repository field.
npm WARN package.json express-cli@0.0.0 No readme data.
Azats-Air:express-cli azat$ ls -lah
total 8
drwxrwxr-x   3 azat  admin   102B May  9 12:19 .
drwxr-xr-x  10 azat  admin   340B May  9 12:18 ..
-rw-rw-r--   1 azat  admin   207B May  9 12:19 package.json
Azats-Air:express-cli azat$
```

Figure 2-2. *The result of running* `$ npm init`

The following is an example of the package.json file with vanilla $ npm init options:

```
{
  "name": "express-cli",
  "version": "0.0.1",
  "description": "",
  "main": "index.js",
  "scripts": {
    "test": "echo \"Error: no test specified\" && exit 1"
  },
  "author": "",
  "license": "BSD"
}
```

Lastly, we install the module using NPM:

```
$ npm install express@4.1.2 --save
```

Or, if we want to be less specific, which is not recommended for this example, use:

```
$ npm install express
```

■ **Note** If you attempt to run the aforementioned $ npm install express command without the package.json file or the node_modules folder, the *smart* NPM will traverse up the directory tree to the folder that has either of these two things. This behavior mimics Git's logic somewhat. For more information on the NPM installation algorithm, please refer to the official documentation at https://npmjs.org/doc/folders.html.

Alternatively, we can update the package.json file by specifying the dependency ("express": "4.1.2" or "express": "4.x") and run $ npm install.

The following is the package.json file with an added Express.js v4.1.2 dependency (the latest as of May 2014):

```json
{
  "name": "expressjsguide",
  "version": "0.0.1",
  "description": "",
  "main": "index.js",
  "scripts": {
    "test": "echo \"Error: no test specified\" && exit 1"
  },
  "dependencies": {
    "express": "4.1.2"
  },
  "author": "",
  "license": "BSD"
}
```
```
$ npm install
```

In Figure 2-3, we show the result of install Express.js v4.1.2 locally, into the node_modules folder. Please notice the path after the express@4.1.2 string in Figure 2-3 is now local and not global, as in the case of express-generator.

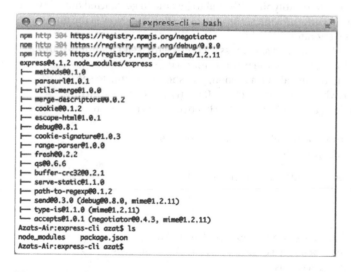

Figure 2-3. The result of running $ npm install

If you want to install Express.js to an existing project and save the dependency (smart thing to do!) into the package.json file, which is already present in that project's folder, run $ npm install express@4.1.2 --save.

To double-check the installation of Express.js and its dependencies, we can run the $ npm ls command, as shown in Figure 2-4.

```
  ● ○ ○              express-cli — bash
Azats-Air:express-cli azat$ npm ls
npm WARN package.json express-cli@0.0.0 No repository field.
npm WARN package.json express-cli@0.0.0 No readme data.
express-cli@0.0.0 /Users/azat/Documents/Code/practicalnode/ch2/express-cli
└─┬ express@4.1.2
  ├─┬ accepts@1.0.1
  │ ├── mime@1.2.11
  │ └── negotiator@0.4.3
  ├── buffer-crc32@0.2.1
  ├── cookie@0.1.2
  ├── cookie-signature@1.0.3
  ├── debug@0.8.1
  ├── escape-html@1.0.1
  ├── fresh@0.2.2
  ├── merge-descriptors@0.0.2
  ├── methods@0.1.0
  ├── parseurl@1.0.1
  ├── path-to-regexp@0.1.2
  ├── qs@0.6.6
  ├── range-parser@1.0.0
  ├─┬ send@0.3.0
  │ ├── debug@0.8.0
  │ └── mime@1.2.11
  ├── serve-static@1.1.0
```

Figure 2-4. *The result of running* $ npm ls

Express.js Scaffolding

So far, we've covered Expres.js installation. When it comes to prototyping, it's vital to be able to get started quickly with the solid app skeleton, which is why many modern frameworks provide some type of scaffolding. Now is the time to explore its rapid app creation mechanism— Express.js Generator!

Comparable with Ruby on Rails and many other web frameworks, Express.js comes with a CLI for jump-starting your development process. The CLI generates a basic foundation for the most common cases.

If you followed the global installation instructions in the installation section, you should be able to see the version number 4.0.0 if you run $ express -V from anywhere on your machine. If we type $ express -h or $ express --help, we should get the list of available options and their usage. The list of options is broken down below to serve readers as a reference.

To generate a skeleton Express.js app, we need to run a terminal command— express [options] [dir|appname]—the options for which are the following:

- -e, --ejs: add EJS (http://embeddedjs.com/) engine support (by default, Jade (http://jade-lang.com/tutorial/) is used)

- -H, --hogan: add Hogan.js engine support

- -c <engine>, --css <engine>: add stylesheet <engine> support, such as LESS (http://lesscss.org/), Stylus (http://learnboost.github.io/stylus/) or Compass (http://compass-style.org/) (by default, plain CSS is used)

- -f, --force: force app generation on a nonempty directory

If the dir/appname option is omitted, Express.js creates files using the current folder as the base for the project. Otherwise, the application is in the folder with the name provided.

Now that we're clear with the command and its options, let's go step by step to create an app with the scaffolding:

1. Check the Express.js version, because the app-generating code is prone to changes.

2. Execute the scaffolding command with options.

3. Run the application locally.

4. Understand the different sections, such as routes, middleware, and configuration.

5. Peek into the Jade template (more on this in Chapter 3).

Express.js Command-Line Interface

Now we can use the CLI to spawn new Express.js apps. For example, to create an app with Stylus support, type the following:

```
$ express -c styl express-styl
```

Then, as the instructions in the terminal tell us (Figure 2-5), type:

```
$ cd express-styl && npm install
$ DEBUG=my-application ./bin/www
```

```
create : express-styl/package.json
create : express-styl/app.js
create : express-styl/public
create : express-styl/public/javascripts
create : express-styl/public/images
create : express-styl/public/stylesheets
create : express-styl/public/stylesheets/style.css
create : express-styl/routes
create : express-styl/routes/index.js
create : express-styl/routes/users.js
create : express-styl/views
create : express-styl/views/index.jade
create : express-styl/views/layout.jade
create : express-styl/views/error.jade
create : express-styl/bin
create : express-styl/bin/www

install dependencies:
  $ cd express-styl && npm install

run the app:
  $ DEBUG=my-application ./bin/www

Azats-Air:ch2 azat$
```

Figure 2-5. *The result of using Express.js Generator*

Open the browser of your choice at http://localhost:3000.

If you don't have computer in front of your right now, here's the full code of express-styl/app.js using Express.js Generator v4.0.0:

```
var express = require('express');
var path = require('path');
var favicon = require('static-favicon');
var logger = require('morgan');
var cookieParser = require('cookie-parser');
var bodyParser = require('body-parser');

var routes = require('./routes/index');
var users = require('./routes/users');
```

```
var app = express();

// view engine setup
app.set('views', path.join(__dirname, 'views'));
app.set('view engine', 'jade');

app.use(favicon());
app.use(logger('dev'));
app.use(bodyParser.json());
app.use(bodyParser.urlencoded());
app.use(cookieParser());
app.use(express.static(path.join(__dirname, 'public')));

app.use('/', routes);
app.use('/users', users);

/// catch 404 and forwarding to error handler
app.use(function(req, res, next) {
    var err = new Error('Not Found');
    err.status = 404;
    next(err);
});

/// error handlers

// development error handler
// will print stacktrace
if (app.get('env') === 'development') {
    app.use(function(err, req, res, next) {
        res.status(err.status || 500);
        res.render('error', {
            message: err.message,
            error: err
        });
    });
}

// production error handler
// no stacktraces leaked to user
app.use(function(err, req, res, next) {
    res.status(err.status || 500);
    res.render('error', {
        message: err.message,
        error: {}
    });
});


module.exports = app;
```

Routes in Express.js

When you open express-styl/app.js, you see two routes in the middle:

```
app.use('/', routes);
app.use('/users', users);
```

The first one basically takes care of all the requests to the home page, such as http://localhost:3000/. The second takes care of requests to /users, such as http://localhost:3000/users. Both of the routes process URLs in a case-insensitive manner and in a same way as with trailing slashes.

By default, Express.js doesn't allow developers to route by query string arguments, such as the following:

```
GET: www.webapplog.com/?id=10233
GET: www.webapplog.com/about/?author=10239
GET: www.webapplog.com/books/?id=10&ref-201
```

However, it's trivial to write your own middleware. It might look like this:

```
app.use(function (req, res, next) {
  if (req.query.id) {
    // process the id, then call next() when done
  else if (req.query.author) {
    // same approach as with id
  else if (req.query.id && req.query.ref) {
    // process when id and ref present
  } else {
    next();
  }
});

app.get('/about', function (req, res, next) {
    // this code is executed after the query string middleware
});
```

The request handler itself (index.js, in this case) is straightforward. Everything from the HTTP request is in req and it writes results to the response in res:

```
exports.list = function(req, res){
  res.send('respond with a resource');
};
```

Middleware as the Backbone of Express.js

Each line/statement above the routes in app.js is middleware:

```
var favicon = require('static-favicon');
var logger = require('morgan');
var cookieParser = require('cookie-parser');
var bodyParser = require('body-parser');
//...
app.use(favicon());
```

```
app.use(logger('dev'));
app.use(bodyParser.json());
app.use(bodyParser.urlencoded());
app.use(cookieParser());
app.use(express.static(path.join(__dirname, 'public')));
```

The middleware includes pass-through functions that either do something useful or add something helpful to the request as it travels along each of them. For example, bodyParser() and cookieParser() add HTTP request payload (req.body) and parsed cookie data (req.cookie), respectively. And in our app.js, app.use(logger('dev')); is tirelessly printing in the terminal pretty logs for each request. In Express.js 3.x, many of these middleware were part of the Express.js module, but not in version 4.x. For this reason, the generator declared and included, and we installed additional modules like static-favicon, morgan, cookie-parser and body-parser.

Configuration of an Express.js App

Here is how we define configuration statements in a typical Express.js app (the app.js file):

```
app.set('views', path.join(__dirname, 'views'));
app.set('view engine', 'jade');
```

And in bin/www:

```
app.set('port', process.env.PORT || 3000);
```

An ordinary setting involves a name, such as views, and a value, such as path.join(__dirname, 'views'), a path to the folder where the templates/views live.

Sometimes there is more than one way to define a certain setting. For example, app.enable('trust proxy') for Boolean flags is identical (aka, sugar-coating) to app.set('trust proxy', true). The Chapter 11 explains why we might need to trust proxy.

Jade Is Haml for Express.js/Node.js

The Jade template engine is akin to the Ruby on Rails' Haml in the way it uses whitespace and indentation, such as layout.jade:

```
doctype html
html
  head
    title= title
    link(rel='stylesheet', href='/stylesheets/style.css')
  body
    block content
```

Other than that, it's possible to use a full-blown JavaScript code inside of Jade templates with the - prefix. More information on Jade and Handlebars template engines is in Chapter 4.

Conclusion About Scaffolding

As you've seen, it's effortless to create web apps with Express.js. The framework is splendid for REST APIs as well. If you feel like the settings and other methods mentioned in this chapter just flew over your head, don't despair! Pro Express.js 4 [2014 Apress] is dedicated solely to Express.js and its interface which can serve as a good reference. For now, the next step is to create a foundation for our project: the Blog app.

The Blog Project Overview

Our Blog app consists of five main parts from the user perspective:

- A home page with a list of articles (Figure 2-6)

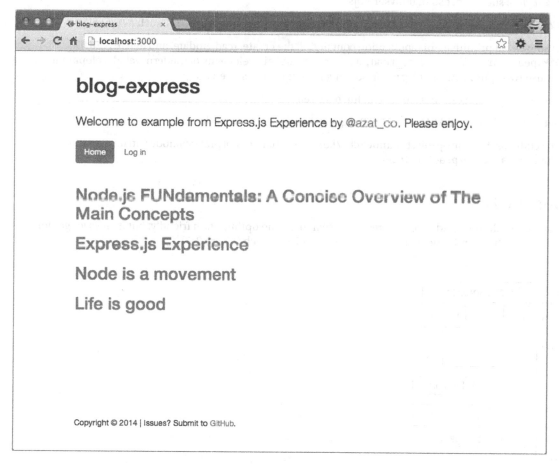

Figure 2-6. *The home page of the Blog app*

- An individual article page with the full-text article
- An admin page for publishing and removing content
- A login page for accessing the aforementioned admin page
- A post article page for adding new content

From a developer's point of view, the app has the following elements:

- *Main file* app.js: settings, inclusions of routes, and other important logic. This is where we run when we start the server.

- *Routes*: all the logic related to pages and abstracted from app.js based on functional meaning, such as getting the data from the database and compiling the data into HTML

- *Node.js project file* package.json: dependencies and other meta data

- *Dependencies in* node_modules: third-party modules installed via package.json

- *Database*: an instance of MongoDB and some seed data

- *Templates*: the *.jade files

- *Static files*: such as *.css or browser *.js

- *Configuration file* config.json: security-insensitive applicationwide settings, such as app title

Although somewhat primitive, this application contains all the create, read, update, and delete (CRUD, http://en.wikipedia.org/wiki/Create,_read,_update_and_delete) elements of modern web development. In addition, we use two approaches in Blog when sending the data to the server:

1. Submit data via traditional forms *with* full page refresh

2. Submit data via REST API (AJAX HTTP requests) *without* page refresh

The source code for this mini-project is under ch2/hello-world folder of practicalnode GitHub repository: https://github.com/azat-co/practicalnode.

Submitting the Data

The first approach is traditional and is considered more search engine optimization friendly, but it takes longer for users (especially on mobile) and is not as smooth as the second approach (Figure 2-7).

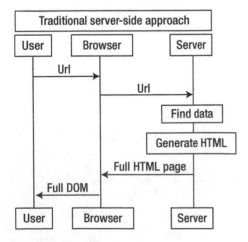

Figure 2-7. *Traditional server-side approach*

Sending and receiving data via REST API/HTTP requests and rendering HTML on the client side is used with front-end frameworks such as Backbone.js, Angular, Ember, and many others (http://todomvc.com/) (Figure 2-8). The use of these frameworks is becoming more and more common nowadays because it allows for more efficiency (HTML is rendered on the client side and only the data are transmitted) and better code organization.

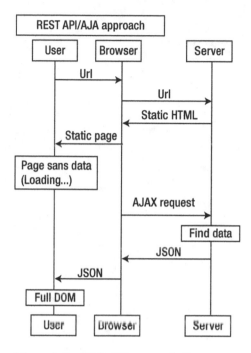

Figure 2-8. REST API approach diagram

Under the hood, virtually all front-end frameworks use jQuery's ajax() method. So, to give you a realistic example, the admin page uses REST API end points via jQuery $.ajax() calls to manipulate the articles, including publish, unpublish, and remove (Figure 2-9).

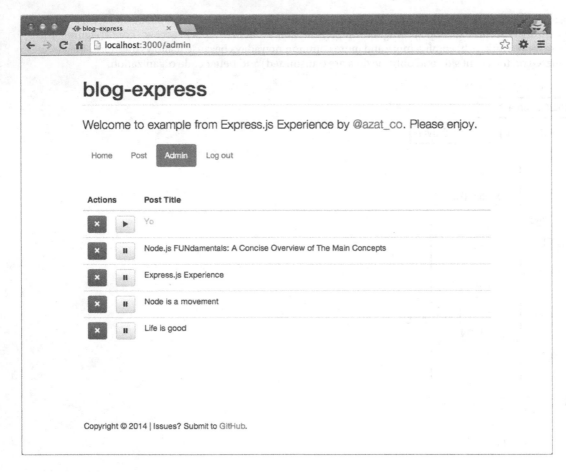

Figure 2-9. *The admin page of Blog*

Unlike the previous section of this chapter, which dealt with scaffolding with CLI, in this practical exercise we intentionally wanted to show how to create an Express.js app manually, because it gives us a better understanding of how things really work together in the framework.

Let's wait no more, and start by creating our project folders.

Express.js 4 Hello World Example

This is the first and the last hello world example in this book! :-) The goal is to show readers how easy is it to create Express.js apps from scratch without generators, fancy modules and middleware. We'll go through these sections:

- Setting up folders
- NPM init and package.json
- Dependency declaration
- The app.js file
- Meet Jade
- Running the app

Setting up Folders

Express.js is very configurable and almost all folders can be renamed. However, there are certain conventions that might help beginners to find their way through many files. Here is a list of the main folders that we use in this chapter, and their meaning:

- node_modules: dependencies (third-party modules) live here as well as Express.js and Connect libraries

- views: Jade (or any other template engine) files

That's it for now, but if you want to create a few more folders for other examples (that we'll cover in the later chapters), be my guest:

- routes: Node.js modules that contain request handlers

- db: seed data and scripts for MongoDB

- public: all the static (front-end) files, including HTML, CSS, JavaScript (browser), and Stylus (or any other CSS-language framework files)

Let's choose a project folder hello-world, and create these directories with Finder or the following terminal command (Figure 2-10):

```
mkdir {public,public/css,public/img,public/js,db,views,views/includes,routes}
```

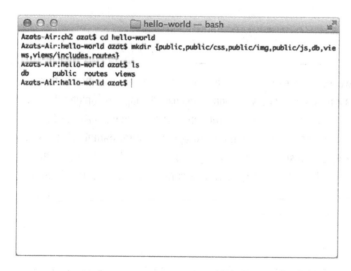

Figure 2-10. *Setting up folders*

Now we're all set to add project metadata with NPM.

NPM Init and package.json

For this example we will be creating the Express.js app from scratch, i.e., without Express.js Generator. We'll start with defining dependencies with package.json and NPM.

NPM is used not only as a registry, but also as a dependency management tool. Therefore, it's essential to set up the project file—package.json. Although it's possible to create the package.json file manually in a text editor, we can use the $ npm init command. Run this command in your project folder and answer all the questions (or leave them blank):

```
$ npm init
```

After the wizard has finished and the package.json file is there (don't worry if there's not much information there yet), we can install modules conveniently and add entries to package.json at the same time with $ npm install <package-name> --save—for example:

```
$ npm install express --save
```

The previous command uses the latest stable version (4.1.2 as of May 2014). We recommend being more specific—which is more robust in the land of the rapidly growing Node.js community—and ask for a specific version:

```
$ npm install express@4.1.2 --save
```

For the Blog app, we need the following modules, which are the latest as of this writing:

- Express.js: 4.1.2
- Jade: 1.3.1
- Mongoskin: 0.6.1
- Stylus: 0.44.0

■ **Warning**   Feel free to update to newer versions. However, your results might vary, because it's very common in the Node.js ecosystem ("userland") to see breaking changes introduced by new versions. This usually happens unintentionally by the dependency of a dependency. For example, even if we include a specific version of Express.js such as 3.4.5, that module includes Jade with a wildcard *, and then on Jade's breaking update, our app will suffer damage. The cure is to commit your node_modules folder along with the rest of the source code to a Git repository and use that instead of fetching modules according to package.json each time on deployment. Or use NPM's shrinkwarp feature. Read more about this issue in Chapter 12.

Dependency Declaration: npm install

Another way to create a package.json file (without using $ npm init) is to type or copy and paste package.json and run $ npm install:

```
{
  "name": "hello-world",
  "version": "0.0.1",
  "private": true,
  "scripts": {
    "start": "node app.js"
  },
  "dependencies": {
```

```
    "express": "4.1.2",
    "jade": "1.3.1",
    "mongoskin": "1.4.1",
    "stylus": "0.44.0"
  }
}
```

In the end, the node_modules folder should be filled with the corresponding libraries.

If you noticed, one of the questions npm init asked was about the so-called entry point. In our case, it's the app.js file, and it's the home for most of the application's logic. To run it, simply use one of the following commands:

- $ node app.js

- $ node app

- $ npm start

Another approach is to name the entry point index.js. In this case, we get the benefit of running the script with the $ node . command.

Let's create the first iteration of app.js.

The App.js File

The app.js file is the main file for this example. A typical structure of the main Express.js file consists of the following areas (this may be a partial repeat from an earlier section, but this is important, so bear with me):

1. Require dependencies

2. Configure settings

3. Connect to database (*optional*)

4. Define middleware

5. Define routes

6. Start the server

7. Start workers with clusters (a term spawn workers is also used for this) (*optional*)

The order here is important, because requests travel from top to bottom in the chain of middleware.

Let's perform a quintessential programming exercise: writing the Hello World application. This app transitions smoothly into the Blog example project, so no effort is wasted!

Open app.js in a code editor of your choice and start writing or just copy the code from GitHub at http://github.com/azat-co/blog-express.

First, all the dependencies need to be included with require():

```
var express = require('express');
var http = require('http');
var path = require('path');
```

Then, the Express.js object is instantiated (Express.js uses a functional pattern):

```
var app = express();
```

One of the ways to configure Express.js settings is to use `app.set()`, with the name of the setting and the value. For example:

```
app.set('appName', hello-world');
```

Let's define a few such configurations in `app.js`:

- `port`: a number on which our server should listen to requests
- `views`: absolute path to the folder with template (views in our example)
- `view engine`: file extension for the template files (for example, `jade`, `html`)

If we want to use the port number provided in the environmental variables (env vars), this is how to access it: `process.evn.PORT`.

So let's write the code for the settings we listed earlier:

```
app.set('port', process.env.PORT || 3000);
app.set('views', path.join(__dirname, 'views'));
app.set('view engine', 'jade');
```

Next comes the middleware section of the application. Middleware is the backbone of the Express.js framework and it comes in two flavors:

1. Defined in external (third-party) modules, such as `bodyParser.json` from Connect/Express.js body-parser: `app.use(bodyParser.json());`

2. Defined in the app or its modules, such as `app.use(function(req, res, next){...});`

Middleware is a way to organize and reuse code, and, essentially, it is nothing more than a function with three parameters: `request`, `response`, and `next`. We'll use more middleware (for example, for authorization and for persistence) in Chapter 6, but for now, its use is minimal.

The next components in the `app.js` file are routes. Routes are processed in the order they are defined. Usually, routes are put after middleware, but some middleware may be placed following the routes. A good example of such middleware, found after a routes, is error handler.

An illustration in Figure 2-11 shows how an HTTP request is processed.

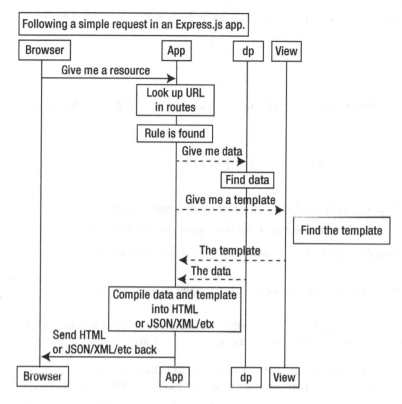

Figure 2-11. *Following a simple request in an Express.js app*

The next section is where we define routes themselves (the order in app.js matters). The way routes are defined in Express.js is with helpers app.VERB(url, fn1, fn2, ..., fn), where fnNs are request handlers, url is on a URL pattern in RegExp, and VERB values are as follows:

- all: catch every request (all methods)
- get: catch GET requests
- post: catch POST requests
- put: catch PUT requests
- del: catch DELETE requests

■ **Note** del and delete methods are aliases, just remember that delete is a valid operator in JavaScript/ECMAScript, and therefore in Node.js. The operator removes a property from an object, e.g., delete books.nodeInAction.

Figure 2-11 shows how a trivial request might travel across the web and the Express.js app, with the dotted lines being the connection inside it.

In this Hello World example a single route is used to catch requests of all methods on all URLs (* wildcard):

```
app.all('*', function(req, res) {
  ...
})
```

Inside the request handler, a template is rendered (res.render() function) with a message msg (property of the second argument):

```
app.all('*', function(req, res) {
    res.render('index', {msg: 'Welcome to the Practical Node.js!'})
})
```

The res.render(viewName, data, callback(error, html)) where parameters mean following:

- viewName: a template name with filename extension or if view engine is set without the extension

- data: an optional object that is passed as locals; for example, to use msg in Jade, we need to have {msg: "..."}

- callback: an optional function that is called with an error and HTML when the compilation is complete

res.render() is not in the Node.js core and is purely an Express.js addition that, if invoked, calls core res.end(), which ends/completes the response. In other words, the middleware chain doesn't proceed after res.render(). res.render is highlighted in chapter 4.

Last but not least are the instructions to start the server, which consist of the core http module and its createServer method. In this method, the system passes the Express.js app object with all the settings and routes:

```
http.createServer(app).listen(app.get('port'), function(){
  console.log('Express server listening on port ' + app.get('port'));
});
```

Here's the full source code of the app.js file for your reference:

```
var express = require('express');

var http = require('http');
var path = require('path');

var app = express();

app.set('port', process.env.PORT || 3000);
app.set('views', path.join(__dirname, 'views'));
app.set('view engine', 'jade');

app.all('*', function(req, res) {
  res.render(
    'index',
    {msg: 'Welcome to the Practical Node.js!'}
  );
});
```

```
http
  .createServer(app)
  .listen(
    app.get('port'),
    function(){
      console.log(
        'Express.js server listening on port ' +
        app.get('port')
      );
    }
  );
```

Before we can run this server, we need to create the index.jade file.

Meet Jade: One Template to Rule Them All

Jade is an absolutely amazing template engine that allows developers to type less code and to execute powerfully almost all JavaScript functions. It also supports top-to-bottom and bottom-to-top inclusion and other useful things. Like its brother from the Ruby world, Haml, Jade uses whitespace/indentation as a part of its language. It's a convention to use two-space indentation.

The Jade syntax and its features are covered more extensively in Chapter 4. For now, just keep in mind that the way Jade works is that the first word is used as an HTML tag (HTML element) and the text that follows (a.k.a., inner text), is put inside this element. For example,

```
h1 hello
p Welcome to the Practical Node.js!
```

Produces the following HTML code:

```
hello</h1>
<p>Welcome to the Practical Node.js!</p>
```

If we want to output a value of a variable (called locals), we use =. For example:

```
p= msg
```

For this example, create index.jade in the views folder that outputs a header and a paragraph with the value of msg variable inside that paragraph (i.e., inner text):

```
h1 hello
p= msg
```

There are more advanced examples of Jade included later in this book; but for now, everything is set for the first demo!

Running the Hello World App

When we run the $ node app command and open browsers at http://localhost:3000, we see what appears in Figure 2-12.

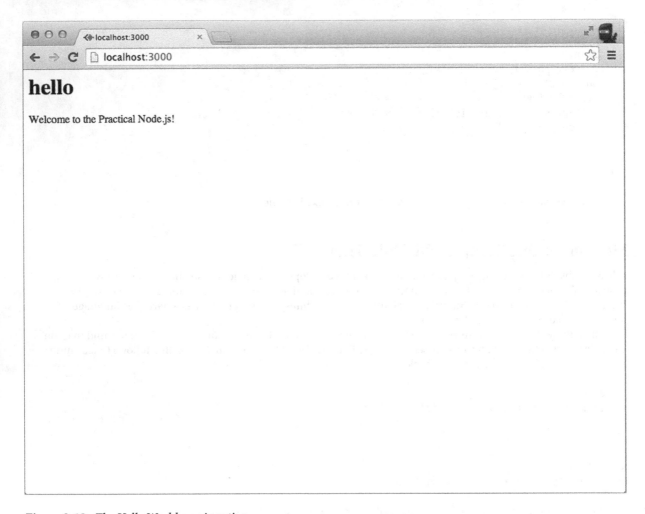

Figure 2-12. *The Hello World app in action*

Nothing fancy so far, but it's worth pointing out that it took us just a few lines (the app.js file) to write a fully functional HTTP server! In the next chapter, we add more new and exciting pages using Jade instructions.

Summary

In this chapter we learned what Express.js is and how it works. We also explored different ways to install it and use its scaffolding (command-line tool) to generate apps. We went through the Blog example with a high-level overview (traditional vs. REST API approaches), and proceeded with creating the project file, folders, and the simple Hello World example, which serves as a foundation for the book's main project: the Blog app. And then lastly, we touched on a few topics such as settings, a typical request process, routes, AJAX versus server side, Jade, templates, and middleware.

CHAPTER 3

■ ■ ■

TDD and BDD for Node.js with Mocha

Test-driven development (TDD), as many of you might know, is one of the main, agile development techniques. The genius of TDD lies in increased quality of code, faster development resulting from greater programmer confidence, and improved bug detection (duh!).

Historically, web apps have been hard to autotest, and developers relied heavily on manual testing. But, certain parts such as standalone services and REST API can be *and should be* tested thoroughly by the TDD. At the same time, rich user interface (UI) / user experience (UX) can be tested with headless browsers such as PhantomJS.

The behavior-driven development (BDD) concept is based on TDD. It differs from TDD in language, which encourages collaboration between product owners and programmers.

Similar to building apps themselves, most of the time software engineers should use a testing framework. To get you started with the Node.js testing framework, Mocha, in this chapter, we cover the following:

- Installing and understanding Mocha
- TDD with the assert
- BDD with Expect.js
- Project: writing the first BDD test for Blog

The source code for this chapter is in the ch3 folder of the practicalnode GitHub repository (https://github.com/azat-co/practicalnode).

Installing and Understanding Mocha

Mocha is a mature and powerful testing framework for Node.js. To install it, simply run:

```
$ npm install -g mocha@1.16.2
```

■ **Note**   We use a specific version (the latest as of this writing is 1.16.2) to prevent inconsistency in this book's examples caused by potential breaking changes in future versions of Mocha.

If you encounter the lack-of-permissions issue, discussed in Chapters 1 and 2, run:

```
$ sudo npm install -g mocha@1.16.2
```

To avoid using sudo, follow the instructions in Chapter 1 on how to install Node.js correctly.

■ **Tip** It's possible to have a separate version of Mocha for each project by simply pointing to the local version of Mocha, which you install like any other NPM module into `node_modules`. The command will be:

```
$ ./node_modules/mocha/bin/mocha test_name
```

for Mac OS X / Linux. For an example, refer to "Putting Configs into a Makefile" later in this chapter.

Most of you have heard about TDD and why it's a good thing to follow. The main idea of TDD is to do the following:

- Define a unit test
- Implement the unit
- Verify that the test passes

BDD is a specialized version of TDD that specifies what needs to be unit-tested from the perspective of business requirements. It's possible to just write test with good old plain core Node.js module `assert`. However, as in many other situations, using a framework is more preferable. For both TDD and BDD, we'll be using the Mocha testing framework because we gain many things for "free." Among them are the following:

- Reporting
- Asynchronous support
- Rich configurability

Here is a list of optional parameters (options) that the `$ mocha [options]` command takes:

- `-h` or `--help`: print help information for the Mocha command
- `-V` or `--version`: print the version number that's being used
- `-r` or `--require <name>`: require a module with the name provided
- `-R` or `--reporter <name>`: use a reporter with the name provided
- `-u` or `--ui <name>`: use the stipulated reporting user interface (such as bdd, tdd)
- `-g` or `--grep <pattern>`: run tests exclusively with a matching pattern
- `-i` or `--invert`: invert the `--grep` match pattern
- `-t` or `--timeout <ms>`: set the test case time out in milliseconds (for example, 5000)
- `-s` or `--slow <ms>`: set the test threshold in milliseconds (for example, 100)
- `-w` or `--watch`: watch test files for changes while hanging on the terminal
- `-c` or `--colors`: enable colors
- `-C` or `--no-colors`: disable colors
- `-G` or `--growl`: enable Mac OS X Growl notifications
- `-d` or `--debug`: enable the Node.js debugger—`$ node --debug`
- `--debug-brk`: enable the Node.js debugger breaking on the first line—`$ node --debug-brk`
- `-b` or `--bail`: exit after the first test failure
- `-A` or `--async-only`: set all tests in asynchronous mode

- `--recursive`: use tests in subfolders

- `--globals <names>`: provide comma-delimited global names

- `--check-leaks`: check for leaks in global variables

- `--interfaces`: print available interfaces

- `--reporters`: print available reporters

- `--compilers <ext>:<module>,...`: provide compiler to use

Figure 3-1 shows an example of nyan cat reporter with the command $ `mocha test-expect.js -R nyan`.

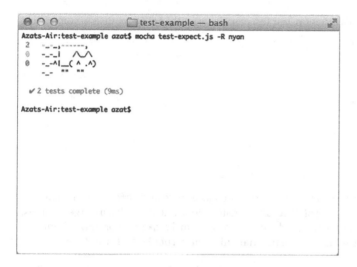

Figure 3-1. *Mocha nyan reporter*

Usually, when it comes to choosing a type of framework, there are a few options. Mocha is one of the more robust and widely used. However, the following alternatives to Mocha are worth considering:

- NodeUnit (`https://github.com/caolan/nodeunit`)

- Jasmine (`http://pivotal.github.com/jasmine/`)

- Vows (`http://vowsjs.org/`)

Understanding Mocha Hooks

A hook is some logic, typically a function or a few statements, which is executed when the associated event happens; for example, in Chapter 7 we'll use hooks to explore the Mongoose library pre hooks. Mocha has hooks that are executed in different parts of suites—before the whole suite, before each test, and so on.

In addition to before and beforeEach hooks, there are after(), and afterEach() hooks. They can be used to clean up the testing setup, such as database data?

All hooks support asynchronous modes. The same is true for tests as well. For example, the following test suite is synchronous and won't wait for the response to finish:

```
describe('homepage', function(){
  it('should respond to GET',function(){
    superagent
      .get('http://localhost:'+port)
      .end(function(res){
        expect(res.status).to.equal(200);
    })
  })
})
```

But, as soon as we add a done parameter to the test's function, our test case waits for the HTTP request to come back:

```
describe('homepage', function(){
  it('should respond to GET',function(done){
    superagent
      .get('http://localhost:'+port)
      .end(function(res){
        expect(res.status).to.equal(200);
        done();
    })
  })
})
```

Test cases (describe) can be nested inside other test cases, and hooks such as before and beforeEach can be mixed in with different test cases on different levels. Nesting of describe constructions is a good idea in large test files.

Sometimes, developers might want to skip a test case/suite (describe.skip() or it.skip()) or make them exclusive (describe.only() or describe.only()). Exclusivity means that only that particular test runs (the opposite of skip).

As an alternative to the BDD interface's describe, it, before, and others, Mocha supports more traditional TDD interfaces:

- suite: analogous to describe
- test: analogous to it
- setup: analogous to before
- teardown: analogous to after
- suiteSetup: analogous to beforeEach
- suiteTeardown: analogous to afterEach

TDD with the Assert

Let's write our first tests with the assert library. This library is part of the Node.js core, which makes it easy to access. It has minimal functionality, but it might be enough for some cases, such as unit tests.

After global Mocha installation is finished, a test file can be created in a test-example folder:

```
$ mkdir test-example
$ subl test-example/test.js
```

■ **Note** subl is a Sublime Text alias command. You can use any other editor, such as Vi (vi) or TextMate (mate).

With the following content:

```
var assert = require('assert');
describe('String#split', function(){
  it('should return an array', function(){
    assert(Array.isArray('a,b,c'.split(',')));
  });
})
```

We can run this simple test.js (inside the test-example folder), which checks for Array type, with:

```
$ mocha test
```

or

```
$ mocha test.js.
```

The results of these Mocha commands are shown in Figure 3-2.

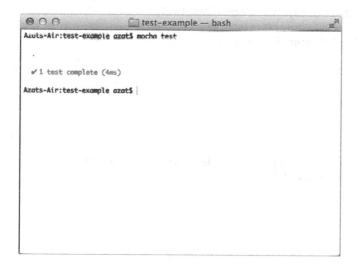

Figure 3-2. Running Array-type test

We can add to our example another test case (it) that asserts equality of array values:

```
var assert = require('assert');
describe('String#split', function(){
  it('should return an array', function(){
    assert(Array.isArray('a,b,c'.split(',')));
  });
```

```
  it('should return the same array', function(){
    assert.equal(['a','b','c'].length, 'a,b,c'.split(',').length, 'arrays have equal length');
    for (var i=0; i<['a','b','c'].length; i++) {
    assert.equal(['a','b','c'][i], 'a,b,c'.split(',')[i], i + 'element is equal');
    };
  });
})
```

As you can see, some code is repeated, so we can abstract it into beforeEach and before constructions:

```
var assert = require('assert');
var expected, current;
before(function(){
  expected = ['a', 'b', 'c'];
})
describe('String#split', function(){
  beforeEach(function(){
    current = 'a,b,c'.split(',');
  })
  it('should return an array', function(){
    assert(Array.isArray(current));
  });
  it('should return the same array', function(){
    assert.equal(expected.length, current.length, 'arrays have equal length');
    for (var i=0; i<expected.length; i++) {
      assert.equal(expected[i], current[i], i + 'element is equal');
    }
  })
})
```

Chai Assert

In the previous example with test.js and assert, we used the Node.js core module assert. Chai is a subset of that library. We can modify our previous example to use chai assert with following code:

```
$ npm install chai@1.8.1
```

And in test-example/test.js:

```
var assert = require('chai').assert;
```

The following are some of the methods from the chai assert library:

- assert(expressions, message): throws an error if the expression is false

- assert.fail(actual, expected, [message], [operator]): throws an error with values of actual, expected, and operator

- assert.ok(object, [message]): throws an error when the object is not double equal (==) to true—aka, truthy (0, and an empty string is false in JavaScript/Node.js)

- `assert.notOk(object, [message])`: throws an error when the object is falsy, i.e., **false, 0** (zero), "" (empty string), **null, undefined** or **NaN**

- `assert.equal(actual, expected, [message])`: throws an error when actual is not double equal (==) to expected

- `asseret.notEqual(actual, expected, [message])`: throws an error when actual is double equal (==)—in other words, not unequal (!=)—to expected

- `.strictEqual(actual, expected, [message])`: throws an error when objects are not triple equal (===)

For the full chai assert API, refer to the official documentation (`http://chaijs.com/api/assert/`).

■ **Note** The chai assert (`chai.assert`) and the Node.js core assert (`assert`) modules are *not 100% compatible*, because the former has more methods. The same is true for chai expect and a standalone expect.js.

BDD with Expect.js

Expect.js is one of the BDD languages. Its syntax allows for chaining and is richer in features than core module assert. There are two options to use expect.js:

1. Install as a local module

2. Install as a part of the chai library

For the former, simply execute the following:

```
$ mkdir node_modules
$ npm install expect.js@0.2.0
```

And, use `var expect = require('expect.js');` inside a Node.js test file. For example, the previous test can be rewritten in expect.js BDD style:

```
var expect = require('expect.js');
var expected, current;
before(function(){
  expected = ['a', 'b', 'c'];
})
describe('String#split', function(){
  beforeEach(function(){
    current = 'a,b,c'.split(',');
  })
  it('should return an array', function(){
    expect(Array.isArray(current)).to.be.true;
  });
```

```
  it('should return the same array', function(){
    expect(expected.length).to.equal(current.length);
    for (var i=0; i<expected.length; i++) {
      expect(expected[i]).equal(current[i]);
    }
  })
})
})
```

For the chai library approach, run the following:

```
$ mkdir node_modules
$ npm install chai@1.8.1
```

And, use var chai = require('chai'); var expect = chai.expect; inside a Node.js test file. For example:

```
var expect = require('chai').expect;
```

■ **Note** $ mkdir node_modules is needed only if you install NPM modules in the folder that has neither the node_modules directory already nor a package.json file. For more information, please refer to Chapter 1.

Expect.js Syntax

The Expect.js library is very extensive. It has nice methods that mimic natural language. Often there are a few ways to write the same assertion, such as expect(response).to.be(true) and expect(response).equal(true). The following lists some of the main Expect.js methods/properties:

- ok: checks for truthyness

- true: checks whether the object is truthy

- to.be, to: chains methods as in linking two methods

- not: chains with a not connotation, such as expect(false).not.to.be(true)

- a/an: checks type (works with array as well)

- include/contain: checks whether an array or string contains an element

- below/above: checks for the upper and lower limits

■ **Note**   Again, there is a slight deviation between the standalone expect.js module and its Chai counterpart.

For the full documentation on chai expect.js, refer to http://chaijs.com/api/bdd/, and for the standalone, refer to https://github.com/LearnBoost/expect.js/.

Project: Writing the First BDD Test for Blog

The goal of this mini-project is to add a few tests for Blog (this book's primary project). We won't get into headless browsers and UI testing, but we can send a few HTTP requests and parse their responses from the app's REST end points (see Chapter 2 for a description of the Blog app).

The source code for this chapter is in the ch3/blog-express folder of the practicalnode GitHub repository (https://github.com/azat-co/practicalnode).

First, let's copy the Hello World project. It will serve as a foundation for Blog. Then, install Mocha in the Blog project folder, and add it to the package.json file at the same time with $ npm install mocha@1.16.2 --save-dev. The --save-dev flag will categorize this module as a development dependency (devDependencies). Modify this command by replacing package name and version number for expect.js (0.2.0) and superagent (0.15.7) (https://npmjs.org/package/superagent). The latter is a library to streamline the making of HTTP requests. Alternatives to superagent include the following:

- request (https://npmjs.org/package/request): the third most starred NPM module (as of this writing)

- *core* http *module*: clunky and very low level

- supertest: a superagent-based assertions library

Here's the updated package.json:

```
{
  "name": "blog-express",
  "version": "0.0.1",
  "private": true,
  "scripts": {
    "start": "node app.js",
    "test": "mocha test"
  },
  "dependencies": {
    "express": "4.1.2",
    "jade": "1.3.1",
    "stylus": "0.44.0"
  },
  "devDependencies": {
    "mocha": "1.16.2",
    "superagent": "0.15.7",
    "expect.js": "0.2.0"
  }
}
```

Now, create a test folder with $ mkdir tests and open tests/index.js in your editor. The test needs to start the server:

```
var boot = require('../app').boot,
  shutdown = require('../app').shutdown,
  port = require('../app').port,
  superagent = require('superagent'),
  expect = require('expect.js');
describe('server', function () {
  before(function () {
    boot();
  });
```

```
describe('homepage', function(){
  it('should respond to GET',function(done){
    superagent
      .get('http://localhost:'+port)
      .end(function(res){
        expect(res.status).to.equal(200);
        done()
    })
  })
});
after(function () {
  shutdown();
});
});
```

In app.js, we expose two methods, boot and shutdown, when the file is imported, in our case, by the test. So, instead of:

```
http.createServer(app).listen(app.get('port'), function(){
  console.log('Express server listening on port ' + app.get('port'));
});
```

we can refactor into:

```
var server = http.createServer(app);
var boot = function () {
  server.listen(app.get('port'), function(){
    console.info('Express server listening on port ' + app.get('port'));
  });
}
var shutdown = function() {
  server.close();
}
if (require.main === module) {
  boot();
}
else {
  console.info('Running app as a module')
  exports.boot = boot;
  exports.shutdown = shutdown;
  exports.port = app.get('port');
}
```

To launch the test, simply run $ mocha tests. The server should boot and respond to the home page request (/ route) as shown in Figure 3-3.

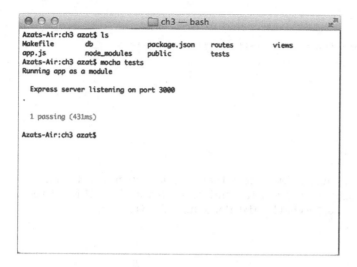

Figure 3-3. Running $ mocha tests

Putting Configs into a Makefile

The mocha accepts many options. It's often a good idea to have these options gathered in one place, which could be a Makefile. For example, we can have test, test-w test all files in the test folder, and have modes for just the module-a.js and module-b.js files to test them separately, this way:

```
REPORTER = list
MOCHA_OPTS = --ui tdd --ignore-leaks

test:
        clear
        echo Starting test ****************************************************
        ./node_modules/mocha/bin/mocha \
        --reporter $(REPORTER) \
        $(MOCHA_OPTS) \
        tests/*.js
        echo Ending test

test-w:
        ./node_modules/mocha/bin/mocha \
        --reporter $(REPORTER) \
        --growl \
        --watch \
        $(MOCHA_OPTS) \
        tests/*.js

test-module-a:
        mocha tests/module-a.js --ui tdd --reporter list --ignore-leaks
```

```
test-module-b:
      clear
      echo Starting test *****************************************************
      ./node_modules/mocha/bin/mocha \
      --reporter $(REPORTER) \
      $(MOCHA_OPTS) \
      tests/module-b.js
      echo Ending test

.PHONY: test test-w test-module-a test-module-b
```

To launch this Makefile, run $ make <mode>—for example, $ make test. For more information on a Makefile please refer to Understanding Make at http://www.cprogramming.com/tutorial/makefiles.html and Using Make and Writing Makefiles at http://www.cs.swarthmore.edu/~newhall/unixhelp/howto_makefiles.html.

For our Blog app, we can keep the Makefile simple:

```
REPORTER = list
MOCHA_OPTS = --ui bdd -c

test:
    clear
    echo Starting test *****************************************************
    ./node_modules/mocha/bin/mocha \
    --reporter $(REPORTER) \
    $(MOCHA_OPTS) \
    tests/*.js
    echo Ending test

.PHONY: test
```

■ **Note** We point to the local Mocha in the Makefile, so the dependency needs to be added to package.json and installed in the node_modules folder.

Now we can run tests with the $ make test command, which allows for more configuration compared with the simple $ mocha tests (Figure 3-4).

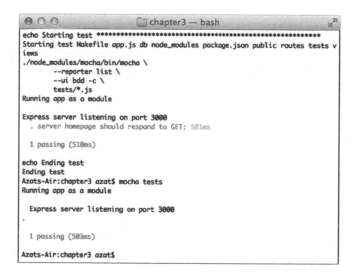

```
echo Starting test ••••••••••••••••••••••••••••••••••••••••••••••••••••••••••••
Starting test Makefile app.js db node_modules package.json public routes tests v
iews
./node_modules/mocha/bin/mocha \
        --reporter list \
        --ui bdd -c \
        tests/*.js
Running app as a module

Express server listening on port 3000
  . server homepage should respond to GET: 501ms

  1 passing (510ms)

echo Ending test
Ending test
Azats-Air:chapter3 azat$ mocha tests
Running app as a module

  Express server listening on port 3000

  .

  1 passing (503ms)

Azats-Air:chapter3 azat$
```

Figure 3-4. Running `make test`

Summary

In this chapter, we installed Mocha as a command-line tool and learned its options, we wrote simple tests with assert and the expect.js libraries, and we created the first test for the Blog app by modifying `app.js` to work as a module. In Chapter 10, we harness TravisCI SaaS by writing a yml config file and using GitHub to trigger continuous multiple tests in the cloud virtual environments. In the next chapter, proceeds the essence of any web app that outputs HTML—template engine. We'll dive deep into Jade and Handlebars, and add pages to Blog.

CHAPTER 4

■ ■ ■

Template Engines: Jade and Handlebars

A template engine is a library or a framework that uses some rules/languages to interpret data and render views. In the case of web applications, views are HTML pages (or parts of them), but they can be JSON or XML files, or, in desktop programs, GUIs. For those of you familiar with the model–view–controller concept, templates belong to the view.

In web apps, it's beneficial to use templates because we can generate an infinite number of pages dynamically with a single template! Another side benefit is when we need to change something; we can do it in one place only.

If we go back to the diagrams in the previous chapter (traditional vs. REST API approaches), we can deduce that templates can be compiled into HTML either server-side (traditional approach) or client-side (REST API approach). No matter which approach we take, the syntax of the libraries themselves remains intact.

In this chapter we cover the following:

- Jade syntax and features

- Jade standalone usage

- Handlebars syntax

- Handlebars standalone usage

- Jade and Handlebars usage in Express.js 4

- Project: adding Jade templates to Blog

Jade Syntax and Features

Jade is a Node.js brother of Haml, in the sense that it uses whitespace and indentation as part of its language. Therefore, we need to be careful to follow the proper syntax.

You can follow the Jade syntax examples in this section, online, at the official web site's demo page (http://jade-lang.com/demo) or at the @naltatis resource (http://naltatis.github.io/jade-syntax-docs/), or by writing standalone Node.js scripts (examples are presented in "Jade Standalone Usage," which appears later in this chapter).

Tags

Any text at the beginning of a line—by default—is interpreted as an HTML tag. The main advantage of Jade is that this text renders both closing and opening tags for the HTML element, as well as the <></>symbols. Therefore, we save many keystrokes as developers writing in Jade!

The text following a tag and a space (e.g., tag `<text>`) is parsed as the inner HTML (i.e., content inside the element). For example, if we have the following Jade code:

```
Body
  div
    h1 Practical Node.js
    p The only book most people will ever need.
  div
    footer &copy; Apress
```

The output of the template above will be:

```
<body>
  <div>
    <h1>Practical Node.js</h1>
    <p>The only book most people will ever need.</p>
  </div>
  <div>
    <footer>&copy; Apress</footer>
  </div>
</body>
```

Variables/Locals

Data that are passed to the Jade template are called *locals*. To output the value of a variable, use =. See the following examples:

Jade code:

```
h1= title
p= body
```

Locals:

```
{
  title: "Express.js Guide",
  body: "The Comprehensive Book on Express.js"
}
```

HTML output:

```
<h1>Express.js Guide</h1>
<p>The Comprehensive Book on Express.js</p>
```

Attributes

Attributes are added by putting them into parentheses right after the tag name. They follow name=value format. In addition, multiple attributes need to be separated by a comma. For example,

```
div(id="content", class="main")
  a(href="http://expressjsguide.com", title="Express.js Guide", target="_blank") Express.js Guide
  form(action="/login")
    button(type="submit, value="save")
  div(class="hero-unit") Lean Node.js!
```

turns into

```
<div id="content" class="main"><a href="http://expressjsguide.com" title="Express.js Guide"
target="_blank">Express.js Guide</a>
  <form action="/login">
    <button type="submit" value="save"></button>
  </form>
  <div class="hero-unit">Learn Node.js</div>
</div>
```

Sometimes, the value of an attribute needs to be dynamic. In this case, just use the variable name! The pipe, or |, allows us to write the content of the HTML node on the new line—in other words, the line with the pipe becomes inner text an example is as follows:

```
a(href=url, data-active=isActive)
label
  input(type="checkbox", checked=isChecked)
  | yes / no
```

The template above is provided with locals:

```
{
  url: "/logout",
  isActive: true,
  isChecked: false
}
```

And they both, i.e., template and locals data, produce output:

```
<a href="/logout" data-active="data-active"></a>
<label>
  <input type="checkbox"/>yes / no
</label>
```

Note that the attribute with the value false is omitted from the HTML output. However, when no value is passed, true is assumed—for example,

```
input(type='radio', checked)
input(type='radio', checked=true)
input(type='radio', checked=false)
<input type="radio" checked="checked"/>
<input type="radio" checked="checked"/>
<input type="radio"/>
```

Literals

For convenience, we can write classes and IDs right after tag names. For example, we can then apply lead and center classes to a paragraph, and create a div element with the side-bar ID and pull-right class (again, the pipe signifies an inner text):

```
div#content
  p.lead.center
    | webapplog: where code lives
    #side-bar.pull-right
    span.contact.span4
      a(href="/contact") contact us
<div id="content">
  <p class="lead center">
    webapplog: where code lives
    <div id="side-bar" class="pull-right"></div>
    <span class="contact span4">
      <a href="/contact">contact us</a>
    </span>
  </p>
</div>
```

Note that if the tag name is omitted, div is used instead.

Text

Outputting raw text is done via | —for example,

```
div
  | Jade is a template engine.
  | It can be used in Node.js and in the browser JavaScript.
```

Script and Style Blocks

Sometimes, developers want to write chunks of content for script or style tags in the HTML! This is possible with a dot. For example, we can write inline front-end JavaScript like this:

```
script.
    console.log('Hello Jade!')
    setTimeout(function(){
     window.location.href='http://rpjs.co'
    },200))
    console.log('Good bye!')
<script>
  console.log('Hello Jade!')
  setTimeout(function(){
   window.location.href='http://rpjs.co'
  },200))
  console.log('Good bye!')
</script>
```

JavaScript Code

Contrary to the previous example, if we want to use *any* JavaScript at template compilation time—in other words, to write executable JavaScript code that manipulates the output of the Jade (i.e., HTML)—we can use the -, =, or != symbols. This might come in handy when we output HTML elements and inject JavaScript. Obviously, these types of things should be done carefully to avoid cross-site scripting (XSS) attacks. For example, if we want to define an array and output <> symbols, we can use !=.

```
- var arr = ['<a>','<b>','<c>']
ul
  - for (var i = 0; i< arr.length; i++)
    li
      span= i
      span!="unescaped: " + arr[i] + " vs. "
      span= "escaped: " + arr[i]
```

produces this:

```
<ul>
  <li><span>0</span><span>unescaped: <a> vs. </span><span>escaped: &lt;a&gt;</span></li>
  <li><span>1</span><span>unescaped: <b> vs. </span><span>escaped: &lt;b&gt;</span></li>
  <li><span>2</span><span>unescaped: <c> vs. </span><span>escaped: &lt;c&gt;</span></li>
</ul>
```

■ **Tip** One of the main differences between Jade and Handlebars is that the former allows pretty much any JavaScript in its code whereas the latter restricts programmers to only a handful of built-in and custom-registered helpers.

Comments

When it comes to comments, we have a choice to output them or not. For the former, use JavaScript style //; for the latter, use //-. For example,

```
// content goes here
p Node.js is a non-blocking I/O for scalable apps.
//- @todo change this to a class
p(id="footer") Copyright 2014 Azat
```

outputs

```
<!-- content goes here-->
<p>Node.js is a non-blocking I/O for scalable apps.</p>
<p id="footer">Copyright 2014 Azat</p>
```

Conditions (if)

Interestingly enough, in addition to the standard JavaScript code where the if statement can be used by prefixing it with -, we can use a minimalistic Jade alternative with no prefix and no parentheses—for example,

```
- var user = {}
- user.admin = Math.random()>0.5
if user.admin
    button(class="launch") Launch Spacecraft
else
  button(class="login") Log in
```

There's also unless, which is equivalent to not or !.

Iterations (each loops)

Similar to conditions, iterators in Jade can be written simply with each—for example,

```
- var languages = ['php', 'node', 'ruby']
div
  each value, index in languages
    p= index + ". " + value
```

The HTML output is as follows:

```
<div>
  <p>0. php</p>
  <p>1. node</p>
  <p>2. ruby</p>
</div>
```

The same construction works with objects as well:

```
- var languages = {'php': -1, 'node': 2, 'ruby':1}
div
  each value, key in languages
    p= key + ": " + value
```

The Jade above is compiled into the HTML output:

```
<div>
  <p>php: -1</p>
  <p>node: 2</p>
  <p>ruby: 1</p>
</div>
```

Filters

Filters are used when there are blocks of texts written in a different language. For example, the filter for Markdown looks like this:

```
p
  :markdown
    # Practical Node.js

    [This book](http://expressjsguide.com) really helps to grasp many components needed for
modern-day web development.
```

■ **Note**   The Markdown modules still need to be installed. The `marked` and markdown NPM packages are often used for this. There's no need for an additional configuration, just install them in the project's local `node_modules` folder.

Interpolation

Interpolation in Jade is achieved via #{name}. For example, to output `title` in a paragraph, do the following:

```
- var title = "Express.js Guide"
p Read the #{title} in PDF, MOBI and EPUB
```

The interpolation is processed at template compilation; therefore, don't use it in executable JavaScript (`-`).:

Case

Here's an example of the `case` statement in Jade:

```
- var coins = Math.round(Math.random()*10)
case coins
  when 0
    p You have no money
  when 1
    p You have a coin
  default
    p You have #{coins} coins!
```

Mixins

Mixins are functions that take parameters and produce some HTML. The declaration syntax is `mixin name(param, param2,...)`, and the usage is `+name(data)`. For example,

```
mixin row(items)
  tr
    each item, index in items
      td= item
```

```jade
mixin table(tableData)
  table
    each row, index in tableData
      +row(row)

- var node = [{name: "express"}, {name: "hapi"}, {name: "derby"}]
+table(node)
- var js = [{name: "backbone"}, {name: "angular"}, {name: "ember"}]
+table(js)
```

The template and data above produce this HTML:

```html
<table>
  <tr>
    <td>express</td>
  </tr>
  <tr>
    <td>hapi</td>
  </tr>
  <tr>
    <td>derby</td>
  </tr>
</table>
<table>
  <tr>
    <td>backbone</td>
  </tr>
  <tr>
    <td>angular</td>
  </tr>
  <tr>
    <td>ember</td>
  </tr>
</table>
```

Include

include is a way to split logic into a separate file for the purpose of reusing it across multiple files. It's a top-to-bottom approach; we dictate what to use in the file that includes another file. The file that includes is processed first (we can define locals there), then the included file is processed (we can use earlier defined locals).

To include a Jade template, use include /path/filename. For example, in file A:

```jade
include ./includes/header
```

Notice there's no need for double or single quotes for the template name and its path.

It's possible to traverse up the tree:

```jade
include ../includes/footer
```

But, there's no way to use a dynamic value for the file and path (use a variable), because includes/partials are handled at compilation (not at runtime).

Extend

extend is a bottom-to-top approach (as oppose to include), in the sense that the included file commands which parts of the main file it wants to replace. The way it works is with extend filename and block blockname statements:

In file_a:

```
block header
  p some default text
block content
  p Loading ...
block footer
  p copyright
```

In file_b:

```
extend file_a
block header
  p very specific text
block content
  .main-content
```

Standalone Jade Usage

Template engines are not always used with Node.js (and frameworks like Express.js). Sometimes, we might just want to use Jade in a standalone manner. The use cases include generating an e-mail template, precompiling Jade before deployment, and debugging. In this section, we do the following:

- Install a Jade module

- Create our first Jade file

- Create a Node.js program that uses the Jade file

- Compare jade.compile, jade.render, and jade.renderFile

To add a jade dependency to your project, or if you're starting from scratch from an empty project folder, do the following:

- Create an empty node_modules folder with $ mkdir node_modules

- Install and add jade to package.json with $ npm install jade –save. See the results in Figure 4-1.

```
● ● ○                        practicalnode — bash
npm WARN package.json css-parse@1.0.4 No repository field.
npm http GET https://registry.npmjs.org/uglify-to-browserify
npm http GET https://registry.npmjs.org/async
npm http 200 https://registry.npmjs.org/optimist
npm http 200 https://registry.npmjs.org/source-map
npm http 200 https://registry.npmjs.org/uglify-to-browserify
npm http GET https://registry.npmjs.org/wordwrap
npm http GET https://registry.npmjs.org/lru-cache
npm http GET https://registry.npmjs.org/sigmund
npm http GET https://registry.npmjs.org/amdefine
npm http 200 https://registry.npmjs.org/sigmund
npm http 200 https://registry.npmjs.org/wordwrap
npm http 200 https://registry.npmjs.org/lru-cache
npm http 200 https://registry.npmjs.org/amdefine
npm http 200 https://registry.npmjs.org/async
jade@0.35.0 node_modules/jade
├── character-parser@1.2.0
├── commander@2.0.0
├── mkdirp@0.3.5
├── monocle@1.1.50 (readdirp@0.2.5)
├── transformers@2.1.0 (promise@2.0.0, css@1.0.8, uglify-js@2.2.5)
├── with@1.1.1 (uglify-js@2.4.0)
└── constantinople@1.0.2 (uglify-js@2.4.8)
Azats-Air:practicalnode azat$
```

Figure 4-1. Installing Jade

Let's say we have some Node.js script that sends e-mail and we need to use a template to generate HTML dynamically for e-mail. This is how it might look (file jade-example.jade):

```
.header
  h1= title
  p
.body
  p= body
.footer
  div= By
    a(href="http://twitter.com/#{author.twitter}")= author.name
  ul
    each tag, index in tags
      li= tag
```

In this case, our Node.js script needs to hydrate, or populate, this template with the following data:

- title: string
- body: string
- author: string
- tags: array

We can extract these variables from multiple sources (databases, file systems, user input, and so on). For example, in the jade-example.js file, we use hard-coded values for title, author, tags, but pass through a command-line argument for body:

```
var jade = require('jade'),
  fs = require('fs');
```

```
var data = {
  title: "Practical Node.js",
  author: {
    twitter: "@azat_co",
    name: "Azat"
  },
  tags: ['express', 'node', 'javascript']
}
data.body = process.argv[2];

fs.readFile('jade-example.jade', 'utf-8', function(error, source){
  var template = jade.compile(source);
  var html = template(data)
  console.log(html)
});
```

In this way, when we run $ node jade-example.js 'email body', we get the output shown in Figure 4-2.

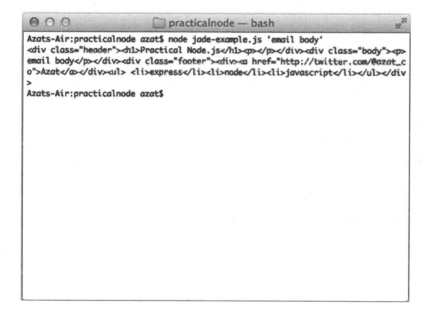

Figure 4-2. *The result of jade-example output*

The "prettified" HTML output is as follows:

```
<div class="header">
    <h1>Practical Node.js</h1>
    <p></p>
</div>
<div class="body">
    <p>email body</p>
</div>
```

```
<div class="footer">
    <div><a href="http://twitter.com/@azat_co"> Azat</a>
    </div>
    <ul>
        <li>express</li>
        <li>node</li>
        <li>javascript</li>
    </ul>
</div>
```

In addition to jade.compile(), the Jade API has the functions jade.render() and jade.renderFile(). For example, the previous file can be rewritten with jade.render():

```
var jade = require('jade'),
  fs = require('fs');

var data = {
  title: "Practical Node.js",
  author: {
    twitter: "@azat_co",
    name: "Azat"
  },
  tags: ['express', 'node', 'javascript']
}
data.body = process.argv[2];

//jade.render
fs.readFile('jade-example.jade', 'utf-8', function(error, source){
  var html = jade.render(source, data)
  console.log(html)
});
```

Furthermore, with jade.renderFile, the jade-example.js file is even more compact:

```
var jade = require('jade'),
  fs = require('fs');

var data = {
  title: "Practical Node.js",
  author: {
    twitter: "@azat_co",
    name: "Azat"
  },
  tags: ['express', 'node', 'javascript']
}
data.body = process.argv[2];

//jade.renderFile

jade.renderFile('jade-example.jade', data, function(error, html){
  console.log(html)
});
```

■ **Note**   Jade can also be used as a command-line tool after installing it with the `-g` or `--global` option via NPM. For more information, run `jade -h` or see the official documentation (`http://jade-lang.com/command-line/`).

To use Jade in a browser, you can use browserify (`https://github.com/substack/node-browserify`) and its jadeify (`https://github.com/substack/node-jadeify`) middleware.

Note   To use the same Jade templates on front-end (browser) and server sides, I recommend `jade-browser` (`https://www.npmjs.org/package/jade-browser`) by Storify, for which I was the maintainer for a time during my work there. `jade-browser` acts as an Express.js middleware and it exposes server-side templates to the browser along with a helpful utility functions.

`https://github.com/storify/jade-browser`

Handlebars Syntax

The Handlebars library is another template engine. It inherits from Mustache and, for the most part, is compatible with Mustache's syntax. However, Handlebars adds more features (i.e., a superset).

Unlike Jade, by design, Handlebars was made so that developers *can't write* a lot of JavaScript logic inside the templates. This helps to keep templates lean and related strictly to the representation of the data (no business logic).

Another drastic difference between Jade and Handlebars is that the latter requires full HTML code (`<`, `>`, and so on), and for this reason it could care less about whitespace and indentation.

Variables

A Handlebars expression is `{{`, some content, followed by `}}`, hence the name of the library (see the resemblance to handlebars on a bicycle?). For example, the Handlebars code:

```
<h1>{{title}}</h1>
<p>{{body}}</p>
```

with data:

```
{
  title: "Express.js Guide",
  body: "The Comprehensive Book on Express.js"
}
```

renders:

```
<h1>Express.js Guide</h1>
<p>The Comprehensive Book on Express.js</p>
```

Iteration (each)

In Handlebars, each is one of the built-in helpers; it allows you to iterate through objects and arrays. Inside the block, we can use @key for the former (objects), and @index for the later (arrays). In addition, each item is referred to as this. When an item is an object itself, this can be omitted and just the property name is used to reference the value of that property.

The following are examples of the each helper block in Handlebars:

```
<div>
{{#each languages}}
  <p>{{@index}}. {{this}}</p>
{{/each}}
</div>
```

The template above is supplied with this data:

```
{languages: ['php', 'node', 'ruby']}
```

And output this HTML upon compilation:

```
<div>
  <p>0. php</p>
  <p>1. node</p>
  <p>2. ruby</p>
</div>
```

Unescaped Output

By default, Handlebars escapes values. If you don't want Handlebars to escape a value, use triple curly braces: {{{ and }}}.

As data, let's use this object that has an array with some HTML tags (angle braces):

```
{
  arr: [
    '<a>a</a>',
    '<i>italic</i>',
    '<strong>bold</strong>'
  ]
}
```

To apply this Handlebars template to our data above (i.e., hydration):

```
<ul>
   {{#each arr}}
   <li>
     <span>{{@index}}</span>
     <span>unescaped: {{{this}}} vs. </span>
     <span>escaped: {{this}}</span>
   </li>
   {{/each}}
</ul>
```

The hydrated template produces this HTML:

```
<ul>
  <li>
    <span>0</span>
    <span>unescaped: <a>a</a> vs. </span>
    <span>escaped: &lt;a&gt;a&lt;/a&gt;</span>
  </li>
  <li>
    <span>1</span>
    <span>unescaped: <i>italic</i> vs. </span>
    <span>escaped: &lt;i&gt;italic&lt;/i&gt;</span>
  </li>
  <li>
    <span>2</span>
    <span>unescaped: <strong>bold</strong> vs. </span>
    <span>escaped: &lt;strong&gt;bold&lt;/strong&gt;</span>
  </li>
</ul>
```

Conditions (if)

if is another built-in helper invoked via #. For example, this Handlebars code:

```
{{#if user.admin}}
  <button class="launch">Launch Spacecraft</button>
{{else}}
    <button class="login"> Log in</button>
{{/if}}
```

populated with data:

```
{
  user: {
    admin: true
  }
}
```

turns into this HTML output:

```
<button class="launch">Launch Spacecraft</button>
```

Unless

To inverse an if not ... (if ! ...) statement (convert negative to positive), we can harness the unless built-in helper block. For example, the previous code snippet can be rewritten with unless.

The Handlebars code that check the truthness of the admin flag (property user.admin):

```
{{#unless user.admin}}
   <button class="login"> Log in</button>
{{else}}
  <button class="launch">Launch Spacecraft</button>
{{/unless}}
```

We supply our template with this data that means that the user is the administrator:

```
{
  user: {
    admin: true
  }
}
```

The HTML output renders the launch button, which is available only to admins:

```
<button class="launch">Launch Spacecraft</button>
```

With

In case there's an object with nested properties, and there are a lot of them, it's possible to use with to pass the context.

We have this Handlebars code that is handling a user's contact and address information:

```
{{#with user}}
  <p>{{name}}</p>
  {{#with contact}}
    <span>Twitter: @{{twitter}}</span>
  {{/with}}
  <span>Address: {{address.city}},
{{/with}}
{{user.address.state}}</span>
```

Then we merge the template with this data. Notice the properties' names are the same as in the Handlebar template, there's only one reference to the user object:

```
{user: {
  contact: {
    email: 'hi@azat.co',
    twitter: 'azat_co'
  },
  address: {
    city: 'San Francisco',
    state: 'California'
  },
  name: 'Azat'
}}
```

The snippets above when compiled, produce HTML:

```
<p>Azat</p>
<span>Twitter: @azat_co</span>
<span>Address: San Francisco, California
</span>
```

Comments

To output comments, use regular HTML <!-- and -->. To hide comments in the final output, use {{! and }} or {{!-- and --}}. For example,

```
<!-- content goes here -->
<p>Node.js is a non-blocking I/O for scalable apps.</p>
{{! @todo change this to a class}}
{{!-- add the example on {{#if}} --}}
<p id="footer">Copyright 2014 Azat</p>
```

outputs

```
<!-- content goes here -->
<p>Node.js is a non-blocking I/O for scalable apps.</p>
<p id="footer">Copyright 2014 Azat</p>
```

Custom Helpers

Custom Handlebars helpers are similar to built-in helper blocks and Jade mixins. To use custom helpers, we need to create them as a JavaScript function and register them with the Handlebars instance.

This Handlebars template uses our custom helper table which we'll register (i.e., define) later in the JavaScript/Node.js code:

```
{{table node}}
```

Here goes the JavaScript/Node.js that tells the Handlebars compiler what to do when it encounters the custom table function (i.e., print an HTML table out of the provided array):

```
Handlebars.registerHelper('table', function(data) {
  var str = '<table>';
  for (var i = 0; i < data.length; i++ ) {
    str += '<tr>';
    for (var key in data[i]) {
      str += '<td>' + data[i][key] + '</td>';
    };
    str += '</tr>';
  };
  str += '</table>';

  return new Handlebars.SafeString (str);
});
```

This is our table data:

```
{
  node:[
    {name: 'express', url: 'http://expressjs.com/'},
    {name: 'hapi', url: 'http://spumko.github.io/'},
    {name: 'compound', url: 'http://compoundjs.com/'},
    {name: 'derby', url: 'http://derbyjs.com/'}
  ]
}
```

The resulting HTML output looks like this:

```
<table>
    <tr>
        <td>express</td>
        <td>http://expressjs.com/</td>
    </tr>
    <tr>
        <td>hapi</td>
        <td>http://spumko.github.io/</td>
    </tr>
    <tr>
        <td>compound</td>
        <td>http://compoundjs.com/</td>
    </tr>
    <tr>
        <td>derby</td>
        <td>http://derbyjs.com/</td>
    </tr>
</table>
```

Includes (Partials)

Includes or partials templates in Handlebars are interpreted by the {{>partial_name}} expression. Partials are akin to helpers and are registered with Handlebars.registerPartial(name, source), where name is a string and source is a Handlebars template code for the partial.

Standalone Handlebars Usage

Developers can install Handlebars via NPM with $ npm install handlebars or $ npm install handlebars --save, assuming there's either node_modules or package.json in the current working directory (see the results of a sample installation in Figure 4-3).

```
  ⊖ ○ ○                      practicalnode — bash                            ⤢
npm http 200 https://registry.npmjs.org/handlebars
npm http GET https://registry.npmjs.org/handlebars/-/handlebars-1.1.2.tgz
npm http 200 https://registry.npmjs.org/handlebars/-/handlebars-1.1.2.tgz
npm http GET https://registry.npmjs.org/optimist
npm http GET https://registry.npmjs.org/uglify-js
npm http 304 https://registry.npmjs.org/optimist
npm http 304 https://registry.npmjs.org/uglify-js
npm http GET https://registry.npmjs.org/wordwrap
npm http GET https://registry.npmjs.org/source-map
npm http GET https://registry.npmjs.org/async
npm http 304 https://registry.npmjs.org/wordwrap
npm http 304 https://registry.npmjs.org/source-map
npm http 304 https://registry.npmjs.org/async
npm http GET https://registry.npmjs.org/amdefine
npm http 304 https://registry.npmjs.org/amdefine
npm WARN package.json css@1.0.8 No repository field.
npm WARN package.json uglify-js@2.2.5 'repositories' (plural) Not supported.
npm WARN package.json Please pick one as the 'repository' field
npm WARN package.json css-stringify@1.0.5 No repository field.
npm WARN package.json css-parse@1.0.4 No repository field.
handlebars@1.1.2 node_modules/handlebars
├── optimist@0.3.7 (wordwrap@0.0.2)
└── uglify-js@2.3.6 (async@0.2.9, source-map@0.1.31)
Azats-Air:practicalnode azat$ |
```

Figure 4-3. *Installing Handlebars*

■ **Note**   Handlebars can be installed via NPM as a command-line tool with the -g or --global options. For more information on how to use Handlebars in this mode, refer to the $ `handlebar` command or the official documentation (`https://github.com/wycats/handlebars.js/#usage-1`).

Here's an example of standalone Node.js Handlebars usage from `handlebars-example.js`:

```javascript
var handlebars = require('handlebars'),
  fs = require('fs');

var data = {
  title: 'practical node.js',
  author: '@azat_co',
  tags: ['express', 'node', 'javascript']
}
data.body = process.argv[2];

fs.readFile('handlebars-example.html', 'utf-8', function(error, source){
  handlebars.registerHelper('custom_title', function(title){
    var words = title.split(' ');
    for (var i = 0; i < words.length; i++) {
      if (words[i].length > 4) {
        words[i] = words[i][0].toUpperCase() + words[i].substr(1);
      }
    }
    title = words.join(' ');
    return title;
  })
```

```
  var template = handlebars.compile(source);
  var html = template(data);
  console.log(html)
});
```

And the `handlebars-example.html` file that uses `custom_title` helper has this content that calls the helper and outputs some other properties:

```
<div class="header">
    <h1>{{custom_title title}}</h1>
</div>
<div class="body">
    <p>{{body}}</p>
</div>
<div class="footer">
    <div><a href="http://twitter.com/{{author.twitter}}">{{autor.name}}</a>
    </div>
    <ul>
      {{#each tags}}
        <li>{{this}}</li>
      {{/each}}
    </ul>
</div>
```

To produce this HTML when we run `$ node handlebars-example.js 'email body'`, use the following:

```
<div class="header">
    <h1>Practical Node.js</h1>
</div>
<div class="body">
    <p>email body</p>
</div>
<div class="footer">
    <div><a href="http://twitter.com/"></a>
    </div>
    <ul>
        <li>express</li>
        <li>node</li>
        <li>javascript</li>
    </ul>
</div>
```

To use Handlebars in the browser, download the library in a straightforward manner from the official web site (http://handlebarsjs.com/) and include it in your pages. Alternatively, it's possible to use just the runtime version from the same web site (which is lighter in size) with precompiled templates. Templates can be precompiled with the Handlebars command-line tool.

Jade and Handlebars Usage in Express.js 4

By default, Express.js 4.x (and 3.x) uses either a template extension provided to the res.render method or the default extension set by the view engine setting, to invoke the require and __express methods on the template library. In other words, for Express.js to utilize a template engine library out of the box, that library needs to have the __express method.

When the template engine library doesn't provide the __express method, or a similar one with (path, options, callback) parameters, it's recommended that you use Consolidate.js (https://github.com/visionmedia/consolidate.js/).

Here is a quick example of Consolidate.js for Express.js 4 (version 4.2.0 and Consolidate version is 0.10.0):

```
var express = require('express'),
  cons = require('consolidate'),
  app = express()

app.engine('html', cons.swig)

app.set('view engine', 'html')
app.set('views', __dirname + '/views')

var platforms = [
  { name: 'node' },
  { name: 'ruby' },
  { name: 'python' }
]

app.get('/', function(req, res){
  res.render('index', {
    title: 'Consolidate This'
  })
})

app.get('/platforms', function(req, res){
  res.render('platforms', {
    title: 'Platforms',
    platforms: platforms
  })
})

app.listen(3000)
console.log('Express server listening on port 3000')
```

Usually, the source code is in the GitHub repository and the snippet is in the ch4/consolidate folder.

For more information on how to configure Express.js settings and use Consolidate.js, refer to the Pro Express.js 4 book (Apress, 2014).

Jade and Express.js

Jade is compatible with Express.js out of the box (in fact, it's the default choice), so to use Jade with Express.js, you just need to install a template engine module jade (https://www.npmjs.org/package/jade) and provide an extension to Express.js via the view engine setting.).

For example, in the main server file we set the setting:

```
app.set('view engine', 'jade');
```

■ Note If you use $ express <app_name> command-line tool, you can add the option for engine support, i.e., –e option for EJS and –H for Hogan. This will add EJS or Hogan automatically to your new project. Without either of these options, the express-generator (versions 4.0.0-4.2.0) will use Jade.

In the route file, we can call the template—for example, views/page.jade (the views folder name is another Express.js default, which can be overwritten with the view setting):

```
app.get('/page', function(req, res, next){
  //get the data dynamically
  res.render('page', data);
});
```

If we don't specify the views engine setting, then the extension must be passed explicitly to res.render():

```
res.render('page.jade', data);
```

Handlebars and Express.js

Contrary to Jade, the Handlebars library from http://handlebarsjs.com/ doesn't come with the __express method, but there are a few options to make Handlebars work with Express.js:).

- consolidate: a Swiss-army knife of Express.js template engine libraries (shown above)

- hbs (https://github.com/donpark/hbs): wrapper library for Handlebars

- express-Handlebars (file://pchns-f01/TECHNOLOGY/BPR/Techutilities/Apress/ Apress%20outline/express3-handlebars): despite the name, this module should work just fine with Express.js 4 as well as version 3.x

Here's how we can use hbs approach (extension hbs). Inside of the typical Express.js app code (i.e., configuration section of the main file that we launch with the $ node command) write the following statements:

```
...
app.set('view engine', 'hbs');
...
```

Or, if another extension is preferable, such as html, we see the following:

```
...
app.set('view engine', 'html');
pp.engine('html', require('hbs').__express);
...
```

The express3-handlebars approach usage is as follows:

```
...
app.engine('handlebars', exphbs({defaultLayout: 'main'}));
app.set('view engine', 'handlebars');
...
```

Project: Adding Jade Templates to Blog

Last, we can continue with Blog. In this section we add main pages using Jade, plus add a layout and some partials:

- layout.jade: global app-wide template
- index.jade: home page with the list of posts
- article.jade: individual article page
- login.jade: page with a login form
- post.jade: page for adding a new article
- admin.jade: page to administer articles after logging in

Because the templates in this mini-project require data, we'll skip the demo until the chapter 5 where we'll plug in the MongoDB database. So the source code for the Jade templates is exactly the same as in the ch5 folder of the GitHub repository practicalnode: https://github.com/azat-co/practicalnode. Feel free to copy it from there or follow the instructions below.

layout.jade

Let's open the project where we left off in the previous chapter and add layout.jade with the document type statement:

```
doctype html
```

■ **Note**   doctype 5 was deprecated around v1.0.

Now we can add the main tags of the page:

```
html
  head
```

The title of the each page is provided from the appTitle variable (aka, local):

```
title= appTitle
```

Then, in the head tag, we list all the front-end assets that we need app-wide (on each page):

```
script(type="text/javascript", src="js/jquery-2.0.3.min.js")
link(rel='stylesheet', href='/css/bootstrap-3.0.2/css/bootstrap.min.css')
link(rel="stylesheet", href="/css/bootstrap-3.0.2/css/bootstrap-theme.min.css")
link(rel="stylesheet", href="/css/style.css")
```

```
script(type="text/javascript", src="/css/bootstrap-3.0.2/js/bootstrap.min.js")
script(type="text/javascript", src="/js/blog.js")
meta(name="viewport", content="width=device-width, initial-scale=1.0")
```

The main content lives in body which has the same level indentation as head:

```
body
```

Inside the body, we write an ID and some classes for the styles that we'll add later:

```
#wrap
  .container
```

The appTitle value is printed dynamically, but the p.lead element only has texts:

```
    h1.page-header= appTitle
    p.lead Welcome to example from Express.js Experience by 
      a(href="http://twitter.com/azat_co") @azat_co
      |. Please enjoy.
```

The block sections can be overwritten by the children templates (templates that extend this file):

```
    block page
    block header
      div
```

Menu is a partial (i.e., an include) that is stored in the views/includes folder. Note the absence of quotation marks:

```
        include includes/menu
```

In this block, we can display messages for users:

```
    block alert
      div.alert.alert-warning.hidden
```

Main content goes in this block:

```
    .content
      block content
```

Lastly, the footer looks as follows:

```
block footer
  footer
    .container
      p
        | Copyright &copy; 2014 | Issues? Submit to
        a(href="https://github.com/azat-co/blog-express/issues") GitHub
        | .
```

The full code of layout.jade is as follows:

```jade
doctype html
html
  head
    title= appTitle
    script(type="text/javascript", src="js/jquery-2.0.3.min.js")
    link(rel="stylesheet", href="/css/bootstrap-3.0.2/css/bootstrap.min.css")
    link(rel="stylesheet", href="/css/bootstrap-3.0.2/css/bootstrap-theme.min.css")
    link(rel="stylesheet", href="/css/style.css")
    script(type="text/javascript", src="/css/bootstrap-3.0.2/js/bootstrap.min.js")
    script(type="text/javascript", src="/js/blog.js")
    meta(name="viewport", content="width=device-width, initial-scale=1.0")
  body
    #wrap
      .container
        h1.page-header= appTitle
        p.lead Welcome to example from Express.js Experience by 
          a(href="http://twitter.com/azat_co") @azat_co
          |. Please enjoy.
        block page
        block header
          div
            include includes/menu
        block alert
          div.alert.alert-warning.hidden
        .content
          block content
    block footer
      footer
        .container
          p
            | Copyright &copy; 2014 | Issues? Submit to
            a(href="https://github.com/azat-co/blog-express/issues") GitHub
            | .
```

index.jade

Now we can look at the home page template index.jade that extends layout:

```jade
extends layout
```

We set the menu variable to index, so the menu include (i.e., menu.jade) can determine which tab to show as active:

```jade
block page
  - var menu = 'index'
```

The main content with the list of articles that comes from locals is as follows:

```
block content
  if (articles.length === 0)
    | There's no published content yet.
    a(href="/login") Log in
    |  to post and publish.
  else
    each article, index in articles
      div
        h2
          a(href="/articles/#{article.slug}")= article.title
```

The full code of index.jade is as follows:

```
extends layout

block page
  - var menu = 'index'
block content
  if (articles.length === 0)
    | There's no published content yet.
    a(href="/login") Log in
    |  to post and publish.
  else
    each article, index in articles
      div
        h2
          a(href="/articles/#{article.slug}")= article.title
```

Figure 4-4 shows how the home page looks after adding style sheets.

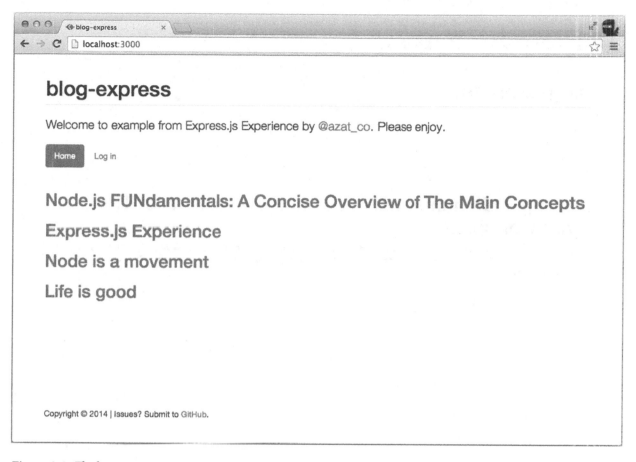

Figure 4-4. *The home page*

article.jade

The individual article page (Figure 4-5) is relatively unsophisticated because most of the elements are abstracted into layout.jade:

```
extends layout

block content
  p
    h1= title
    p= text
```

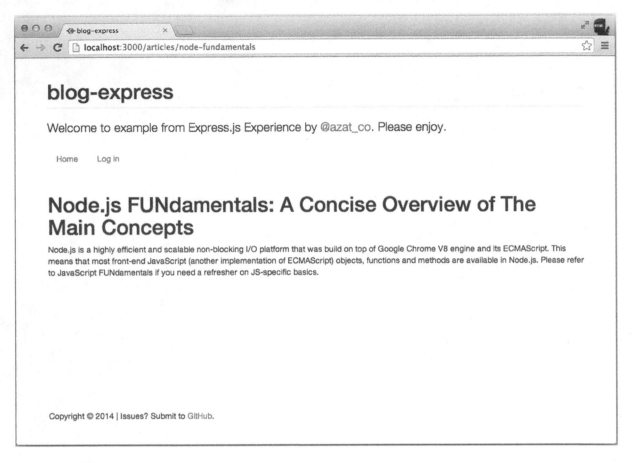

Figure 4-5. *The article page*

login.jade

Similarly, the login page contains only a form and a button (with the Twitter Bootstrap classes/markup):

```
extends layout

block page
  - var menu = 'login'

block content
  .col-md-4.col-md-offset-4
    h2 Log in
    div= error
    div
      form(action="/login", method="POST")
        p
          input.form-control(name="email", type="text", placeholder="hi@azat.co")
```

```
p
    input.form-control(name="password", type="password", placeholder="***")
p
    button.btn.btn-lg.btn-primary.btn-block(type="submit") Log in
```

Figure 4-6 shows how the login page looks.

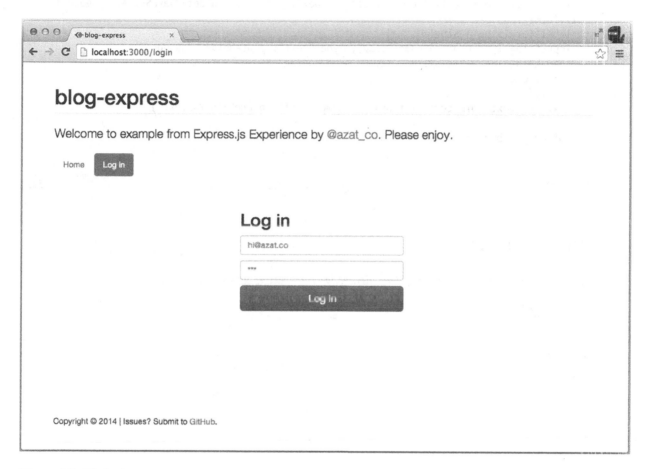

Figure 4-6. *The login page*

post.jade

The post page (Figure 4-7) has another form. This time, the form contains a text area element:

```
extends layout
block page
  - var menu = 'post'
block content
```

```
h2 Post an Article
div= error
div.col-md-8
  form(action="/post", method="POST", role="form")
    div.form-group
      label(for="title") Title
      input#title.form-control(name="title", type="text", placeholder="JavaScript is good")
    div.form-group
      label(for="slug") Slug
      input#slug.form-control(name="slug", type="text", placeholder="js-good")
      span.help-block This string will be used in the URL.
    div.form-group
      label(for="text") Text
      textarea#text.form-control(rows="5", name="text", placeholder="Text")
    p
      button.btn.btn-primary(type="submit") Save
```

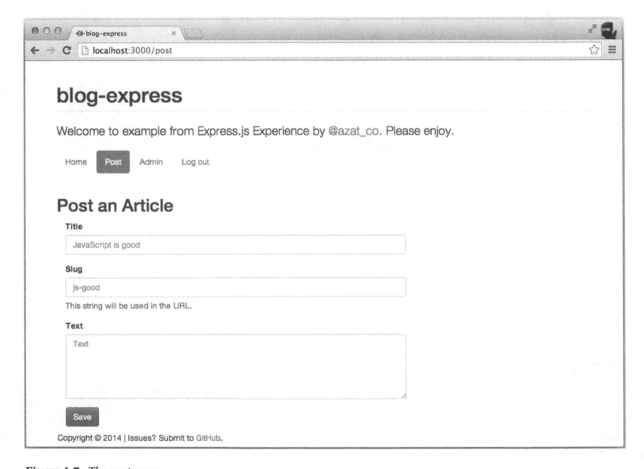

Figure 4-7. *The post page*

admin.jade

The admin page (Figure 4-8) has a loop of articles just like the home page. In addition, we can include a front-end script (js/admin.js) specific to this page:

```
extends layout

block page
  - var menu = 'admin'

block content
  div.admin
    if (articles.length === 0 )
      p
        | Nothing to display. Add a new
        a(href="/post") article
        |.
    else

      table.table.table-stripped
        thead
          tr
            th(colspan="2") Actions
            th Post Title
        tbody
          each article, index in articles
            tr(data-id="#{article._id}", class=(!article.published)?'unpublished':'')
              td.action
                button.btn.btn-danger.btn-sm.remove(type="button")
                  span.glyphicon.glyphicon-remove(title="Remove")
              td.action
                button.btn.btn-default.btn-sm.publish(type="button")
                  span.glyphicon(class=(article.published)?"glyphicon-pause":"glyphicon-play",
title=(article.published)?"Unpublish":"Publish")
              td= article.title
      script(type="text/javascript", src="js/admin.js")
```

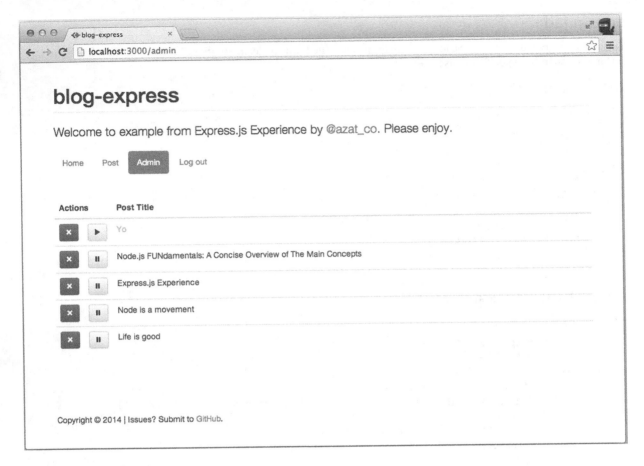

Figure 4-8. *The admin page*

We use interpolation to print article IDs as attributes `data-id`:

```
tr(data-id="#{article._id}", class=(!article.published)?'unpublished':'')
```

And, a conditional (ternary) operator (`https://github.com/donpark/hbs`) is used for classes and title attributes. Remember, it's JavaScript!

```
                span.glyphicon(class=(article.published)?"glyphicon-pause":"glyphicon-play",
title=(article.published)?"Unpublish":"Publish")
```

Summary

You learned about Jade and Handlebars templates (variables, iterations, condition, partials, unescaping, and so forth), and how to use them in a standalone Node.js script or within Express.js. In addition, the main pages for Blog were created using Jade.

In the next chapter we examine an important aspect of modern web development and software engineering: test-driven development. We look at the Mocha module and write some tests for Blog in true TDD/BDD style. In addition, the next chapter deals with adding a database to Blog routes to populate these templates, and shows you how to turn them into working HTML pages!

CHAPTER 5

■ ■ ■

Persistence with MongoDB and Mongoskin

NoSQL databases, also called *non-relational databases*, are more horizontally scalable, usually open source, and better suited for distributed systems. NoSQL databases deal routinely with larger data sizes than traditional ones. The key distinction in implementation comes from the fact that relationships between database entities are not stored in the database itself (no more join queries); they are moved to the application or object-relational mapping (ORM) levels—in our case, to Node.js code. Another good reason to use NoSQL databases is that, because they are schemaless, they are perfect for prototyping and Agile iterations (more pushes!).

MongoDB is a document store NoSQL database (as opposed to key value and wide-column store NoSQL databases, http://nosql-database.org/). It's the most mature and dependable NoSQL database available thus far. In addition to efficiency, scalability, and lightning speed, MongoDB uses JavaScript–like language for its interface! This alone is magical, because now there's no need to switch context between the front end (browser JavaScript), back end (Node.js), and database (MongoDB).

The company behind MongoDB (formerly 10gen, http://en.wikipedia.org/wiki/10gen) is an industry leader and provides education and certification through its online MongoDB University (https://university.mongodb.com/).

To get you started with MongoDB and Node.js, we examine the following in this chapter:

- Easy and proper installation of MongoDB
- How to run the Mongo server
- Data manipulation from the Mongo console
- MongoDB shell in detail
- Minimalistic native MongoDB driver for Node.js example
- Main Mongoskin methods
- Project: storing Blog data in MongoDB with Mongoskin

Easy and Proper Installation of MongoDB

The following steps are better suited for Mac OS X/Linux–based systems, but with some modifications, they can be used for Windows systems as well (i.e., $PATH variable, or the slashes). Next, we look at MongoDB installation from the official package, as well as using HomeBrew for Mac OS X users (recommended). For non-Mac users, there are many other ways to install (http://docs.mongodb.org/manual/installation/).

The HomeBrew installation is recommended and is the easiest path (assuming Mac OS X users have brew installed already, which was covered in Chapter 1): $ brew install mongodb. If this doesn't work, try the manual path described later./).

MongoDB can be downloaded at http://www.mongodb.org/downloads. For the latest Apple laptops, such as MacBook Air, select the OS X 64-bit version. The owners of older Macs should browse the link: http://dl.mongodb.org/dl/osx/i386.

■ **Tip**   If you don't know the architecture type of your processor when choosing a MongoDB package, type $ uname -p in the command line to find this information.

Unpack the package into your web development folder (~/*Documents/Development or any other). If you want, you could install MongoDB into the /usr/local/mongodb folder.

Optional: If you would like to access MongoDB commands from anywhere on your system, you need to add your mongodb path to the $PATH variable. For Mac OS X, you need the open-system paths file with:

```
$ sudo vi /etc/paths
```

Or, if you prefer TextMate:

```
$ mate /etc/paths
```

Then, add the following line to the /etc/paths file:

```
/usr/local/mongodb/bin
```

Create a data folder; by default, MongoDB uses /data/db. Please note this might be different in newer versions of MongoDB. To create the data folder, type and execute the following commands:

```
$ sudo mkdir -p /data/db
$ sudo chown `id -u` /data/db
```

Figure 5-1 shows how this looks onscreen.

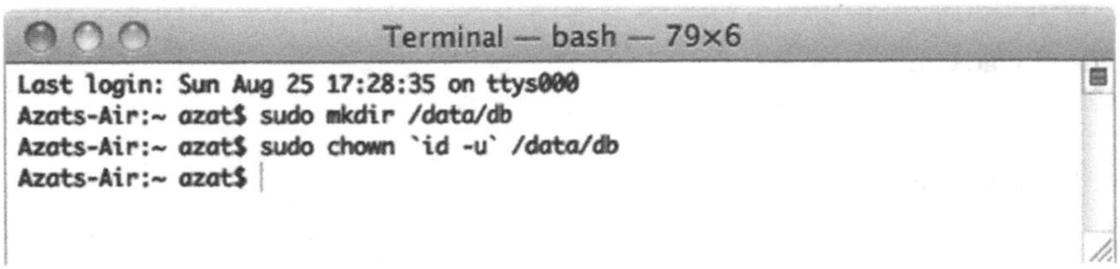

Figure 5-1. *Initial setup for MongoDB: create the data directory*

If you prefer to use path other than /data/db, you can specify it using the --dbpath option to mongod (main MongoDB service).

Detailed instructions for MongoDB installation on various OSs are available at MongoDB.org, "Install MongoDB on OS X" (http://docs.mongodb.org/manual/tutorial/install-mongodb-on-os-x/). For Windows users, there is a good walk-through article titled "Installing MongoDB" (http://www.tuanleaded.com/blog/2011/10/installing-mongodb.

How to Run the Mongo Server

To run the Mongo server, go to the folder where you unpacked MongoDB. That location should have a bin folder in it. From that folder, type the following command:

```
$ ./bin/mongod
```

Or, if you added $PATH for the MongoDB location, type the following:

```
$ mongod
```

■ **Note**   Don't forget to restart the terminal window after adding a new path to the $PATH variable (Figure 5-2).

```
Last login: Sun Aug 25 17:29:16 on ttys000
Azats-Air:~ azat$ mongod
mongod --help for help and startup options
Sun Aug 25 17:31:00
Sun Aug 25 17:31:00 warning: 32-bit servers don't have journaling enabled by default. Please use --journal if you want dur
ability.
Sun Aug 25 17:31:00
Sun Aug 25 17:31:00 [initandlisten] MongoDB starting : pid=738 port=27017 dbpath=/data/db/ 32-bit host=Azats-Air.local
Sun Aug 25 17:31:00 [initandlisten]
Sun Aug 25 17:31:00 [initandlisten] ** NOTE: This is a development version (2.3.0) of MongoDB.
Sun Aug 25 17:31:00 [initandlisten] **       Not recommended for production.
Sun Aug 25 17:31:00 [initandlisten]
Sun Aug 25 17:31:00 [initandlisten] ** NOTE: This is a 32 bit MongoDB binary.
Sun Aug 25 17:31:00 [initandlisten] **       32 bit builds are limited to less than 2GB of data (or less with --journal).
Sun Aug 25 17:31:00 [initandlisten] **       Note that journaling defaults to off for 32 bit and is currently off.
Sun Aug 25 17:31:00 [initandlisten] **       See http://www.mongodb.org/display/DOCS/32+bit
Sun Aug 25 17:31:00 [initandlisten]
Sun Aug 25 17:31:00 [initandlisten] ** WARNING: soft rlimits too low. Number of files is 256, should be at least 1000
Sun Aug 25 17:31:00 [initandlisten]
Sun Aug 25 17:31:00 [initandlisten] db version v2.3.0, pdfile version 4.5
Sun Aug 25 17:31:00 [initandlisten] git version: 86d6c3b316da2fffc1001e665442ba679b51fd26
Sun Aug 25 17:31:00 [initandlisten] build info: Darwin bs-osx-106-i386-1.local 10.8.0 Darwin Kernel Version 10.8.0: Tue Ju
n  7 16:33:36 PDT 2011; root:xnu-1504.15.3~1/RELEASE_I386 i386 BOOST_LIB_VERSION=1_49
Sun Aug 25 17:31:00 [initandlisten] options: {}
Sun Aug 25 17:31:00 [initandlisten] Unable to check for journal files due to: boost::filesystem::directory_iterator::const
ruct: No such file or directory: "/data/db/journal"
Sun Aug 25 17:31:00 [websvr] admin web console waiting for connections on port 28017
Sun Aug 25 17:31:00 [initandlisten] waiting for connections on port 27017
```

Figure 5-2. *Starting up the MongoDB server*

If you see something like

```
MongoDB starting: pid =7218 port=27017...
```

this means the MongoDB database server is running. By default, it's listening to http://localhost:27017. This is the host and port for the scripts and applications to access MongoDB. However, there's a web GUI for humans. If you go to your browser and type http://localhost:28017, you should be able to see the version number, logs, and other useful information. In this case, the MongoDB server is using two different ports (27017 and 28017): one is primary (native) for communications with apps; the other is a web-based GUI for monitoring/statistics. In our Node.js code, we use 27017 only.

Data Manipulation from the Mongo Console

Akin to the Node.js REPL, MongoDB has a console/shell that acts as a client to the database server instance. This means that we have to keep the terminal window with the server open and running while using the console in a different window/tab.

From the folder where you unpacked the archive, launch the mongod service with

```
$ ./bin/mongod
```

Or, if you installed MongoDB globally (recommended), launch the mongod service with

```
$ mongod
```

You should be able to see information in your terminal and in the browser at localhost:28017.

For the MongoDB shell, or mongo, launch in a new terminal window (*important!*) and, in the same folder, type the following commands:

```
$ ./bin/mongo
```

Open another terminal window in the same folder and execute

```
$ ./bin/mongo
```

Or, if you installed mongo globally (recommended), type

```
$ mongo
```

You should see something like this, depending on your version of the MongoDB shell:

```
MongoDB shell version: 2.0.6
connecting to: test
```

Then, type and execute

```
> db.test.save( { a: 1 } )
> db.test.find()
```

Figure 5-3 shows this. If you see that your record is being saved, then everything went well.

```
000                Terminal — mongo — 79×14
Last login: Sun Aug 25 17:30:33 on ttys000
Azats-Air:~ azat$ mongo
MongoDB shell version: 2.3.0
connecting to: test
Welcome to the MongoDB shell.
For interactive help, type "help".
For more comprehensive documentation, see
        http://docs.mongodb.org/
Questions? Try the support group
        http://groups.google.com/group/mongodb-user
> db.test.save( { a: 1} )
> db.test.find()
{ "_id" : ObjectId("521a169d6421d0d4d6f3190f"), "a" : 1 }
>
```

Figure 5-3. Running MongoDB client and storing sample data

Commands find and save do exactly what you might think they do. ;-)

■ **Note**   On Mac OS X (and most Unix systems), to close the process, use control + c. If you use control + z, it puts the process to sleep (or detaches the terminal window). In this case, you might end up with a lock on data files and then have to use the "kill" command (e.g., $ killall node) or Activity Monitor and delete the locked files in the data folder manually. For a vanilla Mac terminal, command + . is an alternative to control + c.

MongoDB Shell in Detail

The most useful MongoDB shell commands are listed here:

- > help: prints a list of available commands
- > show dbs: prints the names of the databases on the database server to which the console is connected (by default, localhost:27017; but, if we pass params to mongo, we can connect to any remote instance)
- > use db_name: switches to db_name
- > show collections: prints a list of collections in the selected database
- > db.collection_name.find(query);: finds all items matching query
- > db.collection_name.findOne(query);: finds one item that matches query
- > db.collection_name.insert(document): adds a document to the collection_name collection
- > db.collection_name.save(document);: saves a document in the collection_name collection—a shorthand of upsert (no _id) or insert (with _id)
- > db.collection_name.update(query,{$set: data});: updates items that match query in the collection_name collection with data object values

- • > db.collection_name.remove(query); removes all items from collection_name that match query criteria

- • > printjson(document);: prints the variable document

It's possible to use good old JavaScript, for example, storing in variable:

```
> var a = db.messages.findOne();
> printjson(a);
> a.text = "hi";
> printjson(a);
> db.messages.save(a);
```

For the purpose of saving time, the API listed here is the bare minimum to get by with MongoDB in this book and its projects. The real interface is richer and has more features. For example, update accepts options such as multi: true, and it's not mentioned here. A full overview of the MongoDB interactive shell is available at mongodb.org, "Overview— The MongoDB Interactive Shell" (http://www.mongodb.org/display/DOCS/Overview +- +The+MongoDB+ Interactive+Shell).

Minimalistic Native MongoDB Driver for Node.js Example

To illustrate the advantages of Mongoskin, let's use Node.js native driver for MongoDB (https://github.com/ christkv/node-mongodb-native) first. We need to write a basic script that accesses the database.

First, however, let's install the MongoDB native driver for Node.js with:

```
$ npm install mongodb@1.3.23
```

Don't forget to include the dependency in the package.json file as well:

```
{
  "name": "node-example",
  "version": "0.0.1",
  "dependencies": {
  "mongodb":"1.3.23",
  ...
  },
  "engines": {
    "node": ">=0.6.x"
  }
}
```

This small example tests whether we can connect to a local MongoDB instance from a Node.js script and run a sequence of statements analogous to the previous section:

1. Declare dependencies

2. Define the database host and port

3. Establish a database connection

4. Create a database document

5. Output a newly created document/object

Here is the code to accomplish these five steps:

```
var mongo = require('mongodb'),
  dbHost  = '127.0.0.1',
  dbPort  = 27017;

var Db = mongo.Db;
var Connection = mongo.Connection;
var Server = mongo.Server;
var db = new Db ('local', new Server(dbHost, dbPort), {safe:true});

db.open(function(error, dbConnection){
  if (error) {
    console.error(error);
    process.exit(1);
  }
  console.log('db state: ', db._state);
  item = {
    name: 'Azat'
  }
  dbConnection.collection('messages').insert(item, function(error, item){
    if (error) {
      console.error(error);
      process.exit(1);
    }
    console.info('created/inserted: ', item);
    db.close();
    process.exit(0);
  });
});
```

The full source code of this script is in the `mongo-native-insert.js` file. Another `mongo-native-insert.js` script looks up any object and modifies it:

1. Get one item from the `message` collection

2. Print it

3. Add a property text with the value `hi`

4. Save the item back to the `message` collection

After we install the library, we can include the MongoDB library in our `mongo-native.js` file:

```
var util = require('util');
var mongodb = require ('mongodb');
```

This is one of the ways to establish a connection to the MongoDB server, in which the db variable holds a reference to the database at a specified host and port:

```
var mongo = require('mongodb'),
  dbHost  = '127.0.0.1',
  dbPort  = 27017;
```

```
var Db = mongo.Db;
var Connection = mongo.Connection;
var Server = mongo.Server;
var db = new Db ('local', new Server(dbHost, dbPort), {safe:true});
```

To open a connection, type the following:

```
db.open(function(error, dbConnection){
  //do something with the database here
  // console.log (util.inspect(db));
  console.log(db._state);
  db.close();
});
```

It's always a good practice to check for any errors and exit gracefully:

```
db.open(function(error, dbConnection){
  if (error) {
    console.error(error);
    process.exit(1);
  }
  console.log('db state: ', db._state);
```

Now we can proceed to the first step mentioned earlier—getting one item from the message collection. This document is in the item variable:

```
dbConnection.collection('messages').findOne({}, function(error, item){
  if (error) {
    console.error(error);
    process.exit(1);
  }
```

The second step, print the value, is as follows:

```
console.info('findOne: ', item);
```

As you can see, methods in the console and Node.js are not much different.
So let's proceed to the remaining two steps: adding a new property and saving the document:

```
item.text = 'hi';
var id = item._id.toString(); // we can store ID in a string
console.info('before saving: ', item);
dbConnection.collection('messages').save(item, function(error, item){
  console.info('save: ', item);
```

To double-check the saved object, we use the ObjectID that we saved before in a string format (in a variable id) with the find method. This method returns a cursor, so we apply toArray() to extract the standard JavaScript array:

```
    dbConnection.collection('messages').find({_id: new mongo.ObjectID(id)}).
toArray(function(error, items){
        console.info('find: ', items);
```

```
          db.close();
          process.exit(0);
        });
      });
    })
});
```

The full source code of this script is available in the mongo-native-insert.js and mongo-native.js files. If we run them with $ node mongo-native-insert and, respectively, $ node mongo-native, while running the mongod service, the scripts should output something similar to the results in Figure 5-4. There are three documents. The first is without the property text; the second and third documents include it.

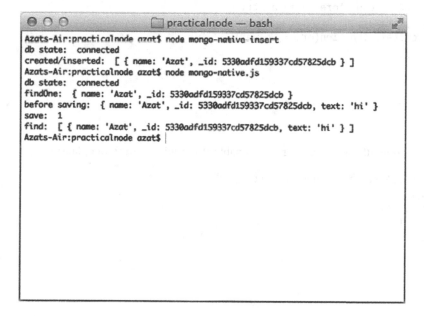

Figure 5-4. Running a simple MongoDB script with a native driver

The full documentation of this library is available at http://mongodb.github.com/node-mongodb-native/api-generated/db.html and on the MongoDB web site (http://docs.mongodb.org/ecosystem/drivers/node-js/).

Main Mongoskin Methods

Mongoskin provides a better API than the native MongoDB driver. To illustrate this, compare this code with the example written using native MongoDB driver for Node.js. As always, to install a module, run NPM with install—for example, $ npm install mongoskin@0.6.1.

The connection to the database is a bit easier:

```
var mongoskin = require('mongoskin'),
  dbHost = '127.0.0.1',
  dbPort = 27017;

var db = mongoskin.db(dbHost + ':' + dbPort + '/local', {safe:true});
```

We can also create our own methods on collections. This might be useful when implementing a model-view-controller-like (MVC-like) architecture by incorporating app-specific logic into these custom methods:

```
db.bind('messages', {
  findOneAndAddText : function (text, fn) {
    db.collection('messages').findOne({}, function(error, item){
      if (error) {
        console.error(error);
        process.exit(1);
      }
      console.info('findOne: ', item);
      item.text = text;
      var id = item._id.toString(); // we can store ID in a string
      console.info('before saving: ', item);
      db.collection('messages').save(item, function(error, count){
        console.info('save: ', count);
        return fn(count, id);
      });
    })
  }
});
```

Lastly, we call the custom method in a straightforward manner (presumably also used in many other places):

```
db.collection('messages').findOneAndAddText('hi', function(count, id){
    db.collection('messages').find({
      _id: db.collection('messages').id(id)
    }).toArray(function(error, items){
      console.info("find: ", items);
      db.close();
      process.exit(0);
    });
});
```

Mongoskin is a subset of the native Node.js MongoDB driver, so most of the methods from the latter are available in the former. Here is the list of the main Mongoskin–only methods:

- `findItems(..., callback)`: finds elements and returns an array instead of a cursor

- `findEach(..., callback)`: iterates through each found element

- `findById(id, ..., callback)`: finds by _id in a string format

- `updateById(_id, ..., callback)`: updates an element with a matching _id

- `removeById(_id, ..., callback)`: removes an element with a matching _id

Alternatives to the native MongoDB driver and Mongoskin include:

- mongoose (http://mongoosejs.com/): an asynchronous JavaScript driver with optional support for modelling

- mongolia (https://github.com/masylum/mongolia): a lightweight MongoDB ORM/driver wrapper

- monk (https://github.com/LearnBoost/monk): a tiny layer that provides simple yet substantial usability improvements for MongoDB use within Node.js

For data validation, these modules often use:

- node-validator (https://github.com/chriso/node-validator): validates data

- express-validator (https://github.com/ctavan/express-validator): validates data in Express.js 3/4

Project: Storing Blog Data in MongoDB with Mongoskin

Let's now return to our Blog project. I've split this feature of storing Blog data in MongoDB with Mongoskin into the following three subprojects:

1. Adding MongoDB seed data

2. Writing Mocha tests

3. Adding persistence

Project: Adding MongoDB Seed Data

First of all, it's not much fun to enter data manually each time we test or run an app. So, in accordance with the Agile principles, we can automate this step by creating a Bash seed data script db/seed.sh:

```
mongoimport --db blog --collection users --file ./db/users.json –jsonArray
mongoimport --db blog --collection articles --file ./db/articles.json --jsonArray
```

This script uses MongoDB's mongoimport feature, which inserts data conveniently into the database straight from JSON files.

The users.json file contains information about authorized users:

```
[{
  "email": "hi@azat.co",
  "admin": true,
  "password": "1"
}]
```

The articles.json file has the content of the blog posts:

```
[{
  "title": "Node is a movement",
  "slug": "node-movement",
  "published": true,
  "text": "In one random deployment, it is often assumed that the number of scattered sensors are
more than that required by the critical sensor density. Otherwise, complete area coverage may not
be guaranteed in this deployment, and some coverage holes may exist. Besides using more sensors to
improve coverage, mobile sensor nodes can be used to improve network coverage..."
}, {
  "title": "Express.js Experience",
  "slug": "express-experience",
  "text": "Work in progress",
  "published": false
},{
  "title": "Node.js FUNdamentals: A Concise Overview of The Main Concepts",
```

```
  "slug": "node-fundamentals",
  "published": true,
  "text": "Node.js is a highly efficient and scalable nonblocking I/O platform that was built on top
of a Google Chrome V8 engine and its ECMAScript. This means that most front-end JavaScript (another
implementation of ECMAScript) objects, functions, and methods are available in Node.js. Please refer
to JavaScript FUNdamentals if you need a refresher on JS-specific basics."
  }]
```

To populate our seed data, simply run $ ./db/seed.sh from the project folder.

Project: Writing Mocha Tests

We can import test data from seed files via require because it's a JSON format:

```
var seedArticles = require('../db/articles.json');
```

Let's add this test to the home page suite to check whether our app shows posts from seed data on the front page:

```
it('should contain posts', function(done) {
  superagent
    .get('http://localhost:'+port)
    .end(function(res){
      seedArticles.forEach(function(item, index, list){
        if (item.published) {
          expect(res.text).to.contain('<h2><a href="/articles/' + item.slug + '">' +
item.title);
        } else {
          expect(res.text).not.to.contain('<h2><a href="/articles/' + item.slug + '">' +
item.title);
        }
        // console.log(item.title, res.text)
      })
      done()
  })
});
```

In a new-article page suite, let's test for presentation of the text with contains:

```
describe('article page', function(){
  it('should display text', function(done){
    var n = seedArticles.length;
    seedArticles.forEach(function(item, index, list){
      superagent
        .get('http://localhost:'+port + '/articles/' + seedArticles[index].slug)
        .end(function(res){
          if (item.published) {
            expect(res.text).to.contain(seedArticles[index].text);
          } else {
            expect(res.status).to.be(401);
          }
```

```
        // console.log(item.title)
        if (index + 1 === n ) {
          done();
        }
      })
    })
  })
})
```

To make sure that Mocha doesn't quit earlier than when superagent calls the response callback, we implemented a countertrick. Instead of it, you can use async (https://www.npmjs.org/package/async). The full source code is in the file tests/index.js under ch5 folder.

Running tests with either $ make test or $ mocha test should fail miserably, but that's expected because we need to implement persistence and then pass data to Jade templates, which we wrote in the previous chapter.

Project: Adding Persistence

This example builds on the previous chapter, with the chapter 3 having the latest code (chapter 4 code is in ch5). Let's go back to our ch3 folder, and add the tests, duplicate them, and then start adding statements to the app.js file.

The full source code of this example is available under ch5 folder. First, the dependencies inclusions need to be reformatted to utilize Mongoskin:

```
var express = require('express'),
  routes = require('./routes'),
  http = require('http'),
  path = require('path'),
  mongoskin = require('mongoskin'),
  dbUrl = process.env.MONGOHQ_URL || 'mongodb://@localhost:27017/blog',
  db = mongoskin.db(dbUrl, {safe: true}),
  collections = {
    articles: db.collection('articles'),
    users: db.collection('users')
  };
```

These statements are needed for the Express.js 4 middleware modules:

```
var session = require('express-session'),
  logger = require('morgan'),
  errorHandler = require('errorhandler'),
  cookieParser = require('cookie-parser'),
  bodyParser = require('body-parser'),
  methodOverride = require('method-override');
```

Then, our usual statements follow, i.e., creating of Express.js instance and assigning the title:

```
var app = express();
app.locals.appTitle = 'blog-express';
```

Now, we add a middleware that exposes Mongoskin/MongoDB collections in each Express.js route via the req object:

```
app.use(function(req, res, next) {
  if (!collections.articles || ! collections.users) return next(new Error('No collections.'))
  req.collections = collections;
  return next();
});
```

Don't forget to call next() in the previous middleware; otherwise, each request stalls.

We set up port number and template engine configurations:

```
app.set('port', process.env.PORT || 3000);
app.set('views', path.join(__dirname, 'views'));
app.set('view engine', 'jade');
```

The configs now include more Connect/Express middleware, the meanings of most of which is to log requests, parse JSON input, use Stylus and server static content:

```
app.use(logger('dev'));
app.use(bodyParser.json());
app.use(bodyParser.urlencoded());
app.use(methodOverride());
app.use(require('stylus').middleware(__dirname + '/public'));
app.use(express.static(path.join(__dirname, 'public')));
```

For development, we use the standart Express.js 4 error handler that we imported earlier with require:

```
if ('development' == app.get('env')) {
  app.use(errorHandler());
}
```

The next section of the app.js file deals with the server routes. So, instead of a single catch-all * route in the ch3 examples, we have the following GET, and POST routes (that mostly render HTML from Jade templates):

```
//PAGES&ROUTES
app.get('/', routes.index);
app.get('/login', routes.user.login);
app.post('/login', routes.user.authenticate);
app.get('/logout', routes.user.logout);
app.get('/admin',  routes.article.admin);
app.get('/post',  routes.article.post);
app.post('/post', routes.article.postArticle);
app.get('/articles/:slug', routes.article.show);
```

REST API routes are used mostly for the admin page. That's where our fancy AJAX browser JavaScript will need them. They use GET, POST, PUT and DELETE methods and don't render HTML from Jade templates, but instead output JSON:

```
//REST API ROUTES
app.get('/api/articles', routes.article.list)
app.post('/api/articles', routes.article.add);
```

```
app.put('/api/articles/:id', routes.article.edit);
app.del('/api/articles/:id', routes.article.del);
```

In the end, we have a 404 catch-all route. It's a good practice to account for the cases when users type a wrong URL. If the request makes to this part of the configuration (top to bottom order), we return the "not found" status:

```
app.all('*', function(req, res) {
  res.send(404);
})
```

The way we start the server is the same as in Chapter 3:

```
var server = http.createServer(app);
var boot = function () {
  server.listen(app.get('port'), function(){
    console.info('Express server listening on port ' + app.get('port'));
  });
}
var shutdown = function() {
  server.close();
}
if (require.main === module) {
  boot();
}
else {
  console.info('Running app as a module')
  exports.boot = boot;
  exports.shutdown = shutdown;
  exports.port = app.get('port');
}
```

Again, for your convenience, the full source code of app.js is under ch5 folder.

We must add index.js, article.js, and user.js files to the routes folder, because we need them in app.js. The user.js file is bare bones for now (we add authentications in Chapter 6).

The method for the GET users route, which should return a list of existing users (which we will implement later) is as follows:

```
exports.list = function(req, res){
  res.send('respond with a resource');
};
```

The method for the GET login page route that renders the login form (login.jade) is as follows:

```
exports.login = function(req, res, next) {
  res.render('login');
};
```

The method for the GET logout route that eventually destroys the session and redirects users to the home page (to be implemented) is as follows:

```
exports.logout = function(req, res, next) {
  res.redirect('/');
};
```

The method for the POST authenticate route that handles authentication and redirects to the admin page (to be implemented) is as follows:

```
exports.authenticate = function(req, res, next) {
  res.redirect('/admin');
};
```

The full code of user.js is:

```
/*
 * GET users listing.
 */

exports.list = function(req, res){
  res.send('respond with a resource');
};

/*
 * GET login page.
 */

exports.login = function(req, res, next) {
  res.render('login');
};

/*
 * GET logout route.
 */

exports.logout = function(req, res, next) {

  res.redirect('/');
};

/*
 * POST authenticate route.
 */

exports.authenticate = function(req, res, next) {
  res.redirect('/admin');

};
```

The most database action happens in the article.js routes.

Let's start with the GET article page where we call findOne with the slug from the req.params object:

```
exports.show = function(req, res, next) {
  if (!req.params.slug) return next(new Error('No article slug.'));
  req.collections.articles.findOne({slug: req.params.slug}, function(error, article) {
    if (error) return next(error);
```

```
    if (!article.published) return res.send(401);
    res.render('article', article);
  });
};
```

The GET articles API route (used in the admin page), where we fetch all articles with the find method and convert the results to an array before sending them back to the requester, is as follows:

```
exports.list = function(req, res, next) {
  req.collections.articles.find({}).toArray(function(error, articles) {
    if (error) return next(error);
    res.send({articles:articles});
  });
};
```

The POST article API routes (used in the admin page), where the insert method is used to add new articles to the articles collection and to send back the result (with _id of a newly created item) is:

```
exports.add = function(req, res, next) {
  if (!req.body.article) return next(new Error('No article payload.'));
  var article = req.body.article;
  article.published = false;
  req.collections.articles.insert(article, function(error, articleResponse) {
    if (error) return next(error);
    res.send(articleResponse);
  });
};
```

The PUT article API route (used on the admin page for publishing), where the updateById shorthand (the same thing can be done with a combination of update and _id query) method is used to set the article document to the payload of the request (req.body):

```
exports.edit = function(req, res, next) {
  if (!req.params.id) return next(new Error('No article ID.'));
  req.collections.articles.updateById(req.params.id, {$set: req.body.article},
function(error, count) {
    if (error) return next(error);
    res.send({affectedCount: count});
  });
};
```

The DELETE article API (used on the admin page) for removing articles in which, again, a combination of remove and _id can be used to achieve similar results:

```
exports.del = function(req, res, next) {
  if (!req.params.id) return next(new Error('No article ID.'));
  req.collections.articles.removeById(req.params.id, function(error, count) {
    if (error) return next(error);
    res.send({affectedCount: count});
  });
};
```

The GET article post page (page is a blank form):

```
exports.post = function(req, res, next) {
  if (!req.body.title)
  res.render('post');
};
```

Next, there's the POST article route for the post page form (the route that actually handles the post addition). In this route we check for the non-empty inputs (`req.body`), construct `article` object and inject it into the database via `req.collections.articles` object exposed to us by middleware. Lastly, we render HTML from the post template:

```
exports.postArticle = function(req, res, next) {
  if (!req.body.title || !req.body.slug || !req.body.text ) {
    return res.render('post', {error: 'Fill title, slug and text.'});
  }
  var article = {
    title: req.body.title,
    slug: req.body.slug,
    text: req.body.text,
    published: false
  };
  req.collections.articles.insert(article, function(error, articleResponse) {
    if (error) return next(error);
    res.render('post', {error: 'Artical was added. Publish it on Admin page.'});
  });
};
```

The `GET admin` page route in which we fetch sorted articles (`{sort: {_id:-1}}`) and manipulate them:

```
exports.admin = function(req, res, next) {
  req.collections.articles.find({},{sort: {_id:-1}}).toArray(function(error, articles) {
    if (error) return next(error);
    res.render('admin',{articles:articles});
  });
}
```

■ **Note** In real production apps that deal with thousands of records, programmers usually use pagination by fetching only a certain number of items at once (5, 10, 100, and so on). To do this, use the `limit` and `skip` options with the `find` method (e.g., HackHall example: https://github.com/azat-co/hackhall/blob/master/routes/posts.js#L37).

Here is the full `article.js` file:

```
/*
 * GET article page.
 */

exports.show = function(req, res, next) {
  if (!req.params.slug) return next(new Error('No article slug.'));
  req.collections.articles.findOne({slug: req.params.slug}, function(error, article) {
```

```
    if (error) return next(error);
    if (!article.published) return res.send(401);
    res.render('article', article);
  });
};

/*
 * GET articles API.
 */

exports.list = function(req, res, next) {
  req.collections.articles.find({}).toArray(function(error, articles) {
    if (error) return next(error);
    res.send({articles:articles});
  });
};

/*
 * POST article API.
 */

exports.add = function(req, res, next) {
  if (!req.body.article) return next(new Error('No article payload.'));
  var article = req.body.article;
  article.published = false;
  req.collections.articles.insert(article, function(error, articleResponse) {
    if (error) return next(error);
    res.send(articleResponse);
  });
};

/*
 * PUT article API.
 */

exports.edit = function(req, res, next) {
  if (!req.params.id) return next(new Error('No article ID.'));
  req.collections.articles.updateById(req.params.id, {$set: req.body.article},
function(error, count) {
    if (error) return next(error);
    res.send({affectedCount: count});
  });
};

/*
 * DELETE article API.
 */
```

```
exports.del = function(req, res, next) {
  if (!req.params.id) return next(new Error('No article ID.'));
  req.collections.articles.removeById(req.params.id, function(error, count) {
    if (error) return next(error);
    res.send({affectedCount: count});
  });
};

/*
 * GET article POST page.
 */

exports.post = function(req, res, next) {
  if (!req.body.title)
  res.render('post');
};

/*
 * POST article POST page.
 */

exports.postArticle = function(req, res, next) {
  if (!req.body.title || !req.body.slug || !req.body.text ) {
    return res.render('post', {error: 'Fill title, slug and text.'});
  }
  var article = {
    title: req.body.title,
    slug: req.body.slug,
    text: req.body.text,
    published: false
  };
  req.collections.articles.insert(article, function(error, articleResponse) {
    if (error) return next(error);
    res.render('post', {error: 'Article was added. Publish it on Admin page.'});
  });
};

/*
 * GET admin page.
 */

exports.admin = function(req, res, next) {
  req.collections.articles.find({},{sort: {_id:-1}}).toArray(function(error, articles) {
    if (error) return next(error);
    res.render('admin',{articles:articles});
  });
}
```

From the project section in Chapter 4, we have the jade files under the views folder. Last, the package.json file looks as follows:

```json
{
  "name": "blog-express",
  "version": "0.0.5",
  "private": true,
  "scripts": {
    "start": "node app.js",
    "test": "mocha test"
  },
  "dependencies": {
    "express": "4.1.2",
    "jade": "1.3.1",
    "stylus": "0.44.0",
    "mongoskin": "1.4.1",
    "cookie-parser": "1.0.1",
    "body-parser": "1.0.2",
    "method-override": "1.0.0",
    "serve-favicon": "2.0.0",
    "express-session": "1.0.4",
    "morgan": "1.0.1",
    "errorhandler": "1.0.1"
  },
  "devDependencies": {
    "mocha": "1.16.2",
    "superagent": "0.15.7",
    "expect.js": "0.2.0"
  }
}
```

For the admin page to function, we need to add some AJAX-iness in the form of the js/admin.js file under the public folder.

In this file, we use ajaxSetup to configure all requests:

```js
$.ajaxSetup({
  xhrFields: {withCredentials: true},
  error: function(xhr, status, error) {
    $('.alert').removeClass('hidden');
    $('.alert').html('Status: ' + status + ', error: ' + error);
  }
});
```

The function findTr is a helper that we can use in our event handlers:

```js
var findTr = function(event) {
  var target = event.srcElement || event.target;
  var $target = $(target);
  var $tr = $target.parents('tr');
  return $tr;
};
```

Overall, we need three event handlers to remove, publish, and unpublish an article. This code snippet that follows, is for removing, and it simply sends a request to our Node.js API route /api/articles/:id, which we wrote a page or two ago:

```
var remove = function(event) {
  var $tr = findTr(event);
  var id = $tr.data('id');
  $.ajax({
    url: '/api/articles/' + id,
    type: 'DELETE',
    success: function(data, status, xhr) {
      $('.alert').addClass('hidden');
      $tr.remove();
    }
  })
};
```

Publishing and unpublishing are coupled together, because they both send PUT to /api/articles/:id:

```
var update = function(event) {
  var $tr = findTr(event);
  $tr.find('button').attr('disabled', 'disabled');
  var data = {
    published: $tr.hasClass('unpublished')
  };
  var id = $tr.attr('data-id');
  $.ajax({
    url: '/api/articles/' + id,
    type: 'PUT',
    contentType: 'application/json',
    data: JSON.stringify({article: data}),
    success: function(dataResponse, status, xhr) {
      $tr.find('button').removeAttr('disabled');
      $('.alert').addClass('hidden');
      if (data.published) {
        $tr.removeClass('unpublished').find('.glyphicon-play').removeClass('glyphicon-play').
addClass('glyphicon-pause');
      } else {
        $tr.addClass('unpublished').find('.glyphicon-pause').removeClass('glyphicon-pause').
addClass('glyphicon-play');
      }
    }
  })
};
```

Then, we attach event listeners in the ready callback:

```
$(document).ready(function(){
  var $element = $('.admin tbody');
  $element.on('click', 'button.remove', remove);
  $element.on('click', 'button', update);
})
```

124

The full source code of the front-end admin.js file is as follows:

```
$.ajaxSetup({
  xhrFields: {withCredentials: true},
  error: function(xhr, status, error) {
    $('.alert').removeClass('hidden');
    $('.alert').html('Status: ' + status + ', error: ' + error);
  }
});

var findTr = function(event) {
  var target = event.srcElement || event.target;
  var $target = $(target);
  var $tr = $target.parents('tr');
  return $tr;
};

var remove = function(event) {
  var $tr = findTr(event);
  var id = $tr.data('id');
  $.ajax({
    url: '/api/articles/' + id,
    type: 'DELETE',
    success: function(data, status, xhr) {
      $('.alert').addClass('hidden');
      $tr.remove();
    }
  })
};

var update = function(event) {
  var $tr = findTr(event);
  $tr.find('button').attr('disabled', 'disabled');
  var data = {
    published: $tr.hasClass('unpublished')
  };
  var id = $tr.attr('data-id');
  $.ajax({
    url: '/api/articles/' + id,
    type: 'PUT',
    contentType: 'application/json',
    data: JSON.stringify({article: data}),
    success: function(dataResponse, status, xhr) {
      $tr.find('button').removeAttr('disabled');
      $('.alert').addClass('hidden');
      if (data.published) {
        $tr.removeClass('unpublished').find('.glyphicon-play').removeClass('glyphicon-play').
addClass('glyphicon-pause');
      } else {
```

```
        $tr.addClass('unpublished').find('.glyphicon-pause').removeClass('glyphicon-pause').
addClass('glyphicon-play');
      }
    }
  })
};

$(document).ready(function(){
  var $element = $('.admin tbody');
  $element.on('click', 'button.remove', remove);
  $element.on('click', 'button', update);
})
```

Running the App

To run the app, simply execute $ node app, but if you want to seed and test it, execute $ make db and $ make test, respectively (Figure 5-5). Don't forget that $ mongod service must be running on the localhost and port 27017. The expected result is that all tests now pass (hurray!), and if users visit http://localhost:3000, they can see posts and even create new ones on the admin page (http://localhost:3000/admin) as shown in Figure 5-6.

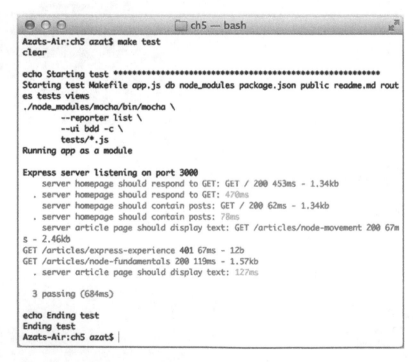

Figure 5-5. *The results of running Mocha tests*

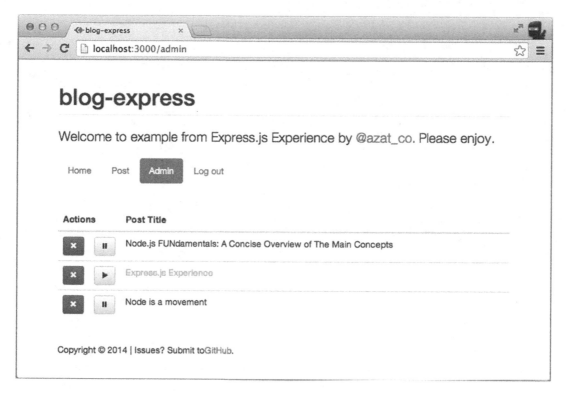

Figure 5-6. *The admin page with seed data*

Of course, in real life, nobody leaves the admin page open to the public. Therefore, in Chapter 6 we'll implement the session-based authorization, and then the password and OAuth authentications.

Summary

In this chapter we learned how to install MongoDB, and use its console and native Node.js driver, for which we wrote a small script and refactored it to see Mongoskin in action. Last, we wrote tests, seeded scripts, and implemented the persistence layer for Blog. In the next chapter, we'll implement authorization and authentication.

CHAPTER 6

■ ■ ■

Using Sessions and OAuth to Authorize and Authenticate Users in Node.js Apps

Security is an important aspect of any real-world web application. This is especially true nowadays, because our apps don't function in silos anymore. We, as developers, can and should leverage numerous third-party services (e.g., Twitter, GitHub) or become service providers ourselves (e.g., provide a public API).

We can makes our apps and communications secure with the usage of various approaches, such as token-based authentication and/or OAuth (http://oauth.net). Therefore, in this practical guide, I dedicate the whole chapter to matters of authorization, authentication, OAuth, and best practices. We'll look at the following topics:

- Authorization with Express.js middleware

- Token-based authentication

- Session-based authentication

- Project: adding e-mail and password login to Blog

- Node.js OAuth

- Project: Adding Twitter OAuth 1.0 sign-in to Blog with Everyauth (https://github.com/bnoguchi/everyauth)

Authorization with Express.js Middleware

Authorization in web apps usually means restricting certain functions to privileged clients. These functions can either be methods, pages, or REST API end points.

Express.js middleware allows us to apply certain rules seamlessly to all routes, groups of routes (namespacing), or individual routes.

- *All routes*: app.get('*', auth)

- *Groups of routes*: app.get('/api/*', auth)

- *Individual routes*: app.get('/admin/users', auth)

For example, if we want to protect all /api/ endpoints, we execute the following:

```
app.all('/api/*', auth);
app.get('/api/users', users.list);
app.post('/api/users', users.create);
...
```

Another way of doing the same thing is to execute:

```
app.get('/api/users', auth, users.list);
app.post('/api/users', auth, users.create);
...
```

In the previous examples, auth() is a function with three parameters: req, res, and next—for example,

```
var auth = function(req, res, next) {
  //authorize user
  //if auth failed, then exit is next(new Error('Not authorized'));
  //or res.send(401);
   return next();
}
```

The next() part is important, because this is how Express.js proceeds to execute subsequent request handlers and routes (if there's a match in a URL pattern).

Token-Based Authentication

For applications to know which privileges a specific client has (e.g., admin), we must add an authentication step. In the previous example, this step goes inside the auth() function.

The most common authentication is a cookie & session–based authentication, and the next section deals with this topic. However, in some cases, more REST-fulness is required, or cookies/sessions are not supported well (e.g., mobile). In this case, it's beneficial to authenticate each request with a token (probably using the OAuth2.0 (http://tools.ietf.org/html/rfc6749) scheme). The token can be passed in a query string or in HTTP request headers. Alternatively, we can send some other authentication combination of information, such as e-mail/username and password, or API key, or API password instead of a token.

So, in our example of token-based authentication, each request can submit a token in a query string (accessed via req.query.token). And, if we have the correct value stored somewhere in our app (database, or in this example just a constant SECRET_TOKEN), we can check the incoming token against it. If the token matches our records, we call next() to proceed with the request executions, if not then we call next(error) which triggers Express.js error handlers execution (see the note below):

```
var auth = function(req, res, next) {
  if (req.query.token && token === SECRET_TOKEN) {
  // Client is fine, proceed to the next route
    return next();
  } else {
    return  next(new Error('Not authorized'));
    // or res.send(401);
  }
};
```

In a more realistic example, we use API keys and secrets to generate HMAC-SHA1 (hash-based message authentication code-secure hash algorithm strings, then compare them with the value in req.query.token.

■ **Note**   Calling next() with an error argument is analogous to throwing in the towel (i.e., to give up). The Express.js app enters the error mode and proceeds to the error handlers.

We just covered token-based authentication, which is often used in REST APIs. However, the user-facing web apps (i.e., browser-enabled users & consumers) come with cookies. We can use cookies to store and send session IDs with each request. Cookies are similar to tokens, but require less work for us, the developers!. This approach is the cornerstone of session-based authentication. The session-based method is the recommended way for basic web apps, because browsers already know what to do with session headers. In addition, in most platforms and frameworks, the session mechanism is built into the core. So, let's jump straight into session-based authentication with Node.js.

Session-Based Authentication

Session-based authentication is done via the session object in the request object req. A web session in general is a secure way to store information about a client so that subsequent requests from that same client can be identified.

In the Express.js 4.x (versions 4.1.2 and 4.2.0 as of this writing), we'll need to import (require()) these modules manually, because Express.js 4.x separated these and some other middleware out of its package. For example, to include and use cookie-parser and express-session:

```
var cookieParser = require('cookie-parser');
var session = require('express-session');
...
app.use(cookieParser());
app.use(session());
```

Needless to say, cookie-parser and express-session must be installed via NPM into the project's node_modules folder.

To use the session in a typical Express.js 3.x app, two pieces of middleware need to be added to the configuration:

1. express.cookieParser(): allows for parsing of the client/request cookies.

2. express.session(): exposes the res.session object in each request handler, and stores data in the app memory or some other persistent store like MongoDB or Redis.

In later examples don't mention Express.js version, assume that it works for both 3.x and 4.x.

The rest is trivial; we can store any data in req.session and it appears automagically on each request from the same client (assuming their browser supports cookies). Hence, the authentication consists of a route that stores some flag (true/false) in the session and of an authorization function in which we check for that flag (if true, then proceed; otherwise, exit). For example,

```
app.post('/login', function(req, res, next) {
  // This function checks for credentials
  // passed in the request's payload
  if (checkForCredentials(req)) {
    req.session.auth = true;
    res.redirect('/dashboard');  // Private resource
  } else {
```

```
    res.send(401); // Not authorized
  }
});
```

■ **Warning**   Avoid storing any sensitive information in cookies. The best practice is not to store any info in cookies manually—except session ID, which Express.js middleware stores for us automatically—because cookies are not secure. Also, cookies have a size limitation (depending on the browser, with Internet Explore being the stringiest) that is very easy to reach.

By default, Express.js uses in-memory session storage. This means that every time an app is restarted or crashes, the sessions are wiped out. To make sessions persistent and available across multiple servers, we can use Redis or MongoDB as session restore.

Project: Adding E-mail and Password Login to Blog

To enable session-based authentication in Blog, we need to do the following:

1. Import and add the session middleware to the configuration part of app.js.

2. Implement the authorization middleware authorize with a session-based authorization so we can re-use the same code for many routes.

3. Add the middleware from #2 (step above) to protected pages and routes in app.js routes, e.g., app.get('/api/, authorize, api.index).

4. Implement an authentication route POST /login, and a logout route, GET /logout in user.js.

Session Middleware

Let's add the automatic cookie parsing and support for session middleware in these two lines by putting them in the middle of configurations in app.js:

```
// Other middleware
app.use(cookieParser('3CCC4ACD-6ED1-4844-9217-82131BDCB239'));
app.use(session({secret: '2C44774A-D649-4D44-9535-46E296EF984F'}));
// Routes
```

For Express.js 3.x:

```
// Other middleware
app.use(express.cookieParser('3CCC4ACD-6ED1-4844-9217-82131BDCB239'));
app.use(express.session({secret: '2C44774A-D649-4D44-9535-46E296EF984F'}));
// Routes
```

■ **Warning**   You should replace randomly generated values with your own ones.

---

session() must be preceded by cookieParser() because session depend on cookies to work properly. For more information about these and other Express.js/Connect middleware, refer to Pro Express.js 4 [Apress, 2014].

cookie-session (express.cookieSession() in Express.js 3.x) can be used in some cases, such as var cookieSession = require('cookie-session'); app.use(cookieSession({secret: process.env.SESSION_SECRET}));. The difference is that express-session uses secure in-memory or Redis storage—and cookies store only for the session ID, i.e., sid—whereas cookie-session uses browser cookies to store session information. In other words, the entire session is serialized into cookie-based storage, not just the session key. This approach should be avoided because of cookie size limitations and security concerns.

It's useful to pass information to the templates regardless of whether the request is authenticated. We can do so by adding middleware that checks the req.session.admin value for truthyness and adds an appropriate property to res.locals:

```
app.use(function(req, res, next) {
  if (req.session && req.session.admin)
    res.locals.admin = true;
  next();
});
```

Authorization in Blog

Authorization is also done via middleware, but we won't set it up right away with app.use like we did in the snippet for res.locals. Instead, we define a function that checks for req.session.admin to be true, and proceeds if it is. Otherwise, the 401 Not Authorized error is thrown and the response is ended.

```
// Authorization
var authorize = function(req, res, next) {
  if (req.session && req.session.admin)
    return next();
  else
    return res.send(401);
};
```

Now we can add this middleware to certain protected end points:

```
...
app.get('/admin', authorize, routes.article.admin);
app.get('/post', authorize, routes.article.post);
app.post('/post', authorize, routes.article.postArticle);
```

We add the authorize middleware to API routes as well:

```
app.all('/api', authorize);
app.get('/api/articles', routes.article.list)
app.post('/api/articles', routes.article.add);
app.put('/api/articles/:id', routes.article.edit);
app.del('/api/articles/:id', routes.article.del);
```

The app.all('/api', authorize); is a more compact alternative to adding authorize to all /api/... routes.

The full source code of the app.js file after adding session support and authorization middleware is as follows (under the ch6/password folder):

```
var express = require('express'),
  routes = require('./routes'),
  http = require('http'),
  path = require('path'),
  mongoskin = require('mongoskin'),
  dbUrl = process.env.MONGOHQ_URL ||
    'mongodb://@localhost:27017/blog',
  db = mongoskin.db(dbUrl, {safe: true}),
  collections = {
    articles: db.collection('articles'),
    users: db.collection('users')
  };

// Express.js Middleware
var session = require('express-session'),
  logger = require('morgan'),
  errorHandler = require('errorhandler'),
  cookieParser = require('cookie-parser'),
  bodyParser = require('body-parser'),
  methodOverride = require('method-override');

var app = express();
app.locals.appTitle = 'blog-express';

// Expose collections to request handlers
app.use(function(req, res, next) {
  if (!collections.articles || ! collections.users)
    return next(new Error('No collections.'));
  req.collections = collections;
  return next();
});

// Express.js configurations
app.set('port', process.env.PORT || 3000);
app.set('views', path.join(__dirname, 'views'));
app.set('view engine', 'jade');

// Express.js middleware configuration
app.use(logger('dev'));
app.use(bodyParser.json());
app.use(bodyParser.urlencoded());
app.use(cookieParser('3CCC4ACD-6ED1-4844-9217-82131BDCB239'));
app.use(session({secret: '2C44774A-D649-4D44-9535-46E296EF984F'}));
app.use(methodOverride());
app.use(require('stylus').middleware(__dirname + '/public'));
app.use(express.static(path.join(__dirname, 'public')));
```

```javascript
// Authentication middleware
app.use(function(req, res, next) {
  if (req.session && req.session.admin)
    res.locals.admin = true;
  next();
});

// Authorization Middleware
var authorize = function(req, res, next) {
  if (req.session && req.session.admin)
    return next();
  else
    return res.send(401);
};

if ('development' == app.get('env')) {
  app.use(errorHandler());
}

// Pages & routes
app.get('/', routes.index);
app.get('/login', routes.user.login);
app.post('/login', routes.user.authenticate);
app.get('/logout', routes.user.logout);
app.get('/admin', authorize, routes.article.admin);
app.get('/post', authorize, routes.article.post);
app.post('/post', authorize, routes.article.postArticle);
app.get('/articles/:slug', routes.article.show);

// REST API routes
app.all('/api', authorize);
app.get('/api/articles', routes.article.list);
app.post('/api/articles', routes.article.add);
app.put('/api/articles/:id', routes.article.edit);
app.del('/api/articles/:id', routes.article.del);

app.all('*', function(req, res) {
  res.send(404);
})

var server = http.createServer(app);
var boot = function () {
  server.listen(app.get('port'), function(){
    console.info('Express server listening on port ' +
      app.get('port'));
  });
}
var shutdown = function() {
  server.close();
}
if (require.main === module) {
  boot();
}
```

```
else {
  console.info('Running app as a module')
  exports.boot = boot;
  exports.shutdown = shutdown;
  exports.port = app.get('port');
}
```

Authentication in Blog

The last step in session-based authorization is to allow users and clients to turn the `req.session.admin` switch on and off. We do this by having a login form and processing the POST request from that form.

For authenticating users as admins we set the appropriate flag (`admin=true`), in the `routes.user.authenticate` in the `user.js` file. This is done in the POST `/login` route which we defined in the app.js— a line that has this statement: `app.post('/login', routes.user.authenticate);`.

In `user.js`, expose the method to the importer, i.e., the file that imports this `user.js` module:

```
exports.authenticate = function(req, res, next) {
```

The form on the login page submits data to this route. In general, a sanity check for the input values is always a good idea. If values are falsy (including empty values), we'll render the login page again with the message `error`. The `return` keyword ensures the rest of the code in this method isn't executed. If the values are non-empty (or otherwise truthy), then the request handler will not terminate yet and proceed to the next statements:

```
if (!req.body.email || !req.body.password)
    return res.render('login',{
       error: 'Please enter your email and password.'
    });
```

Thanks to the database middleware in app.js, we can access database collections in `req.collections`. In our app's architecture, e-mail is a unique identifier (there are no two accounts with the same e-mail), so we use the `findOne` function to find a match of the e-mail and password combination (logical AND):

```
req.collections.users.findOne({
  email: req.body.email,
  password: req.body.password
}, function(error, user){
  ...
```

■ **Warning** In virtually all cases, we don't want to store passwords as a plain text; we should store salts and password hashes instead. In this way, if the database gets compromised, passwords are not seen. For salting, use the core Node.js module crypto.

`findOne` returns an error object and the `user` result object. However, we should still do error processing manually:

```
if (error) return next(error);
if (!user) return res.render('login', {error: 'Incorrect email&password combination.'});
```

If the program has made it thus far (avoided a lot of `return` statements previously), we can authenticate the user as administrator thus enabling the authentication and the `auth` (authorization) method:

```
      req.session.user = user;
      req.session.admin = user.admin;
      res.redirect('/admin');
  })
};
```

The logout route is trivial. We clear the session by calling `destroy()` on `req.session`:

```
exports.logout = function(req, res, next) {
  req.session.destroy();
  res.redirect('/');
};
```

The full source code of `user.js` for your reference is as follows:

```
exports.list = function(req, res){
  res.send('respond with a resource');
};
exports.login = function(req, res, next) {
  res.render('login');
};
exports.logout = function(req, res, next) {
  req.session.destroy();
  res.redirect('/');
};
exports.authenticate = function(req, res, next) {
  if (!req.body.email || !req.body.password)
    return res.render('login', {
      error: 'Please enter your email and password.'
    });
  req.collections.users.findOne({
    email: req.body.email,
    password: req.body.password
  }, function(error, user){
    if (error) return next(error);
    if (!user) return res.render('login', {
      error: 'Incorrect email&password combination.'
    });
    req.session.user = user;
    req.session.admin = user.admin;
    res.redirect('/admin');
  })
};
```

Running the App

Now everything should be set up properly to run Blog. Contrary to the example in Chapter 5, we see protected pages only when we're logged in. These protected pages enable us to create new posts, and to publish and unpublish them. But as soon as we click "Logout" in the menu, we no longer can access the administrator page.

The executable code is under the ch6/password folder of the practicalnode repository:
https://github.com/azat-co/practicalnode.

Node.js OAuth

OAuth—which can be located on NPM (https://www.npmjs.org/package/oauth) and GitHub (https://github.com/ciaranj/node-oauth)—is the powerhouse of OAuth 1.0/2.0 schemes for Node.js. It's a module that generates signatures, encryptions, and HTTP headers, and makes requests. We still need to initiate the OAuth dances (i.e., requests back and forth between consumer, provider and our system), write the callback routes, and store information in sessions or databases. Refer to the service provider's (e.g., Facebook, Twitter, Google) documentation for end points, methods, and parameter names.

It is recommended that node-auth be used when complex integration is needed or when only certain pieces of OAuth are needed (e.g., header signatures are generated by node-auth, but the request is made by the superagent library).

To add OAuth version 0.9.11 (the latest as of this writing) to your project, simply run:

```
$ npm install oauth@0.9.11
```

Twitter OAuth 2.0 Example with Node.js OAuth

OAuth 2.0 is less complicated and, some might argue, less secure than OAuth 1.0. The reasons for this are numerous and better understood when written by Eran Hammer, the person who participated in OAuth2.0 creation: OAuth 2.0 and the Road to Hell.

In essence, OAuth 2.0 is similar to the token-based authorization we examined earlier, for which we have a single token, called a *bearer*, that we pass along with each request. To get that token, all we need to do is exchange our app's token and secret for the bearer.

Usually, this bearer can be stored for a longer time than OAuth 1.x tokens (depends on the rules set by a specific service-provider), and can be used as a single key/password to open protected resources. This bearer acts as our token in the token-based auth.

Here's an ordinary example from Node.js OAuth docs (https://github.com/ciaranj/node-oauth#oauth20). First, we create an oauth2 object that has a Twitter consumer key and secret (replace the values with yours):

```
var OAuth = require('OAuth');
var OAuth2 = OAuth.OAuth2;
var twitterConsumerKey = 'your key';
var twitterConsumerSecret = 'your secret';
var oauth2 = new OAuth2(server.config.keys.twitter.consumerKey,
  twitterConsumerSecret,
  'https://api.twitter.com/',
  null,
  'oauth2/token',
  null
);
```

Then, we request access to the token/bearer from the service provider:

```
oauth2.getOAuthAccessToken(
  '',
  {'grant_type': 'client_credentials'},
  function (e, access_token, refresh_token, results){
```

```
    console.log('bearer: ', access_token);
    // Store bearer
    // Make OAuth2 requests using this bearer to protected endpoints
  }
);
```

Now we can store the bearer for future use and make requests to protected end points with it.

■ **Note** Twitter uses OAuth2.0 for the so called app-only authorizations which are requests to protected resources. Those requests are made on behalf of the applications only (not on behalf of users by the apps). Twitter uses OAuth 1.0 for normal auths, i.e., requests made on behalf of the users by the app). Not all endpoints are available via app-only auth, and quotas/limitations are different. Please refer to the official documentation at `http://dev.twitter.com`.

Everyauth

The Everyauth module allows for multiple OAuth strategies to be implemented and added to any Express.js app in just a few lines of code. Everyauth comes with strategies for most of the service providers, so there's no need to search and implement service provider-specific end points, parameters names, and so forth. Also, Everyauth stores user objects in a session, and database storage can be enabled in a findOrCreate callback using a promise pattern.

■ **Tip** Everyauth has an e-mail and password strategy that can be used instead of the custom-built auth. More information about it can be found in Everyauth documentation at the GitHub repository (`https://github.com/bnoguchi/everyauth#password-authentication`).

Everyauth submodules that enable service provider-specific authorization strategies (as of this writing, take from its GitHub repo (`https://github.com/bnoguchi/everyauth/blob/master/README.md`)) are as follows:

- Password
- Facebook
- Twitter
- Google
- Google Hybrid
- LinkedIn
- Dropbox
- Tumblr
- Evernote
- GitHub
- Instagram
- Foursquare
- Yahoo!

- Justin.tv

- Vimeo

- 37signals (Basecamp, Highrise, Backpack, Campfire)

- Readability

- AngelList

- Dwolla

- OpenStreetMap

- VKontakte (Russian Social Network)

- Mail.ru (Russian Social Network)

- Skyrock

- Gowalla

- TripIt

- 500px

- SoundCloud

- mixi

- Mailchimp

- Mendeley

- Stripe

- Datahero

- Salesforce

- Box.net

- OpenId

- LDAP (experimental; not production tested)

- Windows Azure Access Control Service

Project: Adding Twitter OAuth 1.0 Sign-in to Blog with Everyauth

A typical OAuth 1.0 flow consists of these three steps (simplified):

1. Users go to a page/route to initiate the OAuth dance. There, our app requests a token via GET/POST requests using the signed app's consumer key and secret. For example, /auth/ twitter is added automatically by Everyauth.

2. The app uses the token extracted in step 1 and redirects users to the service-provider (Twitter) and waits for the callback.

3. The service provider redirects users back to the app which catches the redirect in the callback route (e.g., /auth/twitter/callback). Then, the app extracts the access token, the access token secret, and the user information from the Twitter incoming request body / payload.

However, because we're using Everyauth, we don't need to implement requests for the initiate and the callback routes!

Let's add a Sign in with Twitter button to our project. We need the button itself (image or a link), app key, and secret (obtainable at dev.twitter.com), and then we must augment our authorization route to allow for specific Twitter handlers to be administrated on Blog.

Adding a Sign-in with a Twitter Link

By default, Everyauth uses the /auth/:service_provider_name pattern to initiate the three-legged OAuth 1.0 strategy. This, of course, can be customized, but to keep it short and simple (KISS), we can just add this link to menu.jade:

```
li(class=(menu === 'login') ? 'active' : '')
  a(href='/auth/twitter') Sign in with Twitter
```

The whole menu.jade looks like this:

```
.menu
  ul.nav.nav-pills
    li(class=(menu === 'index') ? 'active' : '')
      a(href='/') Home
    if (admin)
      li(class=(menu === 'post') ? 'active' : '')
        a(href="/post") Post
      li(class=(menu === 'admin') ? 'active' : '')
        a(href="/admin") Admin
      li
        a(href="/logout") Log out
    else
      li(class=(menu === 'login')? 'active' : '')
        a(href='/login') Log in
      li
        a(href='/auth/twitter') Sign in with Twitter
```

Configuring the Everyauth Twitter Strategy

To add the Everyauth module (everyauth) to Blog, type the following in the terminal:

```
$ npm install everyauth@0.4.5 --save
```

The configuration of the Everyauth Twitter strategy is implemented in app.js, but in larger apps it's a good idea to abstract these types of strategies into separate files. The most important thing to remember is that Everyauth middleware needs to precede the app.route call.

To procure the Twitter app consumer key and secret, we harness environmental variables via process.env:

```
var TWITTER_CONSUMER_KEY = process.env.TWITTER_CONSUMER_KEY
var TWITTER_CONSUMER_SECRET = process.env.TWITTER_CONSUMER_SECRET
```

To pass these variables we can use Makefile. In the Makefile, add these lines, substituting ABC and XYZ with your values:

```
start:
    TWITTER_CONSUMER_KEY=ABCABC \
    TWITTER_CONSUMER_SECRET=XYZXYZXYZ \
    node app
```

Also, add the start command to .PHONY:

```
.PHONY: test db start
```

As another option, we can create a Bash file start.sh:

```
TWITTER_CONSUMER_KEY=ABCABC \
TWITTER_CONSUMER_SECRET=XYZXYZXYZ \
node app
```

Now we go back to the app.js file, in which we need to import the Everyauth module:

```
everyauth = require('everyauth');
```

It's a good practice to run the module in debug mode the first few times:

```
everyauth.debug = true;
```

Each submodule is enabled using chained commands and promises. To define the previously mentioned key and secret, execute the following:

```
everyauth.twitter
  .consumerKey(TWITTER_CONSUMER_KEY)
  .consumerSecret(TWITTER_CONSUMER_SECRET)
```

Then, to tell the module what to do when Twitter sends back the authorized user object twitterUserMetadata, type

```
.findOrCreateUser( function (session, accessToken, accessTokenSecret, twitterUserMetadata) {
```

We can return the user object right away, but to emulate async writing to a database, let's create a promise

```
var promise = this.Promise();
```

and use the process.nextTick call, which is analogous to setTimeout(callback, 0);, and acts in an asynchronous manner. In a real-world app, you might want to find or save the data to the database:

```
process.nextTick(function(){
```

Change Azat's username to yours:

```
if (twitterUserMetadata.screen_name === 'azat_co') {
```

Store the user object in the in-memory session, just like we did in the /login route:

```
session.user = twitterUserMetadata;
```

The most important, set admin flag to true:

```
session.admin = true;
}
```

Everyauth expects us to fulfill the promise when it's ready:

```
        promise.fulfill(twitterUserMetadata);
    })
    return promise;
    // return twitterUserMetadata
  })
```

After all the steps are done, instruct Everyauth where to redirect the user:

```
  .redirectPath('/admin');
```

Everyauth is so smart that it automatically adds a /logout route, this means our route (app.get('/logout', routes.user.logout);) won't be used. So we need to add some extra logic to the default Everyauth strategy. Otherwise, the session will always keep admin = true. In the handleLogout step, we clear our session by calling the exact same method from user.js:

```
everyauth.everymodule.handleLogout(routes.user.logout);
```

The next line tells Everyauth how to find a user object based on the user argument, but because we stored the whole user object in the session and we don't store user info in findOrCreate, we can just return back the same object:

```
everyauth.everymodule.findUserById( function (user, callback) {
  callback(user);
});
```

Last but not least, the line that follows, enable Everyauth routes and it must go after cookie and session middleware but must come before normal routes (e.g., app.get(), app.post()):

```
app.use(everyauth.middleware());
```

The full source code of the app.js file after adding the Everyauth Twitter OAuth1.0 strategy is as follows:

```
var TWITTER_CONSUMER_KEY = process.env.TWITTER_CONSUMER_KEY;
var TWITTER_CONSUMER_SECRET = process.env.TWITTER_CONSUMER_SECRET;

var express = require('express'),
  routes = require('./routes'),
  http = require('http'),
  path = require('path'),
  mongoskin = require('mongoskin'),
```

```
  dbUrl = process.env.MONGOHQ_URL ||
    'mongodb://@localhost:27017/blog',
  db = mongoskin.db(dbUrl, {safe: true}),
  collections = {
    articles: db.collection('articles'),
    users: db.collection('users')
  }
  everyauth = require('everyauth');

// Express.js Middleware
var session = require('express-session'),
  logger = require('morgan'),
  errorHandler = require('errorhandler'),
  cookieParser = require('cookie-parser'),
  bodyParser = require('body-parser'),
  methodOverride = require('method-override');

everyauth.debug = true;
everyauth.twitter
  .consumerKey(TWITTER_CONSUMER_KEY)
  .consumerSecret(TWITTER_CONSUMER_SECRET)
  .findOrCreateUser(function(
    session,
    accessToken,
    accessTokenSecret,
    twitterUserMetadata) {
      var promise = this.Promise();
      process.nextTick(function(){
        if (twitterUserMetadata.screen_name === 'azat_co') {
          session.user = twitterUserMetadata;
          session.admin = true;
        }
        promise.fulfill(twitterUserMetadata);
      })
      return promise;
    }
  )
  .redirectPath('/admin');

everyauth.everymodule.handleLogout(routes.user.logout);
everyauth.everymodule.findUserById(function (user, callback) {
  callback(user);
});

var app = express();
app.locals.appTitle = 'blog-express';

app.use(function(req, res, next) {
  if (!collections.articles || ! collections.users)
      return next(new Error('No collections.'));
  req.collections = collections;
  return next();
});
```

```javascript
// Express.js configurations
app.set('port', process.env.PORT || 3000);
app.set('views', path.join(__dirname, 'views'));
app.set('view engine', 'jade');

// Express.js middleware configuration
app.use(logger('dev'));
app.use(bodyParser.json());
app.use(bodyParser.urlencoded());
app.use(cookieParser('3CCC4ACD-6ED1-4844-9217-82131BDCB239'));
app.use(session({secret: '2C44774A-D649-4D44-9535-46E296EF984F'}));
app.use(everyauth.middleware());
app.use(methodOverride());
app.use(require('stylus').middleware(__dirname + '/public'));
app.use(express.static(path.join(__dirname, 'public')));

// Authentication middleware
app.use(function(req, res, next) {
  if (req.session && req.session.admin)
    res.locals.admin = true;
  next();
});

// Authorization
var authorize = function(req, res, next) {
  if (req.session && req.session.admin)
    return next();
  else
    return res.send(401);
};

// Development only
if ('development' == app.get('env')) {
  app.use(errorHandler());
}

// Pages and routes
app.get('/', routes.index);
app.get('/login', routes.user.login);
app.post('/login', routes.user.authenticate);
app.get('/logout', routes.user.logout);
app.get('/admin', authorize, routes.article.admin);
app.get('/post', authorize, routes.article.post);
app.post('/post', authorize, routes.article.postArticle);
app.get('/articles/:slug', routes.article.show);

// REST API routes
app.all('/api', authorize);
app.get('/api/articles', routes.article.list);
app.post('/api/articles', routes.article.add);
app.put('/api/articles/:id', routes.article.edit);
app.del('/api/articles/:id', routes.article.del);
```

145

```
app.all('*', function(req, res) {
  res.send(404);
})

var server = http.createServer(app);
var boot = function () {
  server.listen(app.get('port'), function(){
    console.info('Express server listening on port ' +
      app.get('port'));
    }
  );
}
var shutdown = function() {
  server.close();
}
if (require.main === module) {
  boot();
} else {
  console.info('Running app as a module');
  exports.boot = boot;
  exports.shutdown = shutdown;
  exports.port = app.get('port');
}
```

To run the app, execute $ make start, and **don't forget to replace** the Twitter username, consumer key, and secret with yours. Then when you click on "Sign in with Twitter", you'll be redirected to Twitter to authorize this application. Then you'll be redirected back to the localhost app and should see the admin page menu. We have been authorized by a third-party service provider! Also, the user information is available to your app so it can be stored in the database for future usage. If you already gave permissions, the redirect to and from Twitter might happen very fast. The terminal output is shown in Figure 6-1 shows each step of Everyauth process such as getting tokens and sending responses. Each step can be customized to your app's needs.

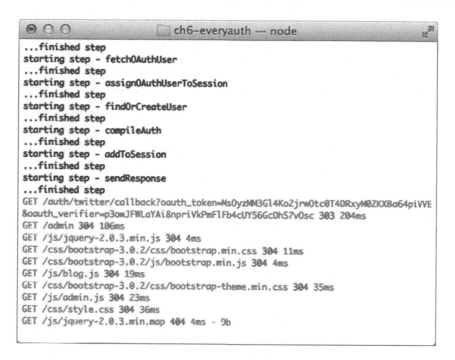

Figure 6-1. Everyauth Twitter strategy with debug mode in action

Summary

In this chapter, we learned how to implement a standard e-mail and password authentication, and used Express.
js middleware to protect sensitive pages and end points in Blog. Then, we covered OAuth 1.0 and OAuth 2.0 with
Everyauth and OAuth modules, respectively.

Now we have a few security options for Blog. In the next chapter we'll explore Mongoose (http://mongoosejs.com)
object-relational mapping (ORM (http://en.wikipedia.org/wiki/Object-relational_mapping)) Node.js library
for MongoDB. This library is a good choice for complex systems with a lot of interdependent business logic between
entities, because it completely abstracts the database and provides developers with tools to operate with data only
via Mongoose objects. The chapter will touch on the main Mongoose classes and methods, explain some of the more
advanced concepts, and re-factor persistence in Blog.

CHAPTER 7

■ ■ ■

Boosting Your Node.js Data with the Mongoose ORM Library

Mongoose is a fully developed object relational mapping (ORM) library for Node.js and MongoDB. The advantages of using ORM are many and go far beyond code organization or the ease of development. Typical ORM is a crucial piece of modern software engineering.

Mongoose abstracts everything from the database, and the application code interacts only with objects and their methods. ORM also allows specifying relationships between different types of objects and putting business logic (related to those objects) in the classes.

In addition, Mongoose has built-in validation and type casting that can be extended and customized according to needs. When used together with Express.js, Mongoose makes the stack truly adherent to the MVC concept.

Mongoose uses a similar interface to those of Mongo shell, native MongoDB driver, and Mongoskin. For this reason, main functions such as find, update, insert, save, remove, and so on, look and act the same, which helps us to get started with Mongoose faster. In this chapter we look at the following:

- Mongoose installation

- Connection establishment in a standalone Mongoose script

- Mongoose schemas

- Hooks for keeping code organized

- Custom static and instance methods

- Mongoose models

- Relationships and joins with population

- Nested documents

- Virtual fields

- Schema type behavior amendment

- Express.js + Mongoose = true MVC

The source code for this chapter is in the ch7/blog-express directory of the practical node GitHub repository (https://github.com/azat-co/practicalnode).

Mongoose Installation

First, we should install Mongoose with NPM. Among many variations, this is one of the ways we can install Mongoose 3.8.4 into an empty folder:

```
$ mkdir node_modules
$ npm install mongoose@3.8.4
```

Connection Establishment in a Standalone Mongoose Script

Mongoose can be used as a standalone MongoDB library. To illustrate this, here's a banal script that establishes a connection, creates a Mongoose model definition, instantiates the practicalNodeBook object, and then saves it to the database.

To have access to the library, we need to include the mongoose module in our program:

```
var mongoose = require('mongoose');
```

Unlike the Node.js native MongoDB driver, which requires us to write a few lines of code, Mongoose can connect to the database server in one line. Mongoose requests are buffered, so we don't have to wait for the established connection (vs. native driver, which usually requires a callback). To do this, just call mongoose.connect(uri(s), [options], [callback]). The uniform resource identifier (URI) or connection string is the only required parameter, and it follows a standard format of type://username:password@host:port/database_name. In our simple example, the host is localhost, the port is 27017 (default), and the database name is test:

```
mongoose.connect('mongodb://localhost/test');
```

For situations that are more advanced, options and callbacks can be passed to connect. The options object supports all properties of the native MongoDB driver (http://mongodb.github.io/node-mongodb-native/driver-articles/mongoclient.html#mongoclient-connect-options).

■ **Note** It's a common practice in Node.js apps (and Mongoose) to open a database connection once, when the program starts, and then to keep it open until termination. This applies to web apps and servers as well.

This is easy so far, right? The next step is an important distinction that Mongoose introduces compared with Mongoskin and other lightweight MongoDB libraries. The step creates a model with the model() function by passing a string and a schema (more on schemas later). The model is usually stored in a capitalized literal:

```
var Book = mongoose.model('Book', { name: String });
```

Now the configuration phase is over and we can create a document that represents a particular instance of the model Book:

```
var practicalNodeBook = new Book({ name: 'Practical Node.js' });
```

Mongoose documents come with very convenient built-in methods (http://mongoosejs.com/docs/api.html#document-js) such as validate, isNew, update, and so on. Just keep in mind that these methods apply to this particular document, not the entire collection or model. The difference between documents and models is that a document is an instance of a model; a model is something abstract. It's like your real MongoDB collection, but it is supported by a schema and is presented as a Node.js class with extra methods and attributes. Collections in Mongoose closely resemble collections in Mongoskin or native driver. Strictly speaking, models, collections, and documents are different Mongoose classes.

Usually we don't use Mongoose collections directly, and we manipulate data via models only. Some of the main model methods look strikingly familiar to the ones from Mongoskin or native MongoDB driver, such as find, insert(), save, and so forth.

To finish our small script and make it write a document to the database, let's use one of the document methods—document.save():

```
practicalNodeBook.save(function (err, results) {
  if (err) {
    console.error(e);
    process.exit(1);
  } else {
    console.log('Saved: ', results);
    process.exit(0);
  }
});
```

Here is the full source code for the mongoose.js file:

```
var mongoose = require('mongoose');
mongoose.connect('mongodb://localhost/test');

var Book = mongoose.model('Book', { name: String });

var practicalNodeBook = new Book({ name: 'Practical Node.js' });
practicalNodeBook.save(function (err, results) {
  if (err) {
    console.error(e);
    process.exit(1);
  } else {
    console.log('Saved: ', results);
    process.exit(0);
  }
});
```

To run this snippet, execute the $ node mongoose.js command (MongoDB server must be running in parallel). The results of the script should output the newly created object, as seen in Figure 7-1.

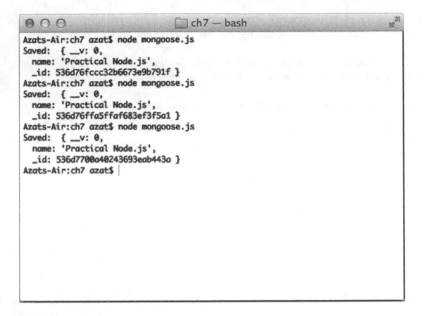

```
Azats-Air:ch7 azat$ node mongoose.js
Saved:  { __v: 0,
  name: 'Practical Node.js',
  _id: 536d76fccc32b6673e9b791f }
Azats-Air:ch7 azat$ node mongoose.js
Saved:  { __v: 0,
  name: 'Practical Node.js',
  _id: 536d76ffa5ffaf683ef3f5a1 }
Azats-Air:ch7 azat$ node mongoose.js
Saved:  { __v: 0,
  name: 'Practical Node.js',
  _id: 536d7700a40243693eab443a }
Azats-Air:ch7 azat$ |
```

Figure 7-1. Running a standalone Mongoose script that creates objects

Mongoose Schemas

Schema is a JSON-ish class that has information about properties/field types of a document. It also can store information about validation and default values, and whether a particular property is required. Schemas can contain business logic and other important information. In other words, schemas serve as blueprints for documents. They are needed for model creation (i.e., schemas are compiled into models). So, before we can use models properly, we need to define their schemas, e.g., the book schema with the name property of string type:

```
var bookSchema = mongoose.Schema({
    name: String
})
```

■ **Warning**   Mongoose ignores those properties that aren't defined in the model's schema.

Mongoose Schema supports these data types:

- String: a standard JavaScript/Node.js string (a sequence of characters) type
- Number: a standard JavaScript/Node number type up to 253 (64-bit); larger numbers with mongoose-long (https://www.npmjs.org/package/mongoose-long) (Git (https://github.com/aheckmann/mongoose-long))
- Boolean: a standard JavaScript/Node Boolean type—true or false
- Buffer: a Node.js binary type (images, PDFs, archives, and so on)
- Date: an ISODate formatted date type, such as 2014-12-31T12:56:26.009Z
- Array: a standard JavaScript/Node array type

- `Schema.Types.ObjectId` a typical, MongoDB 24-character hex string of a 12-byte binary number (e.g., 52dafa354bd71b30fa12c441)

- `Schema.Types.Mixed`: any type of data (i.e., flexible free type)

■ **Warning**   Mongoose does not listen to mixed-type object changes, so call `markModified()` before saving the object to make sure changes in the mixed-type field are persistent.

ObjectId is added automatically as a primary `_id` key if omitted in the `insert` or `save` methods; `_id` key can be used to sort documents chronologically (http://docs.mongodb.org/manual/reference/object-id/). They are available through `Schema.Types` or `mongoose.Schema.Types` (e.g., `Schema.Types.Mixed`).

We have a great deal of flexibility in defining our document schemas—for example,

```
var ObjectId = mongoose.Schema.Types.ObjectId,
  Mixed = mongoose.Schema.Types.Mixed;
var bookSchema = mongoose.Schema({
    name: String,
    created_at: Date,
    updated_at: {type: Date, default: Date.now},
    published: Boolean,
    authorId : { type: ObjectId, required: true },
    description: { type: String, default: null },
    active: {type: Boolean, default: false},
    keywords: { type: [ String ], default: [] }
    description: {
      body: String,
      image: Buffer
    },
    version: {type: Number, default: function() {return 1;}},
    notes: Mixed,
    contributors: [ObjectId]
})
```

It's possible to create and use custom types (e.g., there's a module mongoose-types, https://github.com/bnoguchi/mongoose-types) that already have the rules for the ubiquitous e-mail and URL types.

Mongoose schemas are pluggable, which means, by creating a plugin, certain functionality can be extended across all schemas of the application.

For better code organization and code re-use, in the schema, we can set up static and instance methods, apply plugins, and define hooks.

■ **Tip**   For validation in Node.js, consider using the `validatior.js` and `express-validator` modules.

Hooks for Keeping Code Organized

In a complex application with a lot of interrelated objects, we might want to execute certain logic before saving an object. Hooks are a good place to store such logic. For example, we might want to upload a PDF to the web site before saving a book document:

```
bookSchema.pre('save', function(next) {
    //prepare for saving
    //upload PDF
    return next();
});
```

On the other hand, before removing, we need to make sure there are no pending purchase orders for this book:

```
bookSchema.pre('remove', function(next) {
  //prepare for removing
  return next(e);
});
```

Custom Static and Instance Methods

In addition to dozens of built-in Mongoose model methods, we can add custom ones. For example, to initiate a purchase, we can call the buy method on the document `practicalNodeBook` after we implement the custom instance method buy():

```
bookSchema.method({
  buy: function(quantity, customer, callback) {
    var bookToPurchase = this;
    //create a purchase order and invoice customer
    return callback(results);
  },
  refund: function(customer, callback) {
    //process the refund
    return callback(results);
  }
});
```

Static methods are useful when we either don't have a particular document object or we don't need it:

```
bookSchema.static({
  getZeroInventoryReport: function(callback) {
    //run a query on all books and get the ones with zero inventory
    return callback(books);
  },
  getCountOfBooksById: function(bookId, callback){
    //run a query and get the number of books left for a given book
    return callback(count);
  }
})
```

■ **Note** Hooks and methods must be added to the schemas before compiling them to models—in other words, before calling the `mongoose.model()` method.

Mongoose Models

As in many other ORMs, in Mongoose, the cornerstone object is a model. To compile a schema into a model, use `mongoose.model(name, schema)`—for example,

```
var Book = mongoose.model('Book', bookSchema)
```

The first parameter is just a string, which we can use later to pull the instance of this model. Usually, this string is the same as the object literal for the model (e.g., Book).

Models are used to create documents (actual data). To do so, call new `ModelName(data)`—for example,

```
var practicalNodeBook = new Book({ name: 'Practical Node.js' });
var javascriptTheGoodPartsBook = new Book({ name: "JavaScript The Good Parts"});
```

It's better to assign the initial value through the constructor versus using the `document.set()` method, because Mongoose has to process less function calls and our code remains more compact and better organized. Of course, this is possible only if we know the values when we create the instances.

Don't confuse static with instance model methods. If we call a method on `practicalNodeBook`, it's an instance method; if we call it on the Book object, it's a static class method.

Models have static built-in methods that are very similar to Mongoskin and native MongoDB methods, such as `find()`, `create()`, and `update()`.

A list of the static Mongoose model methods (invoked on a capitalized object, e.g., Book) along with their meaning follows.

- `Model.create(data, [callback (error, doc)])`: creates a new Mongoose document and saves it to the database

- `Model.remove(query, [callback(error)])`: removes documents from the collection that match the query; when finished, calls `callback` with `error`

- `Model.find(query, [fields], [options], [callback(error, docs)])`: finds documents that match the query (as a JSON object); possible to select fields (http://mongoosejs.com/docs/api.html#query_Query-select) and use options (http://mongodb.github.io/node-mongodb-native/api-generated/collection.html#find)

- `Model.update(query, update, [options], [callback(error, affectedCount, raw)])`: updates documents, similar to native update

- `Model.populate(docs, options, [callback(error, doc)])`: populates documents using references to other collections; an alternative to another approach described in the next section

- `Model.findOne(query, [fields], [options], [callback(error, doc)])`: finds the first document that matches the query

- `Model.findById(id, [fields], [options], [callback(error, doc)])`: finds the first element for which `_id` equals the `id` argument (cast based on the schema)

- `Model.findOneAndUpdate([query], [update], [options], [callback(error, doc)])`: finds the first document that matches the query (if present) and updates it, returning the document; uses `findAndModify` (http://mongodb.github.io/node-mongodb-native/api-generated/collection.html#findandmodify)

- `Model.findOneAndRemove(query, [options], [callback(error, doc)])`: finds the first document that matches the query and removes it when returning the document

- `Model.findByIdAndUpdate(id, [update], [options], [callback(error, doc)])`: similar to `findOneAndUpdate` using only the ID

- `Model.findByIdAndRemove(id, [options], [callback(error, doc)])`: similar to `findOneAndRemove` using only the ID

■ **Warning**   Not all the Mongoose model methods trigger hooks. Some of them are executed directly. For example, calling `Model.remove()` does not trigger the `remove` hook, because no Mongoose documents are involved (instances of `Model` that use lowercase literals, e.g., `practicalNodeBook`).

The complete list of the methods is extensive; therefore, refer to the official Mongoose API documentation (`http://mongoosejs.com/docs/api.html#model-js`). The most used instance methods are as follows:

- `doc.model(name)`: returns another Mongoose model

- `doc.remove([callback(error, doc)])`: removes this document

- `doc.save([callback(error, doc, affectedCount)])`: saves this document

- `doc.update(doc, [options], [callback(error, affectedCount, raw)])`: updates the document with `doc` properties, and `options` parameters, and then upon completion fires a callback with `error`, number of `affectedCount` and the database output

- `doc.toJSON([option])`: converts a Mongoose document to JSON (options are listed later)

- `doc.toObject([option])`: converts a Mongoose document to a plain JavaScript object (options are listed later)

- `isModified([path])`: true/false, respectively, if some parts (or the specific path) of the document are or are not modified

- `markModified(path)`: marks a path manually as modified which is useful for mixed (`Schema.Types.Mixed`) data types because they don't trigger the modified flag automatically

- `doc.isNew`: true/false, respectively, whether the document is new or not new

- `doc.id`: returns the document ID

- `doc.set(path, value, [type], [options])`: sets `value` at a `path`

- `doc.validate(callback(error))`: checks validation manually (triggered automatically before `save()`)

Options for `toObject()` and `toJSON()` are as follows:

- `getters`: true/false, calls all getters including path and virtual types

- `virtuals`: true/false, includes virtual getters and can override the getters option

- `minimize`: true/false, removes empty properties/objects (defaults to true)

- `transform`: transforms the function called right before returning the object

For more methods, visit the Mongoose document API (`http://mongoosejs.com/docs/api.html#document-js`).

Relationships and Joins with Population

Although, there are no relationships stored in a NoSQL database such as MongoDB, we can do so in the application layer. Mongoose provides a feature called *population*. It allows us to fill certain parts of the document from a different collection. Let's say we have posts and users collections. We can reference posts in the user schema:

```
var mongoose = require('mongoose'),
  Schema = mongoose.Schema

var userSchema = Schema({
  _id     : Number,
  name: String,
  posts: [{ type: Schema.Types.ObjectId, ref: 'Post' }]
});

var postSchema = Schema({
  _creator: { type: Number, ref: 'User' },
  title: String,
  text: String
});

var Post  = mongoose.model('Post', postSchema);
var User = mongoose.model('User', userSchema);
User.findOne({ name: /azat/i })
  .populate('posts')
  .exec(function (err, user) {
    if (err) return handleError(err);
    console.log('The user has % post(s)', user.posts.length);
  })
```

■ **Note**   ObjectId, Number, String, and Buffer are valid data types to use as references.

In the previous query, we used a regular expression (RegExp), this feature is not exclusive to Mongoose. In fact, the native driver and its other wrappers, along with the mongo console all support RegExps. The syntax is the same as in normal JavaScript/Node.js RegExp patterns. Therefore, in a way, we perform a join query on our Post and User models.

It's possible to return only a portion of populated results. For example, we can limit the number of posts to the first 10 only:

```
.populate({
  path: 'posts',
  options: { limit: 10, sort: 'title' }
})
```

Sometimes it's more practical to return only certain fields instead of the full document. This can be done with `select`:

```
.populate({
  path: 'posts',
  select: 'title',
  options: { limit: 10, sort: 'title' }
})
```

In addition, Mongoose can filter the populated results by a query! For example, we can apply RegExp for "node.js" to the text (a `match` query property):

```
.populate({
  path: 'posts',
  select: '_id title text',
  match: {text: /node\.js/i},
  options: { limit: 10, sort: '_id' }
})
```

Here, it takes selected properties (`select` and then the field names of `_id`, `title`, `text`) and can be as customized as you want it to be. The best practice is to populate only the required fields because this avoids potential leakage of sensitive information and reduces overhead on the system.

The populate method also works on multiple document queries. For example, we can use `find` instead of `findOne`:

```
User.find({}, {limit: 10, sort:{ _id: -1}})
  .populate('posts')
  .exec(function (err, user) {
    if (err) return handleError(err);
    console.log('The user has % post(s)', user.posts.length);
  })
```

■ **Tip**   For custom sorting, we can add properties using `name: -1` or `name: 1` patterns and can pass the resulting object to the `sort` option. Again, this is a standard MongoDB interface and is not exclusive to Mongoose.

Nested Documents

The document storage model in NoSQL databases is well-suited to use nested documents. For example, instead of having two collections—`posts` and `users`—we can have a single collection (`users`), with each item of that collection having `posts`.

The decision of whether to use separate collections or nested documents is more of an architectural question, and its answer depends on usage. For example, if posts are used only in the context of users (their authors)—say, on the users' profile pages—then it's best to use nested documents. However, if the blog features multiple users' posts that need to be queried independently of their user context, then separate collections fit better.

To implement nested documents, we can use the type Schema.Types.Mixed in Mongoose schemas (Schema, e.g., bookSchema or postSchema) or we can create a new schema for the nested document. An example of the former approach is as follows:

```
var userSchema = new mongoose.Schema({
  name: String,
  posts: [mongoose.Schema.Types.Mixed]
});
//attach methods, hooks, etc.
var User = mongoose.model('User', userSchema);
```

However, the latter approach of using a distinct new subschema is more flexible and powerful:

```
var postSchema = new mongoose.Schema({
  title: String,
  text: String
});
//attach methods, hooks, etc., to post schema
var userSchema = new mongoose.Schema({
  name: String,
  posts: [postSchema]
});
//attach methods, hooks, etc., to user schema
var User = mongoose.model('User', userSchema);
```

To create a new user document or to save a post to an existing user when working with a nested posts document, treat the posts property as an array and just use the push method from the JavaScript/Node.js API, or use the MongoDB $push operand (http://docs.mongodb.org/manual/reference/operator/update/push/). For example, we can add a post (newPost) to a user object, which is found by a matching ID (_id is userId):

```
User.update(
  {_id: userId},
  {$push: {posts: newPost}},
  function(error, results) {
    //handle error and check results
  });
```

Virtual Fields

Virtuals are fields that don't exist in the database but act just like normal fields in a Mongoose document. To oversimplify, virtual fields are mock or fake fields that pretend to act and be normal ones.

Virtual fields are awesome for creating aggregate fields. For example, if our system requires to have first name, last name and the full name (which is just a concatenation of the first two names)—there's no need to store the full name values in addition to the first and last name values! All we need to do is concatenate the first and last name in a full name virtual.

Another use case is to make the database backward compatible. For example, we might have thousands of user items in a MongoDB collection and we want to start collecting their locations. We have two options: run a migration script to add the default location ("none") to the thousands of old user documents or use a virtual field and apply defaults at runtime!

To define a virtual we need to

1. Call the `virtual(name)` method to create a virtual type (Mongoose API, http://mongoosejs.com/docs/api.html#schema_Schema-virtual)

2. Apply a getter function with `get(fn)` (Mongoose API, http://mongoosejs.com/docs/api.html#virtualtype_VirtualType-get)

Gravatar (http://en.gravatar.com/) for example, is a service that hosts profile images. The URL is always an md5 hash (http://en.gravatar.com/site/implement/hash/) of the user's e-mail. Therefore, we can get the virtual value (`gravatarUrl`) on the fly by hashing instead of storing the value (less overhead!). In this example, we intentionally made the input email mixed cased and with a trailing space, and then applied `crypto`:

```
Identity.virtual('gravatarUrl')
  .get(function() {
    if (!this.email) return null;
    var crypto = require('crypto'),
      email = "Hi@azat.co ";
    email = email.trim();
    email = email.toLowerCase();
    var hash = crypto
      .createHash('md5')
      .update(email)
      .digest('hex')
    var gravatarBaseUrl = 'https://secure.gravatar.com/avatar/';
    return gravatarBaseUrl + hash;
});
```

Or, the case mentioned earlier—getting a full name out of first and last—is as follows:

```
userSchema.virtual('fullName')
  .get(function(){
    return this.firstName + ' ' + this.lastName;
})
```

Another scenario is when only a subset of the full document is exposed. For example, if the user model has tokens and passwords, we omit these sensitive fields by whitelisting only the fields we want to expose:

```
userSchema.virtual('info')
  .get(function() {
    return {
      service: this.service,
      username: this.username,
      name: this.name,
      date: this.date,
      url: this.url,
      avatar: this.avatar
    };
});
```

Schema Type Behavior Amendment

Mongoose allows us to define/write getters (`get`), setters (`set`), and defaults (`default`) right in the Schema! Same goes for validate and some other useful methods.

Here's an examples of defining set (transform to lower case when the value is assigned), get (when the number is extracted the "thousands" commas are added to it), default (brand new ObjectID is generated), and validate (checks for e-mail patterns and is triggered upon save()) all right in a JSON-like structure of the Schema:

```
postSchema = new mongoose.Schema({
  slug: {
    type: String,
    set: function(slug) {
      return slug.toLowerCase();
    }
  },
  numberOfLikes: {
    type: Number,
    get: function(value) {
      return value.toString().replace(/\B(?=(\d{3})+(?!\d))/g, ",");
    }
  },
  posted_at: {
    type: String,
    get: function(value) {
      if (!value) return null;
      return value.toUTCString();
    }
  },
  authorId: {
    type: ObjectId,
    default: function() {
      return new mongoose.Types.ObjectId()
    }
  },
  email: {
    type: String,
    unique: true,
    validate: [
      function(email) {
        return (email.match(/[a-z0-9!#$%&'*+\/=?^_`{|}~-]+(?:\.[a-z0-9!#$%&'*+\/=?^_`{|}~-]+)*
@(?:[a-z0-9](?:[a-z0-9-]*[a-z0-9])?\.)+[a-z0-9](?:[a-z0-9-]*[a-z0-9])?/i) != null)},
      'Invalid email'
    ]
  }
});
```

If defining custom methods in the Schema definition is not an option for some reason (maybe our system requires us to do it dynamically), there's another approach to amending Schema behavior—to use chained methods:

1. Use Schema.path(name) to get SchemaType (official docs, http://mongoosejs.com/docs/api.html#schema_Schema-path).

2. Use SchemaType.get(fn) to set the getter method (official docs, http://mongoosejs.com/docs/api.html#schematype_SchemaType-get).

For example,

```
userSchema.path('numberOfPosts')
  .get(function(value) {
    if (value) return value;
    return this.posts.length;
  });
```

Path is just a fancy name for the nested field name and its parent objects, for example if we have ZIP code (`zip`) as a child of `contact.address` such as `user.contact.address.zip`, the `contact.address.zip` is a path.

Express.js + Mongoose = True MVC

To avoid rebuilding all other components unrelated to ORM, such as templates, routes, and so forth, we can factor the existing Blog from the previous chapter by making it use Mongoose instead of Mongoskin. This requires minimal effort but produces an abstraction layer between MongoDB and the request handlers. As always, the fully functional code is available on GitHub, in the ch7 folder (https://github.com/azat-co/practicalnode/tree/master/ch7).

The process of refactoring starts with the creation of a new branch: `mongoose`. You can use the final solution in the GitHub repository (https://github.com/azat-co/blog-express/tree/mongoose). First, we need to remove Mongoskin and install Mongoose:

```
$ npm uninstall mongoskin -save
$ npm install mongoose@3.8.4 --save
```

`package.json` is amended to something like this:

```json
{
  "name": "blog-express",
  "version": "0.0.1",
  "private": true,
  "scripts": {
    "start": "node app.js",
    "test": "mocha test"
  },
  "dependencies": {
    "express": "4.1.2",
    "jade": "1.3.1",
    "stylus": "0.44.0",
    "everyauth": "0.4.5",
    "mongoose": "3.8.4",
    "cookie-parser": "1.0.1",
    "body-parser": "1.0.2",
    "method-override": "1.0.0",
    "serve-favicon": "2.0.0",
    "express-session": "1.0.4",
    "morgan": "1.0.1",
    "errorhandler": "1.0.1"
  },
  "devDependencies": {
    "mocha": "1.16.2",
```

```
    "superagent": "0.15.7",
    "expect.js": "0.2.0"
  }
}
```

Now, in the app.js file, we can remove the Mongoskin inclusion (mongoskin = require('mongoskin'),) and add a new one for Mongoose:

```
...
mongoose = require('mongoose'),
```

Let's create a folder models ($ mkdir models) and include it:

```
models = require('./models'),
```

Substitute the connection, and articles and users collections statements:

```
db = mongoskin.db(dbUrl, {safe: true}),
 collections = {
   articles: db.collection('articles'),
   users: db.collection('users')
  }
```

With just the connection statement **leaving out** the collections:

```
db = mongoose.connect(dbUrl, {safe: true}),
```

In the collection middleware, we remove collections:

```
if (!collections.articles || ! collections.users) return next(new Error('No collections.'))
  req.collections = collections;
```

Then, add the models:

```
if (!models.Article || ! models.User) return next(new Error('No models.'))
  req.models = models;
```

That's it! The upgrade from Mongoskin to Mongoose is complete. ;-) Just for your reference, here's the full code of the resulting app.js:

```
var TWITTER_CONSUMER_KEY = process.env.TWITTER_CONSUMER_KEY ||
'MY_TWITTER_CONSUMER_KEY_ABC'
var TWITTER_CONSUMER_SECRET = process.env.TWITTER_CONSUMER_SECRET ||
'MY_TWITTER_CONSUMER_SECRET_XYZXYZ'

var express = require('express'),
  routes = require('./routes'),
  http = require('http'),
  path = require('path'),
  mongoose = require('mongoose'),
  models = require('./models'),
```

```
  dbUrl = process.env.MONGOHQ_URL || 'mongodb://@localhost:27017/blog',
  db = mongoose.connect(dbUrl, {safe: true}),
  everyauth = require('everyauth');

var session = require('express-session'),
  logger = require('morgan'),
  errorHandler = require('errorhandler'),
  cookieParser = require('cookie-parser'),
  bodyParser = require('body-parser'),
  methodOverride = require('method-override');

everyauth.debug = true;
everyauth.twitter
  .consumerKey(TWITTER_CONSUMER_KEY)
  .consumerSecret(TWITTER_CONSUMER_SECRET)
  .findOrCreateUser( function (session, accessToken, accessTokenSecret, twitterUserMetadata) {
    var promise = this.Promise();
    process.nextTick(function(){
      // replace with your Twitter username
      if (twitterUserMetadata.screen_name === 'azat_co') {
        session.user = twitterUserMetadata;
        session.admin = true;
      }
      promise.fulfill(twitterUserMetadata);
    })
    return promise;
})
  .redirectPath('/admin');

//we need it because otherwise the session will be kept alive
everyauth.everymodule.handleLogout(routes.user.logout);

everyauth.everymodule.findUserById( function (user, callback) {
  callback(user);
});

var app = express();
app.locals.appTitle = 'blog-express';

app.use(function(req, res, next) {
  if (!models.Article || ! models.User)
    return next(new Error('No models.'));
  req.models = models;
  return next();
});

app.set('port', process.env.PORT || 3000);
app.set('views', path.join(__dirname, 'views'));
app.set('view engine', 'jade');
```

```javascript
app.use(logger('dev'));
app.use(bodyParser.json());
app.use(cookieParser('3CCC4ACD-6ED1-4844-9217-82131BDCB239'));
app.use(session({secret: '2C44774A-D649-4D44-9535-46E296EF984F'}));
app.use(everyauth.middleware());
app.use(bodyParser.urlencoded());
app.use(methodOverride());
app.use(require('stylus').middleware(__dirname + '/public'));
app.use(express.static(path.join(__dirname, 'public')));

app.use(function(req, res, next) {
  if (req.session && req.session.admin) {
    res.locals.admin = true;
  }
  next();
});

var authorize = function(req, res, next) {
  if (req.session && req.session.admin)
    return next();
  else
    return res.send(401);
};

if ('development' === app.get('env')) {
  app.use(errorHandler());
}

app.get('/', routes.index);
app.get('/login', routes.user.login);
app.post('/login', routes.user.authenticate);
app.get('/logout', routes.user.logout);
app.get('/admin', authorize, routes.article.admin);
app.get('/post', authorize, routes.article.post);
app.post('/post', authorize, routes.article.postArticle);
app.get('/articles/:slug', routes.article.show);

app.all('/api', authorize);
app.get('/api/articles', routes.article.list);
app.post('/api/articles', routes.article.add);
app.put('/api/articles/:id', routes.article.edit);
app.del('/api/articles/:id', routes.article.del);

app.all('*', function(req, res) {
  res.send(404);
})
```

```
var server = http.createServer(app);
var boot = function () {
  server.listen(app.get('port'), function(){
    console.info('Express server listening on port ' + app.get('port'));
  });
}
var shutdown = function() {
  server.close();
}
if (require.main === module) {
  boot();
}
else {
  console.info('Running app as a module')
  exports.boot = boot;
  exports.shutdown = shutdown;
  exports.port = app.get('port');
}
```

There are three files in the models folder:

1. index.js: exposes models to app.js

2. article.js: includes article schemas, methods, and models

3. user.js: includes the user schema and its model

The index.js file is as follows:

```
exports.Article = require('./article');
exports.User = require('./user');
```

The article.js file starts with the inclusion:

```
var mongoose = require('mongoose');
```

Then, the schema itself is:

```
var articleSchema = new mongoose.Schema({
  title: {
    type: String,
    required: true,
    validate: [
      function(value) {
        return value.length<=120
      },
      'Title is too long (120 max)'
    ],
    default: 'New Post'
  },
  text: String,
  published: {
    type: Boolean,
    default: false
  },
```

```
  slug: {
    type: String,
    set: function(value) {
      return value.toLowerCase().replace(' ', '-')
    }
  }
});
```

In the schema above, `title` is required and it's limited to 120 characters with `validate`. The `published` defaults to `false` if not specified upon object creation. The slug should never have spaces due to the `set` method.

To illustrate code reuse, we abstract the `find` method from the routes (`routes/article.js`) into the model (`models/article.js`). This can be done with all database methods:

```
articleSchema.static({
  list: function(callback){
    this.find({}, null, {sort: {_id:-1}}, callback);
  }
})
```

The, we compile the schema and methods into a model:

```
module.exports = mongoose.model('Article', articleSchema);
```

The full source code of `article.js` is as follows:

```
var mongoose = require('mongoose');

var articleSchema = new mongoose.Schema({
  title: {
    type: String,
    required: true,
    validate: [
      function(value) {
        return value.length<=120
      },
      'Title is too long (120 max)'
    ],
    default: 'New Post'
  },
  text: String,
  published: {
    type: Boolean,
    default: false
  },
  slug: {
    type: String,
    set: function(value){
      return value.toLowerCase().replace(' ', '-')
    }
  }
});
```

```
articleSchema.static({
  list: function(callback){
    this.find({}, null, {sort: {_id:-1}}, callback);
  }
})
module.exports = mongoose.model('Article', articleSchema);
```

The models/user.js file also begins with an inclusion and a schema:

```
var mongoose = require('mongoose');

var userSchema = new mongoose.Schema({
  email: {
    type: String,
    required: true,
    set: function(value) {return value.trim().toLowerCase()},
    validate: [
      function(email) {
        return (email.match(/[a-z0-9!#$%&'*+\/=?^_`{|}~-]+(?:\.[a-z0-9!#$%&'*+\/=?^_`{|}~-]+)*
@(?:[a-z0-9](?:[a-z0-9-]*[a-z0-9])?\.)+[a-z0-9](?:[a-z0-9-]*[a-z0-9])?/i) != null)},
      'Invalid email'
    ]
  },
  password: String,
  admin: {
    type: Boolean,
    default: false
  }
});

module.exports = mongoose.model('User', userSchema);
```

The e-mail field is validated with RegExp, then is trimmed and forced to lowercase when it's set.

The routes/article.js file now needs to switch to Mongoose models instead of Mongoskin collections. So, in the show method, this line goes away:

```
req.collections.articles.findOne({slug: req.params.slug}, function(error, article) {
```

Then, this line comes in:

```
req.models.Article.findOne({slug: req.params.slug}, function(error, article) {
```

In the list method, remove:

```
req.collections.articles.find({}).toArray(function(error, articles) {
```

and replace it with:

```
req.models.Article.list(function(error, articles) {
```

In the exports.add method,

```
req.collections.articles.insert(
  article,
  function(error, articleResponse) {
```

is replaced with:

```
req.models.Article.create(article, function(error, articleResponse) {
```

The exports.edit method is trickier, and there are a few possible solutions:

1. Find a Mongoose document (e.g., findById) and use document methods (e.g., update)

2. Use the static model method findByIdAndUpdate

In both cases, this Mongoskin piece of code goes away:

```
req.collections.articles.updateById(
  req.params.id,
  {$set: req.body.article},
  function(error, count) {
```

We'll use the former two-step approach (i.e., find then update), because it's more versatile. So the above snippet is replaced by this code:

```
req.models.Article.findById(
  req.params.id,
  function(error, article) {
    if (error) return next(error);
    article.update({$set: req.body.article}, function(error, count, raw) {
    if (error) return next(error);
    res.send({affectedCount: count});
  })
});
```

Just to show you a more elegant one-step approach (the latter from the new exports.edit implementation list above):

```
req.models.Article.findByIdAndUpdate(
  req.params.id,
  {$set: req.body.article},
  function(error, doc) {
    if (error) return next(error);
    res.send(doc);
  }
);
```

Similarly, with the exports.del request handler:

```
exports.del = function(req, res, next) {
  if (!req.params.id) return next(new Error('No article ID.'));
  req.models.Article.findById(req.params.id, function(error, article) {
    if (error) return next(error);
    if (!article) return next(new Error('article not found'));
    article.remove(function(error, doc){
      if (error) return next(error);
      res.send(doc);
    });
  });
};
```

The exports.postArticle and exports.admin functions look like these (the functions' bodies are the same):

```
req.models.Article.create(article, function(error, articleResponse) {
...
req.models.Article.list(function(error, articles) {
...
```

Again, that's all we have to do to switch to Mongoose for this route. However, to make sure there's nothing missing, here's the full code of the routes/article.js file:

```
exports.show = function(req, res, next) {
  if (!req.params.slug) return next(new Error('No article slug.'));
  req.models.Article.findOne({slug: req.params.slug}, function(error, article) {
    if (error) return next(error);
    if (!article.published && !req.session.admin) return res.send(401);
    res.render('article', article);
  });
};

exports.list = function(req, res, next) {
  req.models.Article.list(function(error, articles) {
    if (error) return next(error);
    res.send({articles: articles});
  });
};

exports.add = function(req, res, next) {
  if (!req.body.article) return next(new Error('No article payload.'));
  var article = req.body.article;
  article.published = false;
  req.models.Article.create(article, function(error, articleResponse) {
    if (error) return next(error);
    res.send(articleResponse);
  });
};
```

```
exports.edit = function(req, res, next) {
  if (!req.params.id) return next(new Error('No article ID.'));
  req.models.Article.findById(req.params.id, function(error, article) {
    if (error) return next(error);
    article.update({$set: req.body.article}, function(error, count, raw){
      if (error) return next(error);
      res.send({affectedCount: count});
    })
  });
};

exports.del = function(req, res, next) {
  if (!req.params.id) return next(new Error('No article ID.'));
  req.models.Article.findById(req.params.id, function(error, article) {
    if (error) return next(error);
    if (!article) return next(new Error('article not found'));
    article.remove(function(error, doc){
      if (error) return next(error);
      res.send(doc);
    });
  });
};

exports.post = function(req, res, next) {
  if (!req.body.title)
  res.render('post');
};

exports.postArticle = function(req, res, next) {
  if (!req.body.title || !req.body.slug || !req.body.text ) {
    return res.render('post', {error: 'Fill title, slug and text.'});
  }
  var article = {
    title: req.body.title,
    slug: req.body.slug,
    text: req.body.text,
    published: false
  };
  req.models.Article.create(article, function(error, articleResponse) {
    if (error) return next(error);
    res.render('post', {error: 'Article was added. Publish it on Admin page.'});
  });
};

exports.admin = function(req, res, next) {
  req.models.Article.list(function(error, articles) {
    if (error) return next(error);
    res.render('admin',{articles:articles});
  });

}
```

The routes/index.js file, which serves the home page, is as follows:

```
exports.article = require('./article');
exports.user = require('./user');

exports.index = function(req, res, next){
  req.models.Article.find({published: true}, null, {sort: {_id:-1}}, function(error, articles){
    if (error) return next(error);
    res.render('index', { articles: articles});
  })
};
```

Lastly, routes/user.js has a single line to change. Instead of:

```
 req.collections.articles.find({}).toArray(function(error, articles) {
```

Now, we have:

```
...
req.models.User.findOne({
...
```

To check if everything went well, simply run Blog as usual with $ node app and navigate the pages on http://localhost:3000/. In addition, we can run Mocha tests with $ mocha test.

Summary

In this chapter, we learned what Mongoose is, how to install it, how to establish a connection to the database, and how to create Mongoose schemas while keeping the code organized with hooks and methods. We also compiled schemas into models and populated references automatically, and used virtual fields and custom schema type properties. Last, we refactored Blog to use Mongoose and made our app gain a true MVC architecture.

Next, we'll cover how to build REST APIs with the two Node.js frameworks: Express.js and Hapi. This is an important topic, because more and more web developments shift towards heavy front-end logic and thin back-end. Some systems even go as far as building/using free-JSON APIs or back-as-a-service services. This tendency allows teams to focus on what is the most important for end-users: user interface, features, as well as what is vital for businesses: reduced iteration cycles, lower costs of maintenance and development.

Another essential piece in this puzzle is test-driven practice. To explore it, we'll cover Mocha, which is a widely used Node.js testing framework. To REST APIs and TDD onward.

CHAPTER 8

■ ■ ■

Building Node.js REST API Servers with Express.js and Hapi

Modern-day web development is moving increasingly toward a structure for which there's a thick client, usually built with frameworks such as Backbone.js, (http://backbonejs.org/) Anglers JS, (https://angularjs.org/) Ember.js, (http://emberjs.com/) and the like, and a thin back-end layer typically represented by a representational state transfer (REST) web application programing interface (API) service. This model has become more and more popular, and we've seen services such as Parse.com and many others pioneer the back end as a service niche. The advantages of this approach are as follows:

- The same back-end REST API can serve multiple client apps/consumers, with web applications being just one of them (mobile and public third-party apps are examples of others).

- There is a separation of concerns, i.e., the clients can be replaced without compromising the integrity of the core business logic, and vice versa.

- User interface / user experience (UI/UX) are inherently hard to test, especially with event-driven, single-page apps, and then there's an added complexity of cross-browser testing; but, with separation of business logic into the back-end REST API, that logic becomes easy to test in both unit and functional testing.

Therefore, the majority of new projects take the REST API and clients approach. Development teams may take this approach even if they have just one client for the time being which is typically a web app, because they realize that otherwise, when they eventually add more apps, they'll have to redo their work.

To get started with Node.js REST servers, in this chapter we cover the following:

- RESTful API basics

- Project dependencies

- Test coverage with Mocha (http://visionmedia.github.io/mocha/) and superagent (http://visionmedia.github.io/superagent/)

- REST API server implementation with Express and Mongoskin (https://github.com/kissjs/node-mongoskin)

- Refactoring: Hapi.js (http://hapijs.com/) REST API Server

The REST API server is able to process the creation of objects, retrieval of objects and collections, make changes to objects and remove objects. For your convenience, all the source code is in the ch8 folder in github.com/azat-co/practicalnode (https://github.com/azat-co/practicalnode).

■ **Note** In this chapter, our examples use a semicolonless style. Semicolons in JavaScript are absolutely optional (http://blog.izs.me/post/2353458699/an-open-letter-to-javascript-leaders-regarding) except in two cases: in the for loop and before expressions/statements that start with a parenthesis (e.g., immediately invoked function expression (http://en.wikipedia.org/wiki/Immediately-invoked_function_expression) (IIFE)). The reason this style is used, is to give you an alternative perspective. Typing fewer semicolons improves speed, looks better and is more consistent because developers tend to miss semicolons from time to time (perfectly running code allows for such sloppiness). Also, some programmers find semicolonless code more readable.

RESTful API Basics

RESTful API[1] became popular because of the demand in distributed systems in which each transaction needs to include enough information about the state of the client. In a sense, this standard is stateless, because no information about the clients' states is stored on the server, making it possible for each request to be served by a different system.

Distinct characteristics of RESTful API (i.e., if API is RESTful, it usually follows these principles) are as follows:

- RESTful API has better scalability support because different components can be deployed independently to different servers.

- It replaced the Simple Object Access Protocol (SOAP[2]) because of the simpler verb and noun structure.

- It uses HTTP methods such as GET, POST, DELETE, PUT, OPTIONS, and so forth.

- JSON is not the only option (although it is the most popular). Unlike SOAP, which is a protocol, the REST methodology is flexible in choosing formats. For example alternative formats might be Extensible Markup Language (XML) or comma-separated values formats (CSV).

In Table 8-1 is an example of a simple create, read, update and delete (CRUD[3]) REST API for message collection.

Table 8-1. *Example of the CRUD REST API Structure*

Method	URL	Meaning
GET	/messages.json	Return list of messages in JSON format
PUT	/messages.json	Update/replace all messages and return status/error in JSON
POST	/messages.json	Create a new message and return its ID in JSON format
GET	/messages/{id}.json	Return message with ID {id} in JSON format
PUT	/messages/{id}.json	Update/replace message with id {id}; if {id} message doesn't exist, create it
DELETE	/messages/{id}.json	Delete message with ID {id}, return status/error in JSON format

---

[1]http://en.wikipedia.org/wiki/Representational_state_transfer#Applied_to_web_services.
[2]http://en.wikipedia.org/wiki/SOAP.
[3]http://en.wikipedia.org/wiki/Create,_read,_update_and_delete.

REST is not a protocol; it's an architecture in the sense that it's more flexible than SOAP, which we know is a protocol. Therefore, REST API URLs could look like /messages/list.html or /messages/list.xml, in case we want to support these formats.

PUT and DELETE are idempotent methods,[4] which means that if the server receives two or more similar requests, the end result is the same.

GET is nullipotent; POST is not idempotent and might affect the state and cause side effects.

More information on REST API[5] can be found at Wikipedia and in the article "A Brief Introduction to REST (http://www.infoq.com/articles/rest-introduction)."

In our REST API server, we perform CRUD operations and harness the Express.js middleware (http://expressjs.com/api.html#middleware) concept with the app.param() and app.use() methods. So, our app should be able to process the following commands using the JSON format (collectionName is the name of the collection, typically pluralized nouns, e.g., messages, comments, users):

- *POST* /collections/{collectionName}: request to create an object; responds with the of newly created object ID

- *GET* /collections/{collectionName}/{id}: request with ID to retrieve an object

- *GET* /collections/{collectionName}/: request to retrieve any items from the collection (items); in our example we'll have this query options: up to 10 items and sorted by ID

- *PUT* /collections/{collectionName}/{id}: request with ID to update an object

- *DELETE* /collections/{collectionName}/{id}: request with ID to remove an object

Project Dependencies

To get started with our project, we need to install packages. In this chapter, we use Mongoskin (https://github.com/kissjs/node-mongoskin), a MongoDB library, which is a better alternative to the plain, good-ol' native MongoDB driver for Node.js (https://github.com/mongodb/node-mongodb-native). In addition, Mongoskin is more lightweight than Mongoose and it is schemaless. For more insights on the library, please check out this Mongoskin comparison blurb, https://github.com/kissjs/node-mongoskin#comparation.

Express.js (http://expressjs.com/) is a wrapper for core Node.js http module (http://nodejs.org/api/http.html) objects. The Express.js framework is built on top of the Connect (https://github.com/senchalabs/connect) middleware library and it provides myriads of convenience. Some people compare the Express.js framework with Ruby's Sinatra because it's non-opinionated and configurable.

First, we need to create a ch8/rest-express folder (or download the source code):

```
$ mkdir rest-express
$ cd rest-express
```

As mentioned in the previous chapter, Node.js/NPM provides multiple ways to install dependencies, including the following:

- Manually, one by one

- As a part of package.json

- By downloading and copying modules

---

[4]http://en.wikipedia.org/wiki/Hypertext_Transfer_Protocol#Idempotent_methods_and_web_application.
[5]http://en.wikipedia.org/wiki/Representational_state_transfer.

To keep things simple, let's just use the package.json approach. You can create the package.json file, or copy the dependencies section or the whole file:

```json
{
  "name": "rest-express",
  "version": "0.0.1",
  "description": "REST API application with Express, Mongoskin, MongoDB, Mocha and Superagent",
  "main": "index.js",
  "directories": {
    "test": "test"
  },
  "scripts": {
    "test": "mocha test -R spec"
  },
  "author": "Azat Mardan",
  "license": "BSD",
  "dependencies": {
    "express": "4.1.2",
    "mongoskin": "1.4.1",
    "body-parser": "1.0.2",
    "morgan": "1.0.1"    },
    "devDependencies": {
      "mocha": "1.16.2",
      "superagent": "0.15.7",
      "expect.js": "0.2.0"
    }
}
```

Then, simply run this command to install modules for the application:

```
$ npm install
```

As a result, the node_modules folder should be created with the superagent, express, mongoskin, and expect libraries. If you change the versions specified in package.json to the later ones, please make sure to update the code according to the packages' change logs.

Test Coverage with Mocha and Superagent

Before the app implementation, let's write functional tests that make HTTP requests to our soon-to-be-created REST API server. In a TDD manner, let's use these tests to build a Node.js free JSON REST API server using the Express.js framework and Mongoskin library for MongoDB.

In this section we walk through the writing of functional tests using the Mocha (http://visionmedia.github.io/mocha/) and superagent[6] libraries. The tests need to perform basic CRUD by posting HTTP requests to our server.

If you know how to use Mocha or just want to jump straight to the Express.js app implementation, feel free to do so. You can use CURL terminal commands for testing, too.

---

[6]http://visionmedia.github.io/superagent/.

Assuming we already have Node.js, NPM, and MongoDB installed, let's create a *new* folder (or, if you wrote the tests, use that folder). Let's use Mocha as a command-line tool, and Expect.js and superagent as local libraries. To install the Mocha CLI (if it's not available via $ mocha -V), run this command from the terminal:

```
$ npm install -g mocha@1.16.2
```

Expect.js and superagent should be available already as part of the installation done in the previous section.

■ **Tip**   Installing Mocha locally gives us the ability to use different versions at the same time. To run tests, simply point to ./node_modules/mocha/bin/mocha. A better alternative is to use Makefile, as described in Chapter 6.

Now let's create a test/index.js file in the same folder (ch8/rest-express), which will have six suites:

1. Create a new object

2. Retrieve an object by its ID

3. Retrieve the whole collection

4. Update an object by its ID

5. Check an updated object by its ID

6. Remove an object by its ID

HTTP requests are a breeze with SuperAgent's chained functions, which we can put inside each test suite. So, we start with dependencies:

```
var superagent = require('superagent')
var expect = require('expect.js')
```

Then, we write our first test case wrapped in the test case (describe and its callback). The idea is simple. We make an HTTP request to a local instance of the server. When we send the request, we pass some data and, of course, the URL path changes from test case to test case. The main thing happens in the request (made by superagent) callback. There, we put multiple assertions that are the bread and butter (or meat and veggies for paleo readers) of TDD. To be strictly correct, this test suite uses BDD language, but this difference is not essential for our project.

```
describe('express rest api server', function(){
  var id
  it('post object', function(done){
    superagent.post('http://localhost:3000/collections/test')
      .send({ name: 'John',
        email: 'john@rpjs.co'
      })
      .end(function(e,res){
        expect(e).to.eql(null)
        expect(res.body.length).to.eql(1)
        expect(res.body[0]._id.length).to.eql(24)
        id = res.body[0]._id
        done()
      })
  })
```

As you may have noticed, we're checking for the following:

- The error object should be null (eql(null))

- The response body array should have one item (to.eql(1))

- The first response body item should have the _id property, which is 24 characters long, i.e., a hex string representation of the standard MongoDB ObjectId type

To finish, we save the newly created object's ID in the id global variable so we can use it later for retrievals, updates, and deletions. Speaking of object retrievals, we test them in the next test case. Notice that the superagent method has changed to get() and the URL path contains the object ID. You can "uncomment" console.log to inspect the full HTTP response body:

```
it('retrieves an object', function(done){
  superagent.get('http://localhost:3000/collections/test/'+id)
    .end(function(e, res){
      expect(e).to.eql(null)
      expect(typeof res.body).to.eql('object')
      expect(res.body._id.length).to.eql(24)
      expect(res.body._id).to.eql(id)
      done()
    })
})
```

The done() callback allows us to test async code. Without it, the Mocha test case ends abruptly, long before the slow server has time to respond.

The next test case's assertion is a bit more interesting because we use the map() function on the response results to return an array of IDs. In this array, we find our ID (saved in id variable) with the contain method. The contain method is a more elegant alternative to native indexOf(). It works because the results, which are limited to 10 records, come sorted by IDs, and our object was created just moments ago.

```
it('retrieves a collection', function(done){
  superagent.get('http://localhost:3000/collections/test')
    .end(function(e, res){
      expect(e).to.eql(null)
      expect(res.body.length).to.be.above(0)
      expect(res.body.map(function (item){
        return item._id
      })).to.contain(id)
      done()
    })
})
```

When the time comes to update our object, we actually need to send some data. We do this by passing an object to superagent's function. Then, we assert that the operation was completed with (msg=success):

```
it('updates an object', function(done){
  superagent.put('http://localhost:3000/collections/test/'+id)
    .send({name: 'Peter',
      email: 'peter@yahoo.com'})
```

```
      .end(function(e, res){
        expect(e).to.eql(null)
        expect(typeof res.body).to.eql('object')
        expect(res.body.msg).to.eql('success')
        done()
      })
  })
```

The last two test cases, which assert retrieval of the updated object and its deletion, use methods similar to those used before. Here is the full source code for the ch8/rest-express/test/index.js file:

```
var superagent = require('superagent')
var expect = require('expect.js')

describe('express rest api server', function(){
  var id
  it('post object', function(done){
    superagent.post('http://localhost:3000/collections/test')
      .send({ name: 'John',
        email: 'john@rpjs.co'
      })
      .end(function(e,res){
        expect(e).to.eql(null)
        expect(res.body.length).to.eql(1)
        expect(res.body[0]._id.length).to.eql(24)
        id = res.body[0]._id
        done()
      })
  })

  it('retrieves an object', function(done){
    superagent.get('http://localhost:3000/collections/test/'+id)
      .end(function(e, res){
        expect(e).to.eql(null)
        expect(typeof res.body).to.eql('object')
        expect(res.body._id.length).to.eql(24)
        expect(res.body._id).to.eql(id)
        done()
      })
  })

  it('retrieves a collection', function(done){
    superagent.get('http://localhost:3000/collections/test')
      .end(function(e, res){
        expect(e).to.eql(null)
        expect(res.body.length).to.be.above(0)
        expect(res.body.map(function (item){
          return item._id
        })).to.contain(id)
        done()
      })
  })
```

```
it('updates an object', function(done){
  superagent.put('http://localhost:3000/collections/test/'+id)
    .send({name: 'Peter',
      email: 'peter@yahoo.com'})
    .end(function(e, res){
      expect(e).to.eql(null)
      expect(typeof res.body).to.eql('object')
      expect(res.body.msg).to.eql('success')
      done()
    })
})

it('checks an updated object', function(done){
  superagent.get('http://localhost:3000/collections/test/'+id)
    .end(function(e, res){
      expect(e).to.eql(null)
      expect(typeof res.body).to.eql('object')
      expect(res.body._id.length).to.eql(24)
      expect(res.body._id).to.eql(id)
      expect(res.body.name).to.eql('Peter')
      done()
    })
})

it('removes an object', function(done){
  superagent.del('http://localhost:3000/collections/test/'+id)
    .end(function(e, res){
      expect(e).to.eql(null)
      expect(typeof res.body).to.eql('object')
      expect(res.body.msg).to.eql('success')
      done()
    })
})
})
})
```

To run the tests, we can use the $ mocha test command, $ mocha test/index.js, or npm test. For now, the tests should fail because we have yet to implement the server!

For those of you who require multiple versions of Mocha, another alternative, which is better, is to run your tests using local Mocha binaries: ./node_modules/mocha/bin/mocha ./test. This, of course, assumes that we have installed Mocha locally into node_modules.

■ **Note** By default, Mocha doesn't use any reporters, and the result output is lackluster. To receive more explanatory logs, supply the -R <name> option (e.g., $ mocha test -R spec or $ mocha test -R list).

REST API Server Implementation with Express and Mongoskin

Create and open ch8/rest-express/index.js, which will be the main application file.

First things first. Let's import our dependencies into the application:

```
var express = require('express'),
  mongoskin = require('mongoskin'),
  bodyParser = require('body-parser'),
  logger = require('morgan')
```

After version 3.x, Express.js streamlined the instantiation of its app instance so that the following line gives us a server object:

```
var app = express()
```

To extract parameters and data from the requests, let's use bodyParser.urlencoded() and bodyParser.json() middleware. We apply them with app.use(), and the code looks more like configuration statements:

```
app.use(bodyParser.urlencoded())
app.use(bodyParser.json())
app.use(logger())
```

express.logger() is optional middleware that allows us to monitor requests. Middleware (in this (http://expressjs.com/api.html#app.use) and other forms (http://expressjs.com/api.html#middleware)) is a powerful and convenient pattern in Express.js and Connect to organize and reuse code.

As with the express.urlencoded() and express.json() methods, which save us from the hurdles of parsing a body object of an HTTP request, Mongoskin makes it possible to connect to the MongoDB database in one effortless line of code:

```
var db = mongoskin.db('mongodb://@localhost:27017/test', {safe:true})
```

■ **Note**   If you wish to connect to a remote database (e.g., MongoHQ (https://www.mongohq.com/home)), substitute the string with your username, password, host, and port values. Here is the format of the uniform resource identifier (URI) string (no spaces): mongodb://[username:password@] host1[:port1][,host2[:port2],... [,hostN[:portN]]] [/[database][?options]]

The next statement is a helper function that converts hex strings into MongoDB ObjectID data types:

```
var id = mongoskin.helper.toObjectID
```

The app.param() method is another form of Express.js middleware. It basically says: Do something every time there is this value in the URL pattern of the request handler. In our case, we select a particular collection when a request pattern contains a string collectionName prefixed with a colon (we see this when we examine routes):

```
app.param('collectionName', function(req, res, next, collectionName){
  req.collection = db.collection(collectionName)
  return next()
})
```

To be user friendly, let's include a root route with a message that asks users to specify a collection name in their URLs:

```
app.get('/', function(req, res, next) {
  res.send('Select a collection, e.g., /collections/messages')
})
```

Now the real work begins. Here is how we retrieve a list of items sorted by _id that has a limit of 10:

```
app.get('/collections/:collectionName', function(req, res, next) {
  req.collection.find({},{
    limit:10, sort: [['_id',-1]]
  }).toArray(function(e, results){
    if (e) return next(e)
    res.send(results)
  })
})
```

Have you noticed a :collectionName string in the URL pattern parameter? This and the previous app.param() middleware are what give us the req.collection object, which points to a specified collection in our database.

The object-creating end point (POST /collections/:collectionName) is slightly easier to grasp because we just pass the whole payload to the MongoDB.

```
app.post('/collections/:collectionName', function(req, res, next) {
  req.collection.insert(req.body, {}, function(e, results){
    if (e) return next(e)
    res.send(results)
  })
})
```

This approach, or architecture, is often called *free JSON REST API*, because clients can throw data structured in any way and the server handles it perfectly (a good example is a back-end as a service called Parse.com, recently acquired by Facebook).

Single-object retrieval functions are faster than find(), but they use a different interface (they return an object directly instead of a cursor—please be aware). We're also extracting the ID from the :id part of the path with req.params.id Express.js magic:

```
app.get('/collections/:collectionName/:id', function(req, res, next) {
  req.collection.findOne({
    _id: id(req.params.id)
  }, function(e, result){
    if (e) return next(e)
    res.send(result)
  })
})
```

The PUT request handler gets more interesting because update() doesn't return the augmented object. Instead, it returns a count of affected objects. Also, {$set:req.body} is a special MongoDB operator (operators tend to start with a dollar sign) that sets values.

The second {safe:true, multi:false} parameter is an object with options that tell MongoDB to wait for the execution before running the callback function and to process only one (the first) item.

```
app.put('/collections/:collectionName/:id', function(req, res, next) {
  req.collection.update({
      _id: id(req.params.id)
    }, {$set:req.body}, {safe:true, multi:false},
    function(e, result){
      if (e) return next(e)
      res.send((result === 1) ? {msg:'success'} : {msg:'error'})
    }
  );
})
```

Last, the DELETE method, which also outputs a custom JSON message (JSON object with msg equals either a success string or the encountered error message):

```
app.del('/collections/:collectionName/:id', function(req, res, next) {
  req.collection.remove({
      _id: id(req.params.id)
    },
    function(e, result){
      if (e) return next(e)
      res.send((result === 1) ? {msg:'success'} : {msg:'error'})
    }
  );
})
```

■ **Note**   app.del() is an alias for app.delete() method in Express.js.

The last line that actually starts the server, on port 3000 in this case, is

```
app.listen(3000, function(){
  console.log ('Server is running')
})
```

Just in case something is not working well, here is the full code of the Express.js 4.1.2 REST API server from the ch8/rest-express/index.js file:

```
var express = require('express'),
  mongoskin = require('mongoskin'),
  bodyParser = require('body-parser'),
  logger = require('morgan')

var app = express()

app.use(bodyParser.urlencoded())
app.use(bodyParser.json())
app.use(logger())

var db = mongoskin.db('mongodb://@localhost:27017/test', {safe:true})
var id = mongoskin.helper.toObjectID
```

```
app.param('collectionName', function(req, res, next, collectionName){
  req.collection = db.collection(collectionName)
  return next()
})

app.get('/', function(req, res, next) {
  res.send('Select a collection, e.g., /collections/messages')
})

app.get('/collections/:collectionName', function(req, res, next) {
  req.collection.find({}, {limit: 10, sort: [['_id', -1]]})
    .toArray(function(e, results){
      if (e) return next(e)
      res.send(results)
    }
  )
})

app.post('/collections/:collectionName', function(req, res, next) {
  req.collection.insert(req.body, {}, function(e, results){
    if (e) return next(e)
    res.send(results)
  })
})

app.get('/collections/:collectionName/:id', function(req, res, next) {
  req.collection.findOne({_id: id(req.params.id)}, function(e, result){
    if (e) return next(e)
    res.send(result)
  })
})

app.put('/collections/:collectionName/:id', function(req, res, next) {
  req.collection.update({_id: id(req.params.id)},
    {$set: req.body},
    {safe: true, multi: false}, function(e, result){
    if (e) return next(e)
    res.send((result === 1) ? {msg:'success'} : {msg:'error'})
  })
})

app.del('/collections/:collectionName/:id', function(req, res, next) {
  req.collection.remove({_id: id(req.params.id)}, function(e, result){
    if (e) return next(e)
    res.send((result === 1) ? {msg:'success'} : {msg:'error'})
  })
})

app.listen(3000, function(){
  console.log ('Server is running')
})
```

Exit your editor and run this command in your terminal:

```
$ node .
```

This is equivalent to `$ node index.`

Then, *in a different terminal window* (without closing the first one), execute the tests:

```
$ mocha test
```

A slightly better execution is as follows (Figure 8-1):

```
$ mocha test -R nyan
```

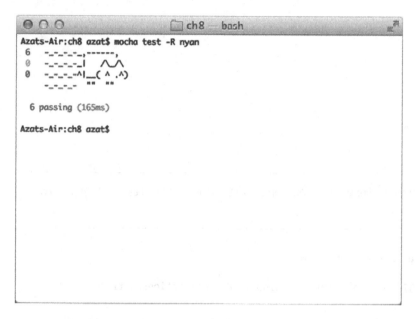

Figure 8-1. *Who wouldn't like a library with Nyan Cat?*

If you really don't like Mocha and/or BDD (and TDD), CURL is always there for you. :-) For example, CURLing is done with the following, as shown in Figure 8-2:

```
curl http://localhost:3000/collections/curl-test
```

Figure 8-2. A GET request made with CURL

■ **Note**   GET requests also work in the browser. For example, open `http://localhost:3000/test` while your server is running.

CURLing data to make a POST request is easy (Figure 8-3):

```
$ curl -d "name=peter&email=peter337@rpjs.co" http://localhost:3000/collections/curl-test
```

```
● ● ●                    🏠 azat — bash
Azats-Air:~ azat$ curl -d "name=peter&email=peter337@rpjs.co" http://localhost:3
000/collections/curl-test
[
  {
    "name": "peter",
    "email": "peter337@rpjs.co",
    "_id": "52f682ab23985a6565000008"
  }
]Azats-Air:~ azat$
```

Figure 8-3. *The result of sending a POST request via CURL*

DELETE or PUT can be sent with `--request NAME` and the ID in the URL, such as:

```
$ curl  --request DELETE http://localhost:3000/collections/curl-test/52f6828a23985a6565000008
```

For a short, nice tutorial on the main CURL commands and options, take a look at CURL Tutorial with Examples of Usage (http://www.yilmazhuseyin.com/blog/dev/curl-tutorial-examples-usage/).

In this chapter, our tests are longer than the app code itself, so abandoning TDD might be tempting, but believe me, *the good habits of TDD save you hours and hours of work* during any serious development, when the complexity of the application on which you are working is high.

You might wonder: Why spend time on TDD in the chapter about REST APIs? The answer is mainly because REST APIs don't have UIs in the form of web pages. APIs are intended for consumption by other programs (i.e., consumers or clients). We, as developers, don't have much choice when it comes to using APIs. We either have to write a client application, or manually send execute CURLs (or jQuery `$.ajax()` calls from the browser console). But, the best way is to use tests, which act as small client apps, if we think categorically!

However, this is not the whole story. TDD is great when it comes to refactoring. The next section is spent changing from Express.js to Hapi. And after we're done, we can rest assured, by running the same tests, that the functionality isn't broken or changed.

Refactoring: Hapi RESP API Server

Hapi (http://spumko.github.io/) (NPM (https://www.npmjs.org/package/hapi) and GitHub (https://github.com/spumko/hapi)) is an enterprise-grade framework. It's more complex and feature rich than Express.js, and it's easier to develop in large teams (http://hueniverse.com/2012/12/hapi-a-prologue/). Hapi is maintained by Eran Hammer (http://hueniverse.com/) of Walmart Labs.

The goal of this section is to show you alternative patterns in implementing the REST API server in Node.js. Now, because we have Mocha tests, we can refactor our code with peace of mind. Here's the `package.json` for this project:

```json
{
  "name": "rest-hapi",
  "version": "0.0.1",
  "description": "REST API application with Express, Mongoskin, MongoDB, Mocha and Superagent",
  "main": "index.js",
  "directories": {
    "test": "test"
  },
  "scripts": {
    "test": "mocha test -R spec"
  },
  "author": "Azat Mardan",
  "license": "BSD",
  "dependencies": {
    "good": "2.0.0",
    "hapi": "2.1.2",
    "mongoskin": "1.4.1"
  },
  "devDependencies": {
    "mocha": "1.16.2",
    "superagent": "0.15.7",
    "expect.js": "0.2.0"
  }
}
```

You can either use package.json with $ npm install or, for Hapi installation only, simply run $ npm install hapi@2.1.2 good@2.0.0 --save from the ch8/rest-hapi folder. hapi is the framework's module and good is its logger. This downloads the modules and unpacks them in the node_modules folder. Next, we need to create a hapi-app.js file and open it in the editor.

As usual, at the beginning of a Node.js program (ch8/rest-hapi/hapi-app.js), we import dependencies:

```js
var hapi = require('hapi'),
  mongoskin = require('mongoskin'),
```

Then, we create the Hapi server object:

```js
server = hapi.createServer('localhost', 3000),
```

and the database (just like in the Express.js example):

```js
var db = mongoskin.db('mongodb://@localhost:27017/test', {safe:true})
var id = mongoskin.helper.toObjectID
```

This function loads the database collection asynchronously based on the provided name argument. Note that loadCollection takes the URL param and gives us the corresponding database collection:

```js
var loadCollection = function(name, callback) {
  callback(db.collection(name))
}
```

This part is the most distinct compared with Express.js. Developers use properties for methods and paths, and instead of res (or response) we use reply inside of the handler property. Every route is an item in the array passed to server.route(). The first such route is for the home page ("/"):

```
server.route([
  {
    method: 'GET',
    path: '/',
    handler: function(req, reply) {
      reply('Select a collection, e.g., /collections/messages')
    }
  },
```

Next item in the array, that is the argument to the route method, is the route that returns a list of items as a response to a GET /collection/:collectionName request. The main logic happens in the handler function again, where we call the loadCollection method, find any objects (find({})), and output limited (up to 10 items) and sorted results:

```
{
method: 'GET',
path: '/collections/{collectionName}',
handler: function(req, reply) {
  loadCollection(req.params.collectionName, function(collection) {
    collection.find({}, {
      limit:10,
      sort: [['_id', -1]]}).toArray(function(e, results){
        if (e) return reply(e)
        reply(results)
      }
    )
  })
  }
},
```

The third route handles the creation of new objects (POST /collections/collectionName). Again, we use loadCollection and then call the insert method with a request body (req.paylod):

```
{
method: 'POST',
path: '/collections/{collectionName}',
handler: function(req, reply) {
  loadCollection(req.params.collectionName, function(collection) {
    collection.insert(req.payload, {}, function(e, results){
      if (e) return reply(e)
      reply(results)
    })
  })
  }
},
```

Please note that each URL parameter is enclosed in {}, unlike the :name convention that Express.js uses. This is, in part, because : is a valid URL symbol, and by using it as a parameter identifier, we eliminate it from our URL addresses.

The next route is responsible for getting a single record by its ID (/collection/collectionName/id). The main logic of using the findOne method is the same as in the Express.js server example:

```
{
method: 'GET',
path: '/collections/{collectionName}/{id}',
handler: function(req, reply) {
  loadCollection(req.params.collectionName, function(collection) {
    collection.findOne({
      _id: id(req.params.id)}, function(e, result){
        if (e) return reply(e)
        reply(result)
      }
    )
  })
}
},
```

This route updates documents in the database and, again, most of the logic in the handler remains the same, as in the Express.js example, except that we call loadCollection to get the right collection based on the URL parameter collectionName:

```
{
method: 'PUT',
path: '/collections/{collectionName}/{id}',
handler: function(req, reply) {
  loadCollection(req.params.collectionName, function(collection) {
    collection.update(
      {_id: id(req.params.id)},
      {$set:req.payload},
      {safe:true, multi:false},
      function(e, result){
        if (e) return reply(e)
        reply((result === 1) ? {msg:'success'} : {msg:'error'})
      }
    )
  })
}
},
```

The last route handles deletions. First, it gets the right collection via the URL parameter (collectionName). Then, it removes the object by its ID and sends back the message (success or error):

```
{
method: 'DELETE',
path: '/collections/{collectionName}/{id}',
handler: function(req, reply) {
  loadCollection(req.params.collectionName, function(collection) {
```

```
            collection.remove({
              _id: id(req.params.id)}, function(e, result){
                if (e) return reply(e)
                reply((result === 1) ? {msg:'success'} : {msg:'error'})
              }
            )
          })
        }
      }
    ])
```

The next configuration deals with logging and is optional:

```
var options = {
  subscribers: {
    'console': ['ops', 'request', 'log', 'error']
  }
};

server.pack.require('good', options, function (err) {
  if (!err) {
      // Plugin loaded successfully
  }
});
```

The last line of hapi-app.js starts the server with the server.start() method:

```
server.start()
```

The following summarizes what we did differently while switching from Express.js to Hapi:

1. Defined routes in an array.

2. Used method, path, and handler properties of the route object.

3. Used the loadCollection method instead of middleware.

4. Used {name} instead of :name for defining URL parameters.

For your convenience, here's the full source code of ch8/rest-hapi/hapi-app.js:

```
var hapi = require('hapi'),
  server = hapi.createServer('localhost', 3000)
  mongoskin = require('mongoskin')

var db = mongoskin.db('mongodb://@localhost:27017/test',
  {safe:true})
var id = mongoskin.helper.toObjectID

var loadCollection = function(name, callback) {
  callback(db.collection(name))
}
```

```
server.route([{
    method: 'GET',
    path: '/',
    handler: function(req, reply) {
      reply('Select a collection, e.g., /collections/messages')
    }
  }, {
    method: 'GET',
    path: '/collections/{collectionName}',
    handler: function(req, reply) {
      loadCollection(req.params.collectionName,
        function(collection) {
          collection.find({}, {
            limit: 10,
            sort: [['_id', -1]]
          }).toArray(function(e, results){
            if (e) return reply(e)
            reply(results)
          })
        }
      )
    }
  }, {
    method: 'POST',
    path: '/collections/{collectionName}',
    handler: function(req, reply) {
      loadCollection(req.params.collectionName,
        function(collection) {
          collection.insert(req.payload, {}, function(e, results){
            if (e) return reply(e)
            reply(results)
          }
        )
      })
    }
  }, {
    method: 'GET',
    path: '/collections/{collectionName}/{id}',
    handler: function(req, reply) {
      loadCollection(req.params.collectionName,
        function(collection) {
          collection.findOne({_id: id(req.params.id)},
            function(e, result){
              if (e) return reply(e)
              reply(result)
            }
          )
        }
      )
    }
```

```
  }, {
    method: 'PUT',
    path: '/collections/{collectionName}/{id}',
    handler: function(req, reply) {
      loadCollection(req.params.collectionName,
        function(collection) {
        collection.update({_id: id(req.params.id)},
          {$set: req.payload},
          {safe: true, multi: false}, function(e, result){
          if (e) return reply(e)
          reply((result === 1) ? {msg:'success'} : {msg:'error'})
        })
      })
    }
  }, {
    method: 'DELETE',
    path: '/collections/{collectionName}/{id}',
    handler: function(req, reply) {
      loadCollection(req.params.collectionName,
        function(collection) {
          collection.remove({_id: id(req.params.id)},
            function(e, result){
              if (e) return reply(e)
              reply(
                (result === 1) ? {msg:'success'} : {msg:'error'}
              )
            }
          )
        }
      )
    }
  }
])

var options = {
  subscribers: {
    'console': ['ops', 'request', 'log', 'error']
  }
};

server.pack.require('good', options, function (err) {
  if (!err) {
    // Plugin loaded successfully
  }
});

server.start()
```

If we run the newly written Hapi server with $ node hapi-app, and then run tests in a separate tab/window, the tests pass! If they don't, for some reason, the source code is in the GitHub repository github.com/azat-co/practicalnode (http://github.com/azat-co/practicalnode).

Summary

The loosely coupled architecture of REST API servers and clients (mobile, web app, or front end) allows for better maintenance and works perfectly with TDD/BDD. In addition, NoSQL databases such as MongoDB are good at handling free REST APIs. We don't have to define schemas, and we can throw any data at it and it is saved!

The Express.js and Mongoskin libraries are great when you need to build a simple REST API server using a few lines of code. Later, if you need to expand the libraries, they also provide a way to configure and organize your code. If you want to learn more about Express.js, take a look at *Pro Express.js [2014, Apress]*. Also, it's good to know that, for more complex systems, the Hapi server framework is there for you!

In this chapter, in addition to Express.js, we used MongoDB via Mongoskin. We also used Mocha and SuperAgent to write functional tests that, potentially, save us hours in testing and debugging when we refactor code in the future. Then, we easily flipped Express.js for Hapi and, thanks to the tests, are confident that our code works as expected! The differences between the Express and Hapi frameworks that we observed are in the way we defined routes and URL parameters, and output the response.

■ ■ ■

CHAPTER 9

Real-Time Apps with WebSocket, Socket.IO, and DerbyJS

Real-time apps are becoming more and more widespread in gaming, social media, various tools, services, and news. The main factor contributing to this trend is that technologies have become much better. They allow for a greater bandwidth to transmit data, and for more calculations to process and retrieve the data.

HTML5 pioneered the new standard of real-time connections called *WebSocket*. At the same time, on the server side, Node.js has a highly efficient, nonblocking input/output platform that is very well suited for the task of being a back-end pair to the browser JavaScript and WebSocket.

To get you started with WebSocket and Node.js, we'll keep things simple stupid (KISS (http://en.wikipedia. org/wiki/KISS_principle)) and cover the following:

- What is WebSocket?

- Native WebSocket and Node.js with the ws module example

- Socket.IO and Express.js example

- Collaborative online editor example with DerbyJS, Express.js, and MongoDB

What Is WebSocket?

WebSocket is a special communication "channel" between browsers (clients) and servers. It's an HTML5 protocol. WebSocket's connection is constant, in contrast to traditional HTTP requests, with the latter usually initiated by the client. Therefore, there's no way for a server to notify the client if there are updates. By maintaining a duplex open connection between the client and the server, updates can be pushed in a timely fashion without clients needing to poll at certain intervals. This main factor makes WebSocket ideal for real-time apps for which data need to be available on the client immediately. For more information on WebSocket, take a look at the extensive resource "About HTML5 WebSocket" (http://www.websocket.org/aboutwebsocket.html).

There's no need to use any special libraries to use WebSocket in modern browsers. The following StackOverflow has a list of such browsers: What browsers support HTML5 WebSockets API? (http://stackoverflow.com/ questions/1253683/what-browsers-support-html5-websocket-api) For older browser support, the workaround includes falling back on polling.

As a side note, polling (both short and long), can also be used to emulate the real-time responsiveness of web apps. In fact, some advanced libraries (Socket.IO) fall back to polling when WebSocket becomes unavailable as a result of connection issues or users not having the latest versions of browsers. Polling is relatively easy and we don't cover it here. It can be implemented with just a setInterval() callback and an end point on the server. However, there's not real-time communication with polling; each request is separate.

Native WebSocket and Node.js with the ws Module Example

Sometimes it's easier to start from the simplest thing and build things on top of it. With this in mind, our mini project includes building a native WebSocket implementation that talks with the Node.js server with the help of the ws module:

- Browser WebSocket implementation
- Node.js server with ws module implementation

Let's examine this with a quick example.

Browser WebSocket Implementation

This is our front-end code (file ch9/basic/index.html) for Chrome version 32.0.1700.77. We start with typical HTML tags:

```
<html>
  <head>
  </head>
  <body>
```

The main code lives in the script tag, where we instantiate an object from global WebSocket:

```
<script type="text/javascript">
  var ws = new WebSocket('ws://localhost:3000');
```

As soon as the connection is established, we send a message to the server:

```
ws.onopen = function(event) {
  ws.send('front-end message: ABC');
};
```

Usually, messages are sent in response to user actions, such as mouse clicks. When we get any message from the WebSocket location, the following handler is executed:

```
ws.onmessage = function(event) {
  console.log('server message: ', event.data);
};
```

A good practice is to have an onerror event handler:

```
ws.onerror = function(event) {
  console.log('server error message: ', event.data);
};
```

We then close the tags and save the file:

```
  </script>
  </body>
</html>
```

To make sure you don't miss anything, here's the full source code of ch9/basic/index.html:

```
<html>
  <head>
  </head>
  <body>
    <script type="text/javascript">
      var ws = new WebSocket('ws://localhost:3000');
      ws.onopen = function(event) {
        ws.send('front-end message: ABC');
      };
      ws.onmessage = function(event) {
        console.log('server message: ', event.data);
      };
    </script>
  </body>
</html>
```

Node.js Server with ws Module Implementation

WebSocket.org provides an echo service for testing the browser WebSocket, but we can build our own small Node.js
server with the help of the ws (http://npmjs.org/ws, GitHub: https://github.com/einaros/ws) library:

```
$ mkdir node_modules
$ npm install ws@0.4.31
```

In the ch9/basic/server.js file, we import ws and initialize the server:

```
var WebSocketServer = require('ws').Server,
  wss = new WebSocketServer({port: 3000});
```

Akin to the front-end code, we use an event pattern to wait for a connection. When the connection is ready, in the
callback we send the string XYZ and attach an event listener on ('message') to listen to incoming messages from the page:

```
wss.on('connection', function(ws) {
    ws.send('XYZ');
    ws.on('message', function(message) {
        console.log('received: %s', message);
    });
});
```

Again, for reference, here's the full code of ch9/basic/server.js:

```
var WebSocketServer = require('ws').Server,
  wss = new WebSocketServer({port: 3000});

wss.on('connection', function(ws) {
    ws.send('XYZ');
    ws.on('message', function(message) {
        console.log('received: %s', message);
    });
});
```

Start the Node.js server with $ node server. Then, open index.html in the browser and you should see this message in the JavaScript console (option + command + j on Macs): server message: XYZ (Figure 9-1).

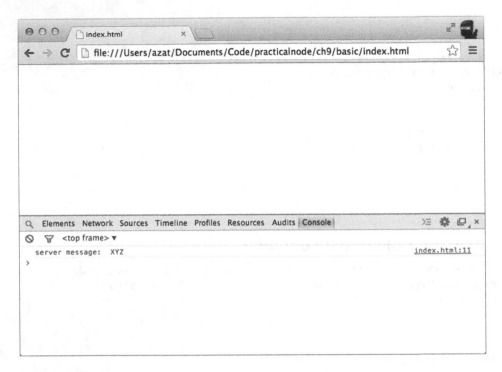

Figure 9-1. *Browser outputs a message received via WebSocket*

While in the terminal, the Node.js server output is received: front-end message: ABC, which is illustrated in Figure 9-2.

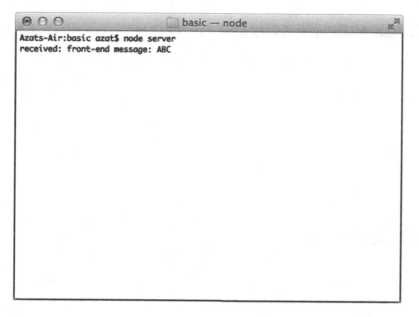

Figure 9-2. The server outputs the browser message received via WebSocket

Native HTML5 WebSocket is an amazing technology. However, WebSocket is a protocol and an evolving standard. This means that each browser implementation might vary. And, of course, if support for older browsers is needed, you should do your research and test.

In addition, often the connection may be lost and may need to be re-established. To handle cross-browser and backward compatibility, as well as re-opening, a lot of developers depend on the Socket.IO library, which we will explore in the next section.

Socket.IO and Express.js Example

Full coverage of the Socket.IO (http://socket.io/) library absolutely deserves its own book. Nevertheless, because it's such a popular library, and getting started with it is very easy with Express.js, we include in this chapter an example that covers the basics. This mini project illustrates duplex-channel communication between browser and server.

As in most real-time web apps, the communication between a server and a client happens in response either to some user actions or as a result of updates from the server. So, in our example, the web page renders a form field in which each character echoes (browser to server and back) in reverse in real time. The example harnesses Express. js command-line tool scaffolding, Socket.IO, and Jade (see screenshots of the working app in Figures 9-3 and 9-4). Of course, you can just download the app from github.com/azat-co/practicalnode (http://github.com/azat-co/practicalnode).

Figure 9-3. *The input of* `!stekcoS` *yields* `Sockets!`

```
⊝ ○ ○                        🗔 socket — node

Azats-Air:socket azat$ node app
   info  - socket.io started
Express server listening on port 3000
GET / 200 350ms - 742b
GET /stylesheets/style.css 200 14ms - 110b
   debug - served static content /socket.io.js
   debug - client authorized
   info  - handshake authorized TD0xgHdxH3sr66zMJ_Xw
   debug - setting request GET /socket.io/1/websocket/TD0xgHdxH3sr66zMJ_Xw
   debug - set heartbeat interval for client TD0xgHdxH3sr66zMJ_Xw
   debug - client authorized for
   debug - websocket writing 1::
   debug - client authorized
   info  - handshake authorized gVQ9UssfFv5xH8SpJ_Xx
   debug - setting request GET /socket.io/1/websocket/gVQ9UssfFv5xH8SpJ_Xx
   debug - set heartbeat interval for client gVQ9UssfFv5xH8SpJ_Xx
   debug - client authorized for
   debug - websocket writing 1::
{ message: '!stekcoS' }
   debug - websocket writing 5:::{"name":"receive","args":["Sockets!"]}
{ message: '!' }
   debug - websocket writing 5:::{"name":"receive","args":["!"]}
{ message: '!' }
   debug - websocket writing 5:::{"name":"receive","args":["!"]}
   debug - emitting heartbeat for client TD0xgHdxH3sr66zMJ_Xw
   debug - websocket writing 2::
   debug - set heartbeat timeout for client TD0xgHdxH3sr66zMJ_Xw
   debug - got heartbeat packet
   debug - cleared heartbeat timeout for client TD0xgHdxH3sr66zMJ_Xw
   debug - set heartbeat interval for client TD0xgHdxH3sr66zMJ_Xw
{ message: '!s' }
   debug - websocket writing 5:::{"name":"receive","args":["s!"]}
{ message: '!st' }
   debug - websocket writing 5:::{"name":"receive","args":["ts!"]}
{ message: '!ste' }
   debug - websocket writing 5:::{"name":"receive","args":["ets!"]}
{ message: '!stek' }
   debug - websocket writing 5:::{"name":"receive","args":["kets!"]}
{ message: '!stekc' }
   debug - websocket writing 5:::{"name":"receive","args":["ckets!"]}
{ message: '!stekco' }
   debug - websocket writing 5:::{"name":"receive","args":["ockets!"]}
{ message: '!stekcoS' }
   debug - websocket writing 5:::{"name":"receive","args":["Sockets!"]}
{ message: '!stekcoS' }
   debug - websocket writing 5:::{"name":"receive","args":["Sockets!"]}
   debug - emitting heartbeat for client gVQ9UssfFv5xH8SpJ_Xx
   debug - websocket writing 2::
   debug - set heartbeat timeout for client gVQ9UssfFv5xH8SpJ_Xx
   debug - got heartbeat packet
   debug - cleared heartbeat timeout for client gVQ9UssfFv5xH8SpJ_Xx
   debug - set heartbeat interval for client gVQ9UssfFv5xH8SpJ_Xx
   debug - emitting heartbeat for client TD0xgHdxH3sr66zMJ_Xw
```

Figure 9-4. Express.js server catching and processing input in real time

To include Socket.IO, we can use `$ npm install socket.io@0.9.16 --save` and repeat it for every module, or we can use `package.json` and `$ npm install`:

```
{
  "name": "socket-express",
  "version": "0.0.1",
  "private": true,
  "scripts": {
    "start": "node ./bin/www"
  },
  "dependencies": {
    "express": "~4.0.0",
    "morgan": "~1.0.0",
    "cookie-parser": "~1.0.1",
    "body-parser": "~1.0.0",
    "debug": "~0.7.4",
    "jade": "~1.3.0",
    "socket.io": "0.9.16"
  }
}
```

Socket.IO, in some way, might be considered another server, because it handles socket connections and not our standard HTTP requests. This is how we refactor autogenerated Express.js code:

```
var http = require('http');
var express = require('express');
var path = require('path');
var logger = require('morgan');
var bodyParser = require('body-parser');
```

The standard Express.js 4.x configuration is as follows:

```
var routes = require('./routes/index');
var app = express();

app.set('views', path.join(__dirname, 'views'));
app.set('view engine', 'jade');

app.use(logger('dev'));
app.use(bodyParser.json());
app.use(bodyParser.urlencoded());
app.use(express.static(path.join(__dirname, 'public')));

app.use('/', routes);
```

Then, the Socket.IO piece is as follows:

```
var server = http.createServer(app);
var io = require('socket.io').listen(server);
```

When the Socket server connection is established, we attach a messageChange event listener that implements logic that is reversing an incoming string:

```
io.sockets.on('connection', function (socket) {
  socket.on('messageChange', function (data) {
    console.log(data);
    socket.emit('receive',
      data.message.split('').reverse().join('')
    );
  })
});
```

We finish by starting the server without standard methods:

```
app.set('port', process.env.PORT || 3000);
server.listen(app.get('port'), function(){
  console.log('Express server listening on port ' + app.get('port'));
});
```

Just in case these snippets are confusing, here's the full content of ch9/socket-express/app.js:

```
var http = require('http');
var express = require('express');
var path = require('path');
var logger = require('morgan');
var bodyParser = require('body-parser');

var routes = require('./routes/index');
var app = express();

app.set('views', path.join(__dirname, 'views'));
app.set('view engine', 'jade');

app.use(logger('dev'));
app.use(bodyParser.json());
app.use(bodyParser.urlencoded());
app.use(express.static(path.join(__dirname, 'public')));

app.use('/', routes);

var server = http.createServer(app);
var io = require('socket.io').listen(server);

io.sockets.on('connection', function (socket) {
  socket.on('messageChange', function (data) {
    console.log(data);
    socket.emit('receive',
      data.message.split('').reverse().join('')
    );
  });
});
```

```
app.set('port', process.env.PORT || 3000);
server.listen(app.get('port'), function(){
  console.log('Express server listening on port ' +
    app.get('port')
  );
});
```

A quick remark about port numbers: by default, WebSocket connections can use the standard ports: 80 for HTTP and 443 for HTTPS.

Last, our app needs some front-end love in index.jade. Nothing fancy; just a form field and some front-end JavaScript in the Jade template:

```
extends layout

block content
  h1= title
  p Welcome to
    span.received-message #{title}
  input(type='text', class='message', placeholder='what is on your mind?', onkeyup='send(this)')
  script(src="/socket.io/socket.io.js")
  script.
    var socket = io.connect('http://localhost');
    socket.on('receive', function (message) {
      console.log('received %s', message);
      document
        .querySelector('.received-message')
        .innerText = message;
    });
    var send = function(input) {
      console.log(input.value);
      var value = input.value;
      console.log('sending %s to server', value);
      socket.emit('messageChange', {message: value});
    };
```

Again, start the server and open the browser to see real-time communication. Typing text in the browser field logs data on the server without messing up HTTP requests and waiting. The approximate browser results are shown in Figure 9-3; the server logs are shown in Figure 9-4.

For more Socket.IO examples, go to socket.io/#how-to-use (http://socket.io/#how-to-use).

Collaborative Online Code Editor Example with DerbyJS, Express.js, and MongoDB

Derby (http://derbyjs.com/) is a new, sophisticated MVC[1] framework designed to be used with Express (http://expressjs.com/) as its middleware, whereas Express.js (http://expressjs.com/) is a popular node framework that uses the middleware concept to enhance the functionality of applications. Derby also comes with the support of Racer (https://github.com/codeparty/racer), a data synchronization engine, and Handlebars (https://github.com/wycats/handlebars.js/) -like template engine, among many other features (http://derbyjs.com/#features).

---

[1]http://en.wikipedia.org/wiki/Model-view-controller.

Meteor (http://meteor.com/) and Sails.js (http://sailsjs.org/) are other reactive (real-time) full-stack MVC Node.js frameworks comparable with DerbyJS. However, Meteor is more opinionated and often relies on proprietary solutions and packages.

The following example illustrates how easy it is to build a real-time application using Express.js, DerbyJS, MongoDB, and Redis.

The structure for this DerbyJS mini project is as follows:

- Project dependencies and package.json
- Server-side code
- DerbyJS app
- DerbyJS view
- Editor tryout

Project Dependencies and package.json

If you haven't installed Node.js, NPM, MongoDB, or Redis, you can do it now by following instructions in these resources:

- Installing Node.js via package manager (https://github.com/joyent/node/wiki/Installing-Node.js-via-package-manager)
- Installing npm (http://howtonode.org/introduction-to-npm)
- Install MongoDB (http://docs.mongodb.org/manual/installation/#install-mongodb)
- Redis Quick Start (http://redis.io/topics/quickstart)

Create a project folder, editor, and a file package.json with the following content:

```json
{
  "name": "editor",
  "version": "0.0.1",
  "description": "Online collaborative code editor",
  "main": "index.js",
  "scripts": {
    "test": "mocha test"
  },
  "git repository": "http://github.com/azat-co/editor",
  "keywords": "editor node derby real-time",
  "author": "Azat Mardan",
  "license": "BSD",
  "dependencies": {
    "derby": "~0.5.12",
    "express": "~3.4.8",
    "livedb-mongo": "~0.3.0",
    "racer-browserchannel": "~0.1.1",
    "redis": "~0.10.0"
  }
}
```

This gets us the derby (DerbyJS), express (Express.js), livedb-mongo, racer-browserchannel, and redis (Redis client) modules. DerbyJS and Express.js are for routing and they use corresponding frameworks (versions 0.5.12 and 3.4.8). Redis, racer-browserchannel, and livedb-mongo allow DerbyJS to use Redis and MongoDB databases.

Server-side Code

As an entry point for our application, create editor/server.js with a single line of code that starts a Derby server we have yet to write:

```
require('derby').run(__dirname + '/server.js');
```

Create and start adding the following lines to editor/server.js. First, import the dependencies:

```
var path = require('path'),
  express = require('express'),
  derby = require('derby'),
  racerBrowserChannel = require('racer-browserchannel'),
  liveDbMongo = require('livedb-mongo'),
```

Then, define the Derby app file:

```
app = require(path.join(__dirname, 'app.js')),
```

Instantiate the Express.js app:

```
expressApp = module.exports = express(),
```

the Redis client:

```
redis = require('redis').createClient(),
```

and the local MongoDB connection URI:

```
mongoUrl = 'mongodb://localhost:27017/editor';
```

Now we create a liveDbMongo object with the connection URI and redis client object:

```
var store = derby.createStore({
  db: liveDbMongo(mongoUrl + '?auto_reconnect', {
    safe: true
  }),
  redis: redis
});
```

Define a public folder with static content:

```
var publicDir = path.join(__dirname, 'public');
```

Then, declare Express.js middleware in chained calls:

```
expressApp
  .use(express.favicon())
  .use(express.compress())
```

It's important to include DerbyJS-specific middleware that exposes Derby routes and model objects:

```
  .use(app.scripts(store))
  .use(racerBrowserChannel(store))
  .use(store.modelMiddleware())
  .use(app.router())
```

Regular Express.js router middleware follows:

```
  .use(expressApp.router);
```

It's possible to mix Express.js and DerbyJS routes in one server—the 404 catchall route:

```
expressApp.all('*', function(req, res, next) {
  return next('404: ' + req.url);
});
```

The full source code of server.js is as follows:

```
var path = require('path'),
  express = require('express'),
  derby = require('derby'),
  racerBrowserChannel = require('racer-browserchannel'),
  liveDbMongo = require('livedb-mongo'),
  app = require(path.join(__dirname, 'app.js')),
  expressApp = module.exports = express(),
  redis = require('redis').createClient(),
  mongoUrl = 'mongodb://localhost:27017/editor';

var store = derby.createStore({
  db: liveDbMongo(mongoUrl + '?auto_reconnect', {
    safe: true
  }),
  redis: redis
});

var publicDir = path.join(__dirname, 'public');

expressApp
  .use(express.favicon())
  .use(express.compress())
  .use(app.scripts(store))
  .use(racerBrowserChannel(store))
```

```
  .use(store.modelMiddleware())
  .use(app.router())
  .use(expressApp.router);

expressApp.all('*', function(req, res, next) {
  return next('404: ' + req.url);
});
```

DerbyJS App

The DerbyJS app (app.js) shares code smartly between the browser and the server, so you can write functions and methods in one place (a Node.js file). However, parts of app.js code become browser JavaScript code (not just Node.js) depending on the DerbyJS rules. This behavior allows for better code reuse and organization, because you don't have to duplicate routes, the helper function, and utility methods. One of the places where the code from the DerbyJS app file becomes browser code only is inside app.ready(), which we will see later.

Declare the variable and create an app (editor/app.js):

```
var app;
app = require('derby').createApp(module);
```

Declare the root route so that when a user visits it, the new snippet is created and the user is redirected to the /:snippetId route:

```
app.get('/', function(page, model, _arg, next) {
  snippetId = model.add('snippets', {
    snippetName: _arg.snippetName,
    code: 'var'
  });
  return page.redirect('/' + snippetId);
});
```

DerbyJS uses a route pattern similar to Express.js, but instead of response (res), we use page, and we get data from the model argument.

The /:snippetId route is where the editor is displayed. To support real-time updates to the Document Object Model (DOM), all we need to do is to call subscribe:

```
app.get('/:snippetId', function(page, model, param, next) {
  var snippet = model.at('snippets.'+param.snippetId);
  snippet.subscribe(function(err){
    if (err) return next(err);
    console.log (snippet.get());
    model.ref('_page.snippet', snippet);
    page.render();
  });
});
```

The model.at method with a parameter in a collection_name.ID pattern is akin to calling findById()—in other words, we get the object from the store/database.

model.ref() allows us to bind an object to the view representation. Usually in the view we would write {{_page.snippet}} and it would update itself reactively. However, to make the editor look beautiful, we use the Ace editor from Cloud9 (http://ace.c9.io/). Ace is attached to the editor object (global browser variable).

Front-end JavaScript code in DerbyJS is written in the app.ready callback. We need to set Ace content from the Derby model on app start:

```
app.ready(function(model) {
  editor.setValue(model.get('_page.snippet.code'));
```

Then, it listens to model changes (coming from other users) and updates the Ace editor with new text (front-end code):

```
model.on('change', '_page.snippet.code', function(){
  if (editor.getValue() !== model.get('_page.snippet.code')) {
    process.nextTick(function(){
      editor.setValue(model.get('_page.snippet.code'), 1);
    })
  }
});
```

process.nextTick is a function that schedules the callback (passed as a parameter to it) in the next event loop iteration. This trick allows us to avoid an infinite loop when the updated model from one user triggers a change event on the Ace editor, and that triggers an unnecessary update on the remote model.

The code that listens to Ace changes (e.g., new character) and updates the DerbyJS model:

```
  editor.getSession().on('change', function(e) {
    if (editor.getValue() !== model.get('_page.snippet.code')) {
      process.nextTick(function(){
        model.set('_page.snippet.code', editor.getValue());
      });
    }
  });
});
```

_page is a special DerbyJS name used for rendering/binding in the views.

For reference, the full source code of editor/app.js is as follows:

```
var app;

app = require('derby').createApp(module);

app.get('/', function(page, model, _arg, next) {
  snippetId = model.add('snippets', {
    snippetName: _arg.snippetName,
    code: 'var'
  });
  return page.redirect('/' + snippetId);
});
```

```
app.get('/:snippetId', function(page, model, param, next) {
  var snippet = model.at('snippets.'+param.snippetId);
  snippet.subscribe(function(err){
    if (err) return next(err);
    console.log (snippet.get());
    model.ref('_page.snippet', snippet);
    page.render();
  });
});

app.ready(function(model) {
  editor.setValue(model.get('_page.snippet.code'));
  model.on('change', '_page.snippet.code', function(){
    if (editor.getValue() !== model.get('_page.snippet.code')) {
      process.nextTick(function(){
        editor.setValue(model.get('_page.snippet.code'), 1);
      });
    }
  });
  editor.getSession().on('change', function(e) {
    if (editor.getValue() !== model.get('_page.snippet.code')) {
      process.nextTick(function(){
        model.set('_page.snippet.code', editor.getValue());
      });
    }
  });
});
```

DerbyJS View

The DerbyJS view (views/app.html) is quite straightforward. It contains built-in tags such as <Title:>, but most of the things are generated dynamically by the Ace editor after the page is loaded.

Let's start by defining the title and head:

```
<Title:>
  Online Collaborative Code Editor
<Head:>
  <meta charset="UTF-8">
  <meta http-equiv="X-UA-Compatible" content="IE=edge,chrome=1">
  <title>Editor</title>
  <style type="text/css" media="screen">
    body {
        overflow: hidden;
    }

    #editor {
        margin: 0;
        position: absolute;
        top: 0px;
        bottom: 0;
```

```
        left: 0;
        right: 0;
    }
  </style>
```

Then, load jQuery and Ace from content delivery networks (CDNs):

```html
<script src="//cdnjs.cloudflare.com/ajax/libs/ace/1.1.01/ace.js"></script>
<script src="//code.jquery.com/jquery-2.1.0.min.js"></script>
```

Apply a hidden input tag and editor element inside the body tag:

```html
<Body:>
  <input type="hidden" value="{_page.snippet.code}" class="code"/>
  <pre id="editor" value="{_page.snippet.code}"></pre>
```

Initialize the Ace editor object as global (the editor variable), then set the theme and language (of course, JavaScript!) with setTheme() and setMode(), respectively:

```html
<script>
    var editor = ace.edit("editor");
    editor.setTheme("ace/theme/twilight");
    editor.getSession().setMode("ace/mode/javascript");
</script>
```

The full source code of views/app.html is as follows:

```html
<Title:>
  Online Collaborative Code Editor
<Head:>
  <meta charset="UTF-8">
  <meta http-equiv="X-UA-Compatible" content="IE=edge,chrome=1">
  <title>Editor</title>
  <style type="text/css" media="screen">
    body {
        overflow: hidden;
    }

    #editor {
        margin: 0;
        position: absolute;
        top: 0px;
        bottom: 0;
        left: 0;
        right: 0;
    }
  </style>
  <script src="//cdnjs.cloudflare.com/ajax/libs/ace/1.1.01/ace.js"></script>
  <script src="//code.jquery.com/jquery-2.1.0.min.js"></script>
<Body:>
  <input type="hidden" value="{_page.snippet.code}" class="code"/>
  <pre id="editor" value="{_page.snippet.code}"></pre>
```

```
<script>
    var editor = ace.edit("editor");
    editor.setTheme("ace/theme/twilight");
    editor.getSession().setMode("ace/mode/javascript");
</script>
```

■ **Note**   It's vital to preserve the same view name (i.e., app.html) as the DerbyJS app file (app.js), because this is how the framework knows what to use.

Editor Tryout

If you followed all the previous steps, there should be app.js, index.js, server.js, views/app.html, and package.json files.

Let's install the modules with $ npm install. Start the databases with $ mongod and $ redis-server, and leave them running. Then, launch the app with $ node . or $ node index.

Open the first browser window at http://localhost:3000/ and it should redirect you to a new snippet (with ID in the URL). Open a second browser window at the same location and start typing (Figure 9-5). You should see the code updating in the first window! Congratulations! In just a few minutes, we built an app that might have taken programmers a few months to build back in the 2000s, when front-end JavaScript and AJAX-y web sites were first gaining popularity.

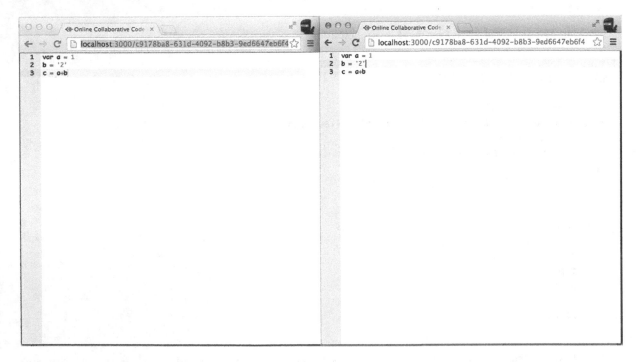

Figure 9-5. *Collaborative online code editor*

The working project is available on GitHub at https://github.com/azat-co/editor.

Summary

In this chapter, we saw that there's native support for WebSocket in modern HTML5 browsers, and we learned how to get started with Socket.IO and Express.js to harness the power of WebSocket in Node.js. In addition, we explored the mighty full-stack framework of DerbyJS in the editor example.

In the next chapter we'll move to the essential part of any real-world project which is getting Node.js apps to a production level readiness by adding extra configuration, monitoring, logging and other things.

■ ■ ■

CHAPTER 10

Getting Node.js Apps Production Ready

Getting Node.js apps to a production-ready state is probably the most under covered and skipped topic in the Node.js literature, but it's one of the most important in my humble opinion.

Yes, the apps differ in structures, frameworks they use, and goals they try to achieve; however, there are a few commonalities worth knowing about, for example, environmental variables, multithreading, logging and error handling. So, in this chapter we cover the following topics:

- Environment variables

- Express.js in production

- Socket.IO in production

- Error handling

- Node.js domains for error handling

- Multithreading with Cluster

- Multithreading with Cluster2

- Event logging and monitoring

- Building tasks with Grunt

- Git for version control and deployments

- Running tests in Cloud with TravisCI

Environment Variables

Before deployment to the production environment, it's good to prepare our app's code. Let's start with information that needs to be private and can't be shared in a version control system. Sensitive information such as API keys, passwords, and database URIs are best stored in environment variables (http://en.wikipedia.org/wiki/environment_variable), not in the source code itself. Node.js makes it fairly easy to access these variables:

```
console.log (process.env.NODE_ENV,
  process.env.API_KEY,
  process.env.DB_PASSWORD)
```

Then, before the application is started, set these variables:

```
$ NODE_ENV=test API_KEY=XYZ DB_PASSWORD=ABC node envvar.js
```

■ **Note**   There's no space between NAME and value (NAME=VALUE).

Typically, the environment variable setting is a part of the deployment or operations setup. In the next chapter, we deal with putting these variables on the server.

Express.js in Production

In Express.js 4.x, use if/else statements to check for NODE_ENV values:

```
var errorHandler = require('errorhandler');
if (process.env.NODE_ENV === 'development') {
  app.use(errorHandler({
    dumpExceptions: true,
    showStack: true
  }));
} else if (process.env.NODE_ENV === 'production') {
  app.use(errorHandler());
}
```

Express.js 3.x provides app.configure(), the so-called sugarcoating methods for different modes: development, test, stage, production, and so on.

```
app.configure('development', function(){
  app.use(express.errorHandler({
    dumpExceptions: true,
    showStack: true
  }));
});

app.configure('production', function(){
  app.use(express.errorHandler());
});
```

Each app.configure pattern is equivalent to a series of if/else statements:

```
if (process.env.NODE_ENV === 'development') {
  app.use(express.errorHandler({
    dumpExceptions: true,
    showStack: true
  }));
} else if (process.env.NODE_ENV === 'production') {
  app.use(express.errorHandler());
}
```

To run the server in a specific mode, just set an environment variable. For example,

```
$ NODE_ENV=production node app.js
```

or:

```
$ export NODE_ENV=production
$ node app.js
```

■ **Note** By default, Express.js falls back to development mode as we see in the source code (`http://bit.ly/117UEi6`).

When using in-memory session store (the default choice), the data can't be shared across different processes/servers (which we want in production mode). Conveniently, Express.js and Connect notify us about this as we see in this source code (`http://bit.ly/1nnvvhf`) with this message:

```
Warning: connect.session() MemoryStore is not
designed for a production environment, as it will leak
memory, and will not scale past a single process.
```

This problem is solved easily by using a shared Redis instance as a session store. For example, for Express.js 4, execute the following:

```
var session = require('express-session'),
  RedisStore = require('connect-redis')(session);

app.use(session({
  store: new RedisStore(options),
  secret: 'keyboard cat'
}));
```

The more advanced example with session options is as follows:

```
var SessionStore = require('connect-redis');
var session = require('express-session');

app.use(session({
  key: '92A7-9AC',
  secret: '33D203B7-443B',
  store: new SessionStore({
    cookie: { domain: '.webapplog.com' },
    db: 1, // Redis DB
    host: 'webapplog.com'
}));
```

For Express.js 3.x application use this middleware configuration:

```
var SessionStore = require('connect-redis');
```

```
app.configure(function(){
  this.use(express.session({
    key: '92A7-9AC',
    secret: '33D203B7-443B',
    store: new SessionStore({
      cookie: { domain: '.webapplog.com' },
      db: 1, // Redis DB
      host: 'webapplog.com'
    })
  }));
});
```

Options for connect-redis are client, host, port, ttl, db, pass, prefix, and url. For more information, please refer to the official connect-redis documentation (https://github.com/visionmedia/connect-redis).

Socket.IO in Production

Akin to Express.js 3.x, the Socket.IO library has configure() method that can be used to define different rules for different environments:

```
var io = require('socket.io').listen(80);

io.configure('production', function(){
  io.enable('browser client etag');
  io.set('log level', 1);
  io.set('transports', [
    'websocket',
    'flashsocket',
    'htmlfile',
    'xhr-polling',
    'jsonp-polling'
  ]);
});

io.configure('development', function(){
  io.set('transports', ['websocket']);
});
```

Often, WebSockets data are stored in a high-performance database such as Redis. In this example, you can use environment variables for values of port and hostname:

```
var sio = require('socket.io'),
  RedisStore = sio.RedisStore,
  io = sio.listen();

io.configure(function () {
  io.set('store', new RedisStore({ host: 'http://webapplog.com' }));
});

var redis = require('redis'),
  redisClient = redis.createClient(port, hostname),
  redisSub = redis.createClient(port, hostname);
```

```
redisClient.on('error', function (err) {
  console.error(err);
});

redisSub.on('error', function (err) {
  console.error(err);
});

io.configure(function () {
  io.set('store', new RedisStore({
    nodeId: function () { return nodeId; },
    redisPub: redisPub,
    redisSub: redisSub,
    redisClient: redisClient
  }));
});
```

Error Handling

As a rule of thumb, listen to all error events from http.Server and https.Server (i.e., always have onerror event listeners doing something):

```
server.on('error', function (err) {
  console.error(err);
  ...
})
```

Then, have a catchall event listener (uncaughtException) for unforeseen cases. These cases won't make it to the onerror handlers:

```
process.on('uncaughtException', function (err) {
  console.error('uncaughtException: ', err.message);
  console.error(err.stack);
  process.exit(1);
});
```

Alternatively, you can use the addListener method:

```
process.addListener('uncaughtException', function (err) {
  console.error('uncaughtException: ', err.message);
  console.error(err.stack);
  process.exit(1);
});
```

The following snippet is devised to catch uncaught exceptions, log them, notify development and operations (DevOps) via e-mail/text messages, and then exit:

```
process.addListener('uncaughtException', function (e) {
  server.statsd.increment('errors.uncaughtexception');
  log.sub('uncaughtException').error(e.stack || e.message);
  if(server.sendgrid && server.set('env') === 'production') {
```

```
    server.notify.error(e);
  }
  exit();
});
```

You might wonder what to do in the event of these uncaught exceptions (the server.notify.error() method). It depends. Typically, at a minimum, we want them to be recorded, most likely in the logs. For this purpose, later we'll cover a more advanced alternative to console.log—the Winston library (https://github.com/flatiron/winston). At a maximum, you can implement text message alerts effortlessly using the Twilio API (http://www.twilio.com). The following is an example in which helpers can send HipChat (https://www.hipchat.com) messages via their REST API and send an e-mail containing an error stack:

```
var sendHipChatMessage = function(message, callback) {
  var fromhost = server
    .set('hostname')
    .replace('-','')
    .substr(0, 15); //truncate the string
  try {
    message = JSON.stringify(message);
  } catch(e) {}
  var data = {
    'format': 'json',
    auth_token: server.config.keys.hipchat.servers,
    room_id: server.config.keys.hipchat.serversRoomId,
    from: fromhost,
    message: 'v'
      + server.set('version')
      + '\nmessage: '
      + message
  };
  request({
    url:'http://api.hipchat.com/v1/rooms/message',
    method:'POST',
    qs: data}, function (e, r, body) {
      if (e) console.error(e);
      if (callback) return callback();
  });
};

server.notify = {};
server.notify.error = function(e) {
  var message = e.stack || e.message || e.name || e;
  sendHipChatMessage(message);
  console.error(message);
  server.sendgrid.email({
    to: 'error@webapplog.com',
    from: server.set('hostname') + '@webapplog.com',
    subject: 'Webapp '
      + server.set('version')
      + ' error: "'
      + e.name
      + '"',
```

```
      category: 'webapp-error',
      text: e.stack || e.message
    }, exit);
    return;
}
```

Node.js Domains for Error Handling

Because Node.js allows developers to write asynchronous code, and that's what we usually do, and because state changes during different async parts of code, sometimes it's harder to trace errors and have a meaningful state and context in which the application was during that exception. To mitigate this, we have domains in Node.js.

Contrary to its more popular homonym (domain as in webapplog.com or google.com), domain is a core Node. js module (http://nodejs.org/api/domain.html). It aids developers in tracking and isolating errors that could be a juggernaut task. Think of domains as a smarter version of try/catch statements (https://developer.mozilla.org/en-US/docs/web/javaScript/reference/statements/try...catch).

When it comes to Express.js (and other frameworks), we can apply domains in error-prone routes. A route can become error prone if it has pretty much any nontrivial code (i.e., any route can be prone to error), but usually developers can just analyze logs and determine which URL and path are causing the crashes. Typically, these routes rely on third-party modules, some communication, or file system/database input/output.

Before defining the routes, we need to define custom handlers to catch errors from domains. In Express.js 4.x we do the following:

```
var express = require('express');
var domain = require('domain');
var defaultHandler = require('errorhandler');
```

In Express.js 3.x, we execute:

```
var express = require('express');
var domain = require('domain');
var defaultHandler = express.errorHandler();
```

Then, for Express.js 4.x and 3.x, we add middleware:

```
app.use(function (error, req, res, next) {
  if (domain.active) {
    console.info('caught with domain');
    domain.active.emit("error", error);
  } else {
    console.info('no domain');
    defaultHandler(error, req, res, next);
  }
});
```

Here is a "crashy route" in which the error-prone code goes inside the d.run callback:

```
app.get('/e', function (req, res, next) {
  var d = domain.create();
  d.on('error', function (error) {
    console.error(error.stack);
```

```
    res.send(500, {'error': error.message});
  });
  d.run(function () {
    // Error-prone code goes here
    throw new Error('Database is down.');
  });
});
```

On the other hand, we can call next with an error object (e.g., when an error variable comes from other nested calls):

```
app.get('/e', function (req, res, next) {
  var d = domain.create();
  d.on('error', function (error) {
    console.error(error.stack);
    res.send(500, {'error': error.message});
  });
  d.run(function () {
    // Error-prone code goes here
    next(new Error('Database is down.'));
  });
});
```

After you launch this example with $ node app, go to the /e URL. You should see the following information in your logs:

```
caught with domain { domain: null,
  _events: { error: [Function] },
  _maxListeners: 10,
  members: [] }
Error: Database is down.
    at /Users/azat/Documents/Code/practicalnode/ch10/domains/app.js:29:10
    at b (domain.js:183:18)
    at Domain.run (domain.js:123:23)
```

The stack trace information (lines after Error: Database is down.) might be very handy in debugging async code. And the browser should output a nice JSON error message:

```
{"error":"Database is down."}
```

The working (or should we write *crashing*) example of Express.js 4.1.2 and domains in routes is in the ch10/domains folder on GitHub (https://github.com/azat-co/practicalnode/tree/master/ch10/domains). The package.json for this example looks like this:

```
{
  "name": "express-domains",
  "version": "0.0.1",
  "private": true,
  "scripts": {
    "start": "node app.js"
  },
```

```
  "dependencies": {
    "express": "4.1.2",
    "jade": "1.3.1",
    "errorhandler": "1.0.1"
  }
}
```

For your convenience, here's the full content of practicalnode/ch10/domains/app.js:

```
var express = require('express');
var routes = require('./routes');
var http = require('http');
var path = require('path');
var errorHandler = require('errorhandler');

var app = express();

app.set('port', process.env.PORT || 3000);
app.set('views', __dirname + '/views');
app.set('view engine', 'jade');
app.use(express.static(path.join(__dirname, 'public')));

var domain = require('domain');
var defaultHandler = errorHandler();
app.get('/', routes.index);

app.get('/e', function (req, res, next) {
  var d = domain.create();
  d.on('error', function (error) {
    console.error(error.stack);
    res.send(500, {'error': error.message});
  });
  d.run(function () {
    // Error-prone code goes here
    throw new Error('Database is down.');
    // next(new Error('Database is down.'));
  });
});

app.use(function (error, req, res, next) {
  if (domain.active) {
    console.info('caught with domain', domain.active);
    domain.active.emit('error', error);
  } else {
    console.info('no domain');
    defaultHandler(error, req, res, next);
  }
});

http.createServer(app).listen(app.get('port'), function () {
  console.log('Express server listening on port '
    + app.get('port'));
});
```

For more ways to apply domains with Express.js, take a look at the *Node.js domains your friends and neighbors* by Forrest L Norvell (http://twitter.com/othiym23) & Domenic Denicola (http://domenicdenicola.com/) presentation from NodeConf 2013 slide 4-1(http://othiym23.github.io/nodeconf2013-domains/#/4/1).

■ **Warning**   The domain module is in the *experimental* stage, which means that it's likely that methods and behavior will change. Therefore, stay updated and use exact versions in the package.json file.

Multithreading with Cluster

There are a lot of opinions out there against Node.js that are rooted in the myth that Node.js-based systems *have* to be single threaded. Although a single Node.js process *is* single threaded, nothing can be further from the truth about the systems. And with the core cluster module (http://nodejs.org/api/cluster.html), we can spawn many Node.js processes effortlessly to handle the system's load. These individual processes use the same source code and they can listen to the same port. Typically, each process uses one machine's CPU. There's a master process that spawns all other processes and, in a way, controls them (can kill, restart, and so on).

Here is a working example of an Express.js (version 4.x or 3.x) app that runs on four processes. At the beginning of the file, we import dependencies:

```
var cluster = require('cluster');
var http = require('http');
var numCPUs = require('os').cpus().length;
var express = require('express');
```

The cluster module has a property that tells us whether the process is master or child (master controls children). We use it to spawn four workers (the default workers use the same file, but this can be overwritten with setupMaster (http://nodejs.org/docs/v0.9.0/api/cluster.html#cluster_cluster_setupmaster_settings)). In addition, we can attach event listeners and receive messages from workers (e.g., kill).

```
if (cluster.isMaster) {
  console.log (' Fork %s worker(s) from master', numCPUs)
  for (var i = 0; i < numCPUs; i++) {
    cluster.fork();
  };
  cluster.on('online', function(worker) {
    console.log ('worker is running on %s pid', worker.process.pid)
  });
  cluster.on('exit', function(worker, code, signal) {
    console.log('worker with %s is closed', worker.process.pid);
  });
}
```

The worker code is just an Express.js app with a twist. Let's get the process ID:

```
} else if (cluster.isWorker) {
  var port = 3000;
  console.log('worker (%s) is now listening to http://localhost:%s',
    cluster.worker.process.pid, port);
  var app = express();
  app.get('*', function(req, res) {
```

```
    res.send(200, 'cluser '
      + cluster.worker.process.pid
      + ' responded \n');
  })
  app.listen(port);
}
```

The full source code of practicalnode/ch10/cluster.js is as follows:

```
var cluster = require('cluster');
var numCPUs = require('os').cpus().length;
var express = require('express');

if (cluster.isMaster) {
  console.log (' Fork %s worker(s) from master', numCPUs);
  for (var i = 0; i < numCPUs; i++) {
    cluster.fork();
  }
  cluster.on('online', function(worker) {
    console.log ('worker is running on %s pid', worker.process.pid);
  });
  cluster.on('exit', function(worker, code, signal) {
    console.log('worker with %s is closed', worker.process.pid);
  });
} else if (cluster.isWorker) {
  var port = 3000;
  console.log('worker (%s) is now listening to http://localhost:%s',
    cluster.worker.process.pid, port);
  var app = express();
  app.get('*', function(req, res) {
    res.send(200, 'cluser '
      + cluster.worker.process.pid
      + ' responded \n');
  });
  app.listen(port);
}
```

As usual, to start an app, run $ node cluster. There should be four (or two, depending on your machine's architecture) processes, as shown in Figure 10-1.

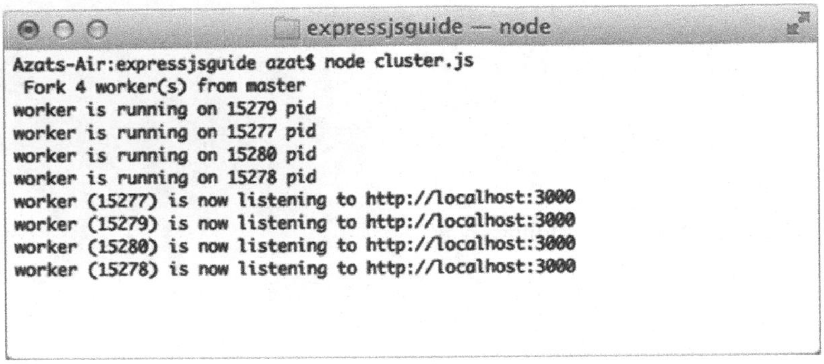

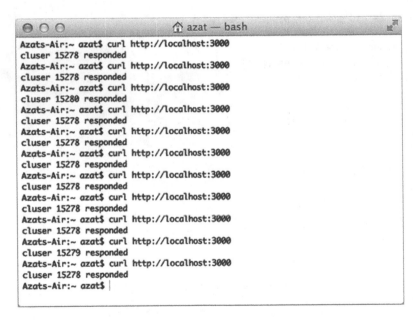

Figure 10-1. *Starting four processes with Cluster*

When we CURL with $ `curl http://localhost:3000`, there are different processes that listen to the *same* port and respond to us (Figure 10-2).

Figure 10-2. *Server response is rendered by different processes*

Multithreading with Cluster2

If you prefer ready solutions to low-level libraries (such as `cluster`), check out the real-world production library created and used by eBay: `cluster2` (GitHub (https://github.com/cubejs/cluster2), NPM (https://www.npmjs.org/package/cluster2)) which is a wrapper for the core cluster module. Cluster2 provides handy utility functions and is battle-tested on a large-scale production deployment.

To install Cluster2, run:

```
$ npm install cluster2
```

To use Cluster2 with Express.js, use `listen()` on an instance of the cluster object:

```
var Cluster2 = require('cluster2'),
    express = require('express');

var app = express.createServer();
// Other Express.js configurations and routes
app.get('/', function(req, res) {
  res.send('hello');
});

var cluster2 = new Cluster2({
  port: 3000
  // Other Cluster2 options
});
cluster2.listen(function(callback) {
  callback(app);
});
```

Event Logging and Monitoring

When things go south (e.g., overloads, crashes), there are two things software engineers can do:

1. Monitor via dashboard and health statuses (monitoring and REPL).

2. Analyze postmortems after the events have happened (Winston and Papertrail).

Monitoring

When going to production, software and development operations engineers need a way to get current status quickly. Having a dashboard or just an end point that spits out JSON-formatted properties is a good idea, including properties such as the following:

- memoryUsage: memory usage information

- uptime: number of seconds the Node.js process is running

- pid: process ID

- connections: number of connections

- loadavg: load average

- sha: Secure Hash Algorithm (SHA) of the Git commit deploy and /or version tag of the deploy

Here's an example of the Express.js route /status:

```
app.get('/status', function(req, res){
  res.send({
    pid: process.pid,
    memory: process.memoryUsage(),
    uptime: process.uptime()
  })
})
```

A more informative example with connections and other information is as follows:

```
var os = require('os'),
  exec = require('child_process').exec,
  async = require('async'),
  started_at = new Date();

module.exports = function(req, res, next) {
  var server = req.app;
  if(req.param('info')) {
    var connections = {},
      swap;

    async.parallel([
      function(done) {
        exec('netstat -an | grep :80 | wc -l', function(e, res) {
          connections['80'] = parseInt(res,10);
          done();
        });
      },
      function(done) {
        exec(
          'netstat -an | grep :'
            + server.set('port')
            + ' | wc -l',
          function(e, res) {
            connections[server.set('port')] = parseInt(res,10);
            done();
          }
        );
      },
      function(done) {
        exec('vmstat -SM -s | grep "used swap" | sed -E "s/[^0-9]*([0-9]{1,8}).*/\1/"',
        function(e, res) {
          swap = res;
          done();
        });
      }], function(e) {
      res.send({
        status: 'up',
        version: server.get('version'),
        sha: server.et('git sha'),
        started_at: started_at,
        node: {
          version: process.version,
          memoryUsage: Math.round(process.memoryUsage().rss / 1024 / 1024)+"M",
          uptime: process.uptime()
        },
        system: {
          loadavg: os.loadavg(),
          freeMemory: Math.round(os.freemem()/1024/1024)+"M"
        },
```

```
            env: process.env.NODE_ENV,
            hostname: os.hostname(),
            connections: connections,
            swap: swap
        });
    });
  }
  else {
    res.send({status: 'up'});
  }
}
```

REPL in Production

What can be better than poking around a live process and its context using the REPL tool? We can do this easily with production apps if we set up REPL as a server:

```
var net = require('net'),
  options = {name: 'azat'};

net.createServer(function(socket) {
  repl.start(options.name + "> ", socket).context.app = app;
}).listen("/tmp/repl-app-" + options.name);
```

Then, connect to the remote machine by using Secure Shell (SSH). Once on the remote machine, run:

```
$ telnet /tmp/repl-app-azat
```

You should be prompted with a standard >, which means you're in the REPL.

Or, if you want to connect to the remote server right away, i.e., by-passing the SSH step, you can modify the code to this:

```
var repl = require('repl');
var net = require('net'),
  options = { name: 'azat' };

app = {a: 1};
net.createServer(function(socket) {
  repl.start(options.name + "> ", socket).context.app = app;
}).listen(3000);
```

Please use iptable to restrict the Internet protocol addresses (IPs) when using this approach. Then, straight from your local machine (where the hostname is the IP of the remote box), execute:

```
$ telnet hostname 3000
```

Winston

Winston provides a way to have one interface for logging events while defining multiple transports, e.g., e-mail, database, file, console, Software as a Service (SaaS), and so on. The list of transports supported by Winston include the following:

- Console
- File
- Loggly (http://www.loggly.com/)
- Riak
- MongoDB
- SimpleDB
- Mail
- Amazon SNS
- Graylog2
- Papertrail
- Cassandra

It's easy to get started with Winston:

```
$ npm install winston
```

In the code, execute the following:

```
var winston = require('winston');
winston.log('info', 'Hello distributed log files!');
winston.info('Hello again distributed logs');
```

To add and remove transporters, use the `winston.add()` and `winston.remove()` functions. To add, use:

```
winston.add(winston.transports.File, {filename: 'webapp.log'});
```

To remove, use:

```
winston.remove(winston.transports.Console);
```

For more information, go to the official documentation (https://github.com/flatiron/winston#working-with-transports).

Papertrail App for Logging

Papertrail (https://papertrailapp.com) is a SaaS that provides centralized storage and a web GUI to search and analyze logs. To use Papertrail with the Node.js app, do the following:

1. Write logs to a file and remote_sync (https://github.com/papertrail/remote_syslog) them to Papertrail.

2. Send logs with winston (https://github.com/flatiron/winston#working-with-transports), which is described earlier, and winston-papertrail (https://github.com/kenperkins/winston-papertrail) directly to the service.

Building Tasks with Grunt

Grunt is a Node.js-based task runner. It performs compilations, minifications, linting, unit testing, and other important tasks for automation.

Install Grunt globally with NPM:

```
$ npm install -g grunt-cli
```

Grunt uses Gruntfile.js to store its tasks. For example,

```
module.exports = function(grunt) {

  // Project configuration
  grunt.initConfig({
    pkg: grunt.file.readJSON('package.json'),
    uglify: {
      options: {
        banner: '/*! <%= pkg.name %> <%= grunt.template.today("yyyy-mm-dd") %> */\n'
      },
      build: {
        src: 'src/<%= pkg.name %>.js',
        dest: 'build/<%= pkg.name %>.min.js'
      }
    }
  });

  // load the plugin that provides the "uglify" task
  grunt.loadNpmTasks('grunt-contrib-uglify');

  // Default task
  grunt.registerTask('default', ['uglify']);

};
```

package.json should have plugins required by the grunt.loadNpmTasks() method. For example,

```
{
  "name": "grunt-example",
  "version": "0.0.1",
  "devDependencies": {
    "grunt": "~0.4.2",
    "grunt-contrib-jshint": "~0.6.3",
    "grunt-contrib-uglify": "~0.2.2",
    "grunt-contrib-coffee": "~0.10.1",
    "grunt-contrib-concat": "~0.3.0"
  }
}
```

Let's move to the more complex example in which we use jshint, uglify, coffee, and concat plugins in the default task in Gruntfile.js.

Start by defining package.json:

```
module.exports = function(grunt) {

  grunt.initConfig({
    pkg: grunt.file.readJSON('package.json'),
```

And then the coffee task:

```
coffee: {
  compile: {
    files: {
```

The first parameter is the destination and the second is source:

```
      'source/<%= pkg.name %>.js': ['source/**/*.coffee']
      // Compile and concatenate into single file
    }
  }
},
```

concat merges multiple files into one to reduce the number of HTTP requests:

```
concat: {
  options: {
    separator: ';'
  },
```

This time, our target is in the build folder:

```
  dist: {
    src: ['source/**/*.js'],
    dest: 'build/<%= pkg.name %>.js'
  }
},
```

The uglify method minifies our *.js file:

```
uglify: {
  options: {
    banner: '/*! <%= pkg.name %> <%= grunt.template.today("dd-mm-yyyy") %> */\n'
  },
  dist: {
    files: {
```

Again, the first value is the destination; the second dynamic name is from the concat task:

```
      'build/<%= pkg.name %>.min.js': ['<%= concat.dist.dest %>']
    }
  }
},
```

jshint is a linter and shows errors if the code is not compliant:

```
   jshint: {
     files: ['Gruntfile.js', 'source/**/*.js'],
     options: {
       // options here to override JSHint defaults
       globals: {
         jQuery: true,
         console: true,
         module: true,
         document: true
       }
     }
   }
 });
```

Load the modules to make them accessible for Grunt:

```
grunt.loadNpmTasks('grunt-contrib-uglify');
grunt.loadNpmTasks('grunt-contrib-jshint');
grunt.loadNpmTasks('grunt-contrib-concat');
grunt.loadNpmTasks('grunt-contrib-coffee');
```

Last, define the default task as sequence of subtasks:

```
grunt.registerTask('default', [ 'jshint', 'coffee','concat', 'uglify']);
};
```

To run the task, simply execute $ grunt or $ grunt default.
Gruntfile.js is as follows:

```
module.exports = function(grunt) {

  grunt.initConfig({
    pkg: grunt.file.readJSON('package.json'),
    coffee: {
      compile: {
        files: {
          'source/<%= pkg.name %>.js': ['source/**/*.coffee'] // compile and concat into single file
        }
      }
    },
    concat: {
      options: {
        separator: ';'
      },
      dist: {
        src: ['source/**/*.js'],
        dest: 'build/<%= pkg.name %>.js'
      }
```

```
    },
    uglify: {
      options: {
        banner: '/*! <%= pkg.name %> <%= grunt.template.today("dd-mm-yyyy") %> */\n'
      },
      dist: {
        files: {
          'build/<%= pkg.name %>.min.js': ['<%= concat.dist.dest %>']
        }
      }
    },

    jshint: {
      files: ['Gruntfile.js', 'source/**/*.js'],
      options: {
        // options here to override JSHint defaults
        globals: {
          jQuery: true,
          console: true,
          module: true,
          document: true
        }
      }
    }
  });

  grunt.loadNpmTasks('grunt-contrib-uglify');
  grunt.loadNpmTasks('grunt-contrib-jshint');
  grunt.loadNpmTasks('grunt-contrib-concat');
  grunt.loadNpmTasks('grunt-contrib-coffee');

  grunt.registerTask('default', [ 'jshint', 'coffee','concat', 'uglify']);

};
```

The results of running $ grunt are shown in Figure 10-3.

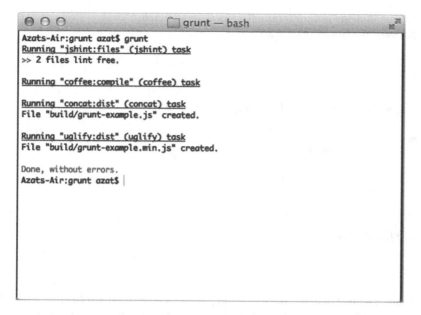

```
Azats-Air:grunt azat$ grunt
Running "jshint:files" (jshint) task
>> 2 files lint free.

Running "coffee:compile" (coffee) task

Running "concat:dist" (concat) task
File "build/grunt-example.js" created.

Running "uglify:dist" (uglify) task
File "build/grunt-example.min.js" created.

Done, without errors.
Azats-Air:grunt azat$ |
```

Figure 10-3. *The results of the Grunt default task*

Git for Version Control and Deployments

Git has become not only a standard version control system, but also—because of its distributed nature—Git has become the default transport mechanism of deployment (i.e., enables you to send source code).

Platform as a service (PaaS) solutions often leverage Git for deploys, because it's already a part of many development flows. Instead of "pushing" your code to GitHub or BitBucket, the destination becomes a PaaS-like Heroku, Azure, or Nodejitsu. Git is also used for continuous deployment and continuous integration (e.g., TravisCI, CircleCI).

Even when IaaS solutions are used, systems such as Chef (http://docs.opscode.com) can be used.

Installing Git

To install Git for your OS, download a package from the official website (http://git-scm.com/downloads). Then, follow these steps:

1. In your terminal, type these commands, *substituting* "John Doe" and johndoe@example.com with your name and e-mail address:

    ```
    $ git config --global user.name "John Doe"
    $ git config --global user.email johndoe@example.com
    ```

2. To check the installation, run:

    ```
    $ git version
    ```

3. You should see something like the following in your terminal window, as shown in Figure 10-4 (your version might vary; in our case it's 1.8.3.2):

```
git version 1.8.3.2
```

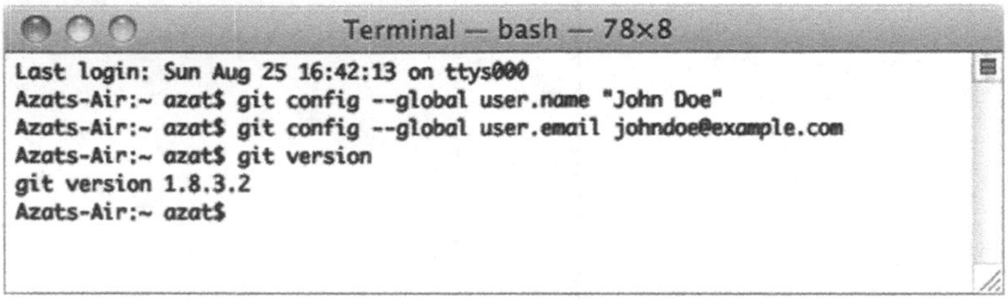

```
● ● ●                    Terminal — bash — 78×8
Last login: Sun Aug 25 16:42:13 on ttys000
Azats-Air:~ azat$ git config --global user.name "John Doe"
Azats-Air:~ azat$ git config --global user.email johndoe@example.com
Azats-Air:~ azat$ git version
git version 1.8.3.2
Azats-Air:~ azat$
```

Figure 10-4. *Configuring and testing the Git installation*

Generating SSH Keys

SSH keys provide a secure connection without the need to enter username and password every time. For GitHub repositories, the latter approach is used with HTTPS URLs (e.g., https://github.com/azat-co/rpjs.git) and the former with SSH URLs (e.g., git@github.com:azat-co/rpjs.git).

To generate SSH keys for GitHub on Mac OS X/Unix machines, do the following:

1. Check for existing SSH keys:

```
$ cd ~/.ssh
$ ls -lah
```

2. If you see some files like id_rsa (please refer to Figure 10-5 for an example), you can delete them or back them up into a separate folder by using the following commands:

```
$ mkdir key_backup
$ cp id_rsa* key_backup
$ rm id_rsa*
```

```
0 0 0                           Terminal — bash — 105×28
Azats-Air:~ azat$ ssh-keygen -t rsa -C "johny@example.com"
Generating public/private rsa key pair.
Enter file in which to save the key (/Users/azat/.ssh/id_rsa):
Created directory '/Users/azat/.ssh'.
Enter passphrase (empty for no passphrase):
Enter same passphrase again:
Your identification has been saved in /Users/azat/.ssh/id_rsa.
Your public key has been saved in /Users/azat/.ssh/id_rsa.pub.
The key fingerprint is:
df:08:f9:a0:0c:87:ed:e8:38:33:92:11:54:c3:bb:0f johny@example.com
The key's randomart image is:
+--[ RSA 2048]----+
|  oo             |
| . ..            |
|.  .             |
|.  . o  .        |
| .  + o S        |
|.  E * . = o     |
| o + +   + .     |
|o +o .           |
| ..+.            |
+-----------------+
Azats-Air:~ azat$ open id_rsa.pub
The file /Users/azat/id_rsa.pub does not exist.
Azats-Air:~ azat$ open ~/.ssh/id_rsa.pub
No application knows how to open /Users/azat/.ssh/id_rsa.pub.
Azats-Air:~ azat$ pbcopy < ~/.ssh/id_rsa.pub
Azats-Air:~ azat$
```

Figure 10-5. Generating an RSA (Ron Rivest, (http://en.wikipedia.org/wiki/ron_rivest), Adi Shamir (http://en.wikipedia.org/wiki/adi_shamir) and Leonard Adleman (http://en.wikipedia.org/wiki/leonard_adleman)) key pair for SSH and copying the public RSA key to a clipboard

3. Now we can generate a new SSH key pair using the ssh-keygen command, assuming we are in the ~/.ssh folder:

    ```
    $ ssh-keygen -t rsa -C "your_email@youremail.com"
    ```

4. Next, answer the questions. It's better to keep the default name id_rsa. Then, copy the content of the id_rsa.pub file to your clipboard:

    ```
    $ pbcopy < ~/.ssh/id_rsa.pub
    ```

    Alternatively, you can open the id_rsa.pub file in the default editor:

    ```
    $ open id_rsa.pub
    ```

    or in TextMate:

    ```
    $ mate id_rsa.pub
    ```

■ **Tip** SSH connections are also used to connect to IaaS remote machines.

After you have copied the public key, go to github.com (http://github.com), log in, go to your account settings, select "SSH key," and add the new SSH key. Assign a name (e.g., the name of your computer) and paste the value of your *public* key.

To check whether you have an SSH connection to GitHub, type and execute the following command in your terminal:

```
$ ssh -T git@github.com
```

If you see something such as,

```
Hi your-GitHub-username! You've successfully authenticated,
but GitHub does not provide shell access.
```

then everything is set up.

While connecting to GitHub for the first time, you may receive the warning "authenticity of host . . . can't be established." Please don't be confused with this message; just proceed by answering yes, as shown in Figure 10-6.

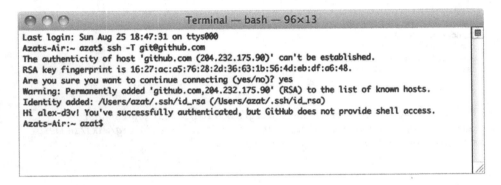

Figure 10-6. *Testing the SSH connection to GitHub for the very first time*

If, for some reason, you have a different message, please repeat steps 3 and 4 from the previous section on SSH Keys and/or reupload the content of your *.pub file to GitHub.

■ **Warning**   Keep your id_rsa file private. Don't share it with anybody!

More instructions are available at GitHub: Generating SSH Keys (https://help.github.com/articles/generating-ssh-keys). Windows users might find useful the SSH key generator feature in PuTTY (http://www.putty.org).

In case you've never used Git and/or GitHub, or you've forgotten how to commit code, the next section provides a short tutorial.

Creating a Local Git Repository

To create a GitHub repository, go to github.com (http://github.com/), log in, and create a new repository. There will be an SSH address; copy it. In your terminal window, navigate to the project folder to which you would like to push GitHub. Then, do the following:

1. Create a local Git and .git folder in the root of the project folder:

   ```
   $ git init
   ```

2. Add all the files to the repository and start tracking them:

   ```
   $ git add
   ```

3. Make the first commit:

   ```
   $ git commit -m "initial commit"
   ```

Pushing the Local Repository to GitHub

You can create a new repository in github.com via a web interface. Then, copy your newly created repo's to the Git SSH URI, which looks something like git@github.com:username/reponame.

1. Add the GitHub remote destination:

   ```
   $ git remote add your-github-repo-ssh-url
   ```

   It might look something like this:

   ```
   $ git remote add origin git@github.com:azat co/simple-message-board.git
   ```

2. Now everything should be set to push your local Git repository to the remote destination on GitHub with the following command:

   ```
   $ git push origin master
   ```

3. You should be able to see your files at github.com (http://github.com/) under your account and repository.

   Later, when you make changes to the file, there is no need to repeat all these steps. Just execute:

   ```
   $ git add
   $ git commit -am "some message"
   $ git push origin master
   ```

   If there are no new untracked files that you want to start tracking, type the following:

   ```
   $ git commit -am "some message"
   $ git push origin master
   ```

To include changes from individual files, run the following:

```
$ git commit filename -m "some message"
$ git push origin master
```

To remove a file from the Git repository, execute:

```
$ git rm filename
```

For more Git commands, go to:

```
$ git --help
```

■ **Note**   We advise against committing the node_modules folder to the repository for a project intended to be used in other applications, i.e., for a module. On the other hand, it's a good practice to commit that folder along with all the dependencies for a standalone application, because future updates might break something unintentionally.

Running Tests in Cloud with TravisCI

TravisCI is an SaaS continuous integration system that allows you to automate testing on each GitHub push (e.g., $ git push origin master). Alternative services include Codeship (https://www.codeship.io), CircleCI (https://circleci.com), and many others www.quora.com (http://bit.ly/1ipdxxt).

　　TravisCI is more common among open-source projects and has a similar configuration to other systems, i.e., a YAML file. In case of Node.js programs, it can look like this:

```
language: node_js
node_js:
  - "0.11"
  - "0.10"
```

　　In this configuration, 0.11 and 0.10 are versions of Node.js to use for testing. These multiple Node.js versions are tested on a separate set of virtual machines (VMs). The following configuration file can be copied and used (it's recommended by TravisCI):

```
language: node_js
node_js:
  - "0.11"
  - "0.10"
  - "0.8"
  - "0.6"
```

　　NPM's package.json has a property scripts.test that is a string to execute scripts, so we can put the mocha command in it:

```
echo '{"scripts": {"test": "mocha test-expect.js"}}' > package.json
```

The previous line yields the following package.json file:

```
{"scripts": {"test": "mocha test-expect.js"}}
```

Then, we can run $ npm test successfully.

On the other hand, we can use any other command that invokes the execution of the test, such as the Makefile command $ make test:

```
echo '{"scripts": {"test": "make test"}}' > package.json
```

TravisCI uses this NPM instruction to run the tests.

After all the preparation is done in the form of the YAML file and the package.json property, the next step is to sign up for TravisCI (free for open-source project/public repositories on GitHub) and select the repository from the web interface on travis-ci.org (http://travis-ci.org).

For more information on the TravisCI configuration, follow the project in this chapter or see *Building a Node.js* project (http://about.travis-ci.org/docs/user/languages/javascript-with-nodejs/) (http://docs.travis-ci.com/user/languages/javascript-with-nodejs).

TravisCI Configuration

There's no database in our application yet, but it's good to prepare the TravisCI configuration right now. To add a database to the TravisCI testing instance, use:

```
services:
  - mongodb
```

By default, TravisCI starts the MongoDB instance for us on the local host, port 27017:

```
language: node_js
node_js:
  - "0.11"
  - "0.10"
  - "0.8"
  - "0.6"
services:
  - mongodb
```

That's it! The test build will be synched on each push to GitHub.

If your tests fail even locally right now, don't despair, because that's the whole point of TDD. In the next chapter, we hook up the database and write more tests for fun.

Because of the GitHub hooks to TravisCI, the test build should start automatically. On their completion, contributors can get e-mail / Internet Relay Chat (IRC) notifications.

Summary

In this chapter, we briefly touched on environment variables, went through the basics of Git, and generated SSH keys. We used Grunt for predeploy tasks such as concatenation, minification, and compilation; implemented clusters, monitoring, error handling, and logging; and configured TravisCI to run tests.

In the next chapter, we'll proceed to cover the deployment of the app to PaaS (Heroku) and IaaS (Amazon Web Services). We'll also show basic examples of Nginx, Varnish Cache and Upstart configurations.

CHAPTER 11

■ ■ ■

Deploying Node.js Apps

As we approach the end of the book, there's a vital step we have to explore: the deployment itself. To help you navigate between PaaS and IaaS options, and have some scripts you can use on your servers, we cover the following topics:

- Deploying to Heroku (PaaS)

- Deploying to Amazon Web Services (AWS)

- Keeping Node.js apps alive with forever, Upstart, and init.d

- Serving static resources properly with Nginx

- Caching with Varnish

Deploying to Heroku

Heroku (http://www.heroku.com) is a polyglot Agile application deployment Platform as a Service (PaaS). The benefits of using PaaS over other cloud solutions include the following:

1. It's easy to deploy, i.e., just one Git command to deploy $ git push heroku master.

2. It's easy to scale, e.g., log in to Heroku.com and click a few options.

3. It's easy to secure and maintain, e.g., no need to set up startup scripts manually.

Heroku works similarly to Windows Azure (http://azure.microsoft.com/en-us), Nodejitsu (https://www.nodejitsu.com), and many others in the sense that you can use Git to deploy applications. In other words, Heroku uses ubiquitous Git as its deployment mechanism. This means that after becoming familiar with Heroku and comfortable with Git, and after creating accounts with Windows Azure, Nodejitsu, and other PaaSs, it's fairly easy to deploy Node.js apps to them as well.

To get started with the process, we need to follow these steps:

1. Install Heroku Toolbelt (https://toolbelt.heroku.com)—a bundle that includes Git and other tools.

2. Log in to Heroku, which should upload a public SSH key file (e.g., id_rsa.pub) to the cloud (i.e., heroku.com).

To set up Heroku, follow these steps:

1. Sign up at `http://heroku.com`. Currently, they have a free account. To use it, select all options as minimum (0) and the database as shared.

2. Download Heroku Toolbelt at `https://toolbelt.heroku.com`. Toolbelt is a package of tools, i.e., libraries, that consists of Heroku, Git, and Foreman (`https://github.com/ddollar/foreman`). For users of older Macs, get this client (`http://assets.heroku.com/heroku-client/heroku-client.tgz`) directly. If you use another OS, browse Heroku Client GitHub (`https://github.com/heroku/heroku`).

3. After the installation is done, you should have access to the `heroku` command. To check it and log in to Heroku, type:

    ```
    $ heroku login
    ```

The system asks you for Heroku credentials (username and password), and if you've already created the SSH key, it uploads it automatically to the Heroku web site, as shown in Figure 11-1.

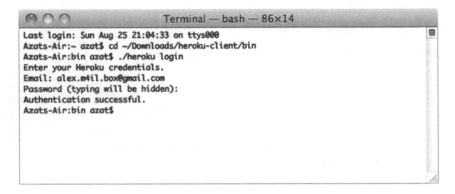

```
Last login: Sun Aug 25 21:04:33 on ttys000
Azats-Air:~ azat$ cd ~/Downloads/heroku-client/bin
Azats-Air:bin azat$ ./heroku login
Enter your Heroku credentials.
Email: alex.m4il.box@gmail.com
Password (typing will be hidden):
Authentication successful.
Azats-Air:bin azat$
```

Figure 11-1. *The response to a successful $ `heroku login` command*

4. If everything went well, to create a Heroku application inside your specific project folder, you should be able to run:

    ```
    $ heroku create
    ```

Official instructions are available at Heroku: Quickstart (`https://devcenter.heroku.com/articles/quickstart`) and Heroku: Node.js (`https://devcenter.heroku.com/articles/getting-started-with-nodejs`).

Then, for each app we need to deploy, perform the following setup steps:

1. Create the local Git repository.

2. Initialize the Heroku app with $ `heroku create` (adds a Git remote destination to Heroku cloud).

Last, initial deployment as well as each change is deployed by (1) staging the commit with $ `git add`, (2) committing the changes to the local repository with $ `git commit`, and (3) pushing the changes to the Heroku remote $ `git push heroku master`.

On deployment, Heroku determines which stack to use (Node.js, in our case). For this reason, we need to provide the mandatory files package.json, which tells Heroku what dependencies to install; Procfile, which tells Heroku what process to start; and Node.js app files (e.g., server.js). The content of Procfile can be as minimalistic as web: node server.js.

Here is a step-by-step breakdown using Git to deploy to Heroku:

1. Create a local Git repository and .git folder if you haven't done so already:

```
$ git init
```

2. Add files:

```
$ git add
```

3. Commit files and changes:

```
$ git commit -m "my first commit"
```

4. Create the Heroku Cedar stack application (Cedar stack is a special technology that Heroku uses to create and run its apps) and add the Git remote destination with this command:

```
$ heroku create
```

If everything went well, the system should tell you that the remote has been added and the app has been created, and it should give you the app name.

5. To look up the remote type and execute (*optional*), do the following:

```
$ git remote show
```

6. Deploy the code to Heroku with:

```
$ git push heroku master
```

Terminal logs should tell you whether the deployment went smoothly (i.e., succeeded). If you have a different branch you'd like to use, you can use $ git push heroku branch_name, just like you would do with any other Git destination (e.g., GitHub).

7. To open the app in your default browser, type:

```
$ heroku open
```

or just go to the URL of your app and type something like: http://yourappname-NNNN.herokuapp.com.

8. To look at the Heroku logs for this app, type:

```
$ heroku logs
```

To update the app with the new code, type the following *only*:

```
$ git add -A
$ git commit -m "commit for deploy to heroku"
$ git push heroku master
```

■ **Note** You'll be assigned a new application URL each time you create a new Heroku app with the command
`$ heroku create`.

To propagate environment variables to the Heroku cloud, use the `heroku config` set of commands:

- `$ heroku config`: list of environment variables
- `$ heroku config:get NAME`: value of `NAME` environment variable
- `$ heroku config:set NAME=VALUE`: setting the value of `NAME` to `VALUE`
- `$ heroku config:unset NAME`: removal of the environment variable

■ **Note** Configuration variable data are limited to 16KB for each app.

To use the same environment variables locally, you can store them in the `.env` file in the root of your project. The format is `NAME=VALUE`. For example:

```
DB_PASSWORD=F2C9C45
API_KEY=7C311DA3126F
```

■ **Warning** There shouldn't be any spaces between the name, equal sign, and the value.

After the data are in `.env`, just use Foreman (part of Heroku Toolbelt):

```
$ foreman start
```

■ **Tip** Don't forget to add your `.env` to `.gitignore` to avoid sharing it in the version control system.

As an alternative to Foreman and the `.env` file, it's possible just to set environment variables before starting an app:

```
$ DB_PASSWORD=F2C9C45 API_KEY=7C311DA3126F node server
```

or in your profile file (e.g., `~/.bashrc`):

```
export DB_PASSWORD=F2C9C45
export API_KEY=7C311DA3126F
```

Needless to say, if you have more than one app and/or API key, then you can use names such as `APPNAME_API_KEY`.

To sync your local .env seamlessly with cloud variables, use the heroku-config plugin (https://github.com/ddollar/heroku-config). To install it, run:

```
$ heroku plugins:install git://github.com/ddollar/heroku-config.git
```

To get variables from the cloud to the local file, type:

```
$ heroku config:pull
```

To overwrite cloud data with local variables, type:

```
$ heroku config:push
```

For official information on setting up environment variables in Heroku, see Configuration and Config Vars (https://devcenter.heroku.com/articles/config-vars). The article might require Heroku login.

There are a multitude of add-ons for Heroku (https://addons.heroku.com). Each add-on is like a mini service associated with a particular Heroku app. For example, MongoHQ (https://addons.heroku.com/mongohq) provides MongoDB database, while the Postgres add-on (https://addons.heroku.com/heroku-postgresql) does the same for the PostgreSQL database, and SendGrid (https://addons.heroku.com/sendgrid) allows sending transactional e-mails. In Figure 11-2, you can see the beginning of the long list of Heroku add-ons:

Figure 11-2. *There are a multitude of add-ons for Heroku applications*

Most of the add-ons pass information to the Node.js app (and others such as Rails) via environment variables. For example, the MongoHQ URI is provided in

```
process.env.MONGOHQ_URL
```

To make our Node.js apps work locally and remotely, all we need to do is to specify the local URI to which to fall back (when the environment variable is not set):

```
var databaseUrl = process.env.MONGOHQ_URL || "mongodb://@127.0.0.1:27017/practicalnode";
```

The same thing goes for the server port number:

```
var port = process.env.PORT || 5000;
app.listen(port);
```

■ **Note**   It's possible to copy a database connection string (and other data) from the Heroku web interface. However, it's not recommended that you do so.

Some useful Git and Heroku commands are as follows:

- `git remote -v`: list defined remote destinations
- `git remote add NAME URL`: add a new remote destination with NAME and URL (usually SSH or HTTPS protocols)
- `heroku start`: start the app in the cloud
- `heroku info`: pull the app's info

Deploying to Amazon Web Services

Cloud is eating the world of computing. There are private and public clouds. AWS, probably the most popular choice among the public cloud offerings, falls under the IaaS category. The advantages of using an IaaS such as AWS over PaaS-like Heroku are as follows:

1. It's more configurable (any services, packages, or operation systems).

2. It's more controllable. There are no restrictions or limitations.

3. It's cheaper to maintain. PaaS can quickly cost a fortune for high-performance resources.

In this tutorial, we use 64-bit Amazon Linux AMI (http://aws.amazon.com/amazon-linux-ami) with CentOS. It might be easier to use the Extra Packages for Enterprise Linux (EPEL) package manager to install Node.js and NPM. If you don't have EPEL, skip to the manual C++ build instructions.

Assuming you have your Elastic Compute Cloud (EC2) instance up and running, make an SSH connection into it and see if you have yum with EPEL (https://fedoraproject.org/wiki/EPEL). To do so, just see if this command says epel:

```
yum repolist
```

If there are no mentions of epel, run:

```
rpm -Uvh http://download-i2.fedoraproject.org/pub/epel/6/i386/epel-release-6-8.noarch.rpm
```

Then, to install both Node.js and NPM, simply run this command:

```
sudo yum install nodejs npm --enablerepo=epel
```

This might take a while. Answer with y as the process goes. In the end, you should see something like this (your results may vary):

```
Installed:
  nodejs.i686 0:0.10.26-1.el6           npm.noarch 0:1.3.6-4.el6
Dependency Installed:
...
Dependency Updated:
...
Complete!
```

You probably know this, but just in case, to check installations, type the following:

```
$ node -V
$ npm -v
```

For more information on using yum, see Managing Software with yum (https://www.centos.org/docs/5/html/yum) and Tips on securing your EC2 instance (http://aws.amazon.com/articles/1233).

So, if the previous EPEL option didn't work for you, follow these build steps. On your EC2 instance, install all system updates with yum:

```
sudo yum update
```

Then, install the C++ compiler (again with yum):

```
sudo yum install gcc-c++ make
```

Do the same with openssl:

```
sudo yum install openssl-devel
```

Then install Git, which is needed for delivering source files to the remote machine. When Git is unavailable, rsync (http://ss64.com/bash/rsync.html) can be used:

```
sudo yum install git
```

Last, clone the Node repository straight from GitHub:

```
git clone git://github.com/joyent/node.git
```

and build Node.js:

```
cd node
git checkout v0.10.12
./configure
make
sudo make install
```

■ **Note** For a different version of Node.js, you can list them all with $ `git tag -l` and check out the one you need.

To install NPM, run:

```
git clone https://github.com/isaacs/npm.git
cd npm
sudo make install
```

Relax and enjoy the build. The next step is to configure AWS ports / firewall settings. Here's a short example of `server.js`, which outputs "Hello readers" and looks like this:

```
var http = require('http')
http.createServer(function(req, res) {
  res.writeHead(200, {'Content-Type': 'text/plain'});
  console.log ('responding');
  res.end('Hello readers!'
    + 'If you see this, then your Node.js server '
    + 'is running on AWS EC2!');
}).listen(80);
console.log ('server is up');
```

On the EC2 instance, either configure the firewall to redirect connections (e.g., port to Node.js 3000, but this is too advanced for our example) or disable the firewall (okay for our quick demonstration and development purposes):

```
$ service iptables save
$ service iptables stop
$ chkconfig iptables off
```

In the AWS console, find your EC2 instance and apply a proper rule to allow for inbound traffic, as shown in Figure 11-3. For example,

```
Type: HTTP
```

Figure 11-3. *Allowing inbound HTTP traffic on port 80*

The other fields fill automatically:

```
Protocol: TCP
Port Range: 80
Source: 0.0.0.0/0
```

Or we can just allow all traffic (again, for development purposes only), as shown in Figure 11-4.

Figure 11-4. *Allowing all traffic for development mode only*

Now, while the Node.js app is running, executing $ `netstat -apn | grep 80`, the remote machine should show the process. For example,

```
tcp        0        0 0.0.0.0:80              0.0.0.0:*               LISTEN      1064/node
```

And from your local machine, i.e., your development computer, you can either use the public IP or the public DNS (the Domain Name System) domain, which is found and copied from the AWS console under that instance's description. For example,

```
$ curl XXX.XXX.XXX.XXX -v
```

Or, just open the browser using the public DNS.

For the proper `iptables` setup, please consult experienced development operations engineers and manuals, because this is an important security aspect and it is out of the scope of this book. However, here are some commands to redirect traffic to, say, port 3001:

```
sudo iptables -A PREROUTING -t nat -i eth0 -p tcp --dport 80 -j REDIRECT --to-port 8080
sudo iptables -t nat -A INPUT -p tcp --dport 80 -j     REDIRECT --to-ports 3001
sudo iptables -t nat -A OUTPUT -p tcp --dport 80 -j     REDIRECT --to-ports 3001
```

You can also use commands such as the following:

```
$ service iptables save
$ service iptables start
$ service iptables restart
$ chkconfig iptables on
```

It's worth mentioning that AWS supports many other operating systems via its AWS Marketplace (`https://aws.amazon.com/marketplace`). Although AWS EC2 is a very popular and affordable choice, some companies opt for special Node.js tools available in the SmartOS (`http://smartos.org`), e.g., DTrace (`http://dtrace.org/blogs`), built on top of Solaris by Joyent (`http://www.joyent.com`), the company that maintains Node.js.

Keeping Node.js Apps Alive with forever, Upstart, and init.d

This section relates only to IaaS deployment—another advantage to PaaS deployments. The reason why we need this step is to bring the application back to life in case it crashes. Even if we have a master–child system, something needs to keep an eye on the master itself. You also need a way to stop and start processes for maintenance, upgrades, and so forth.

Luckily, there's no shortage of solutions to monitor and restart our Node.js apps:

- *forever* (`https://github.com/nodejitsu/forever`): probably the easiest method. The forever module is installed via NPM and works on almost any Unix OS. Unfortunately, if the server itself fails (not our Node.js server, but the big Unix server), then nothing resumes forever.

- *Upstart* (`http://upstart.ubuntu.com`): the most recommended option. It solves the problem of starting daemons on startups, but it requires writing an Upstart script and having the latest Unix OS version support for it. We'll show you an Upstart script example for CentOS.

- *init.d* (`http://www.unix.com/man-page/opensolaris/4/init.d`): an outdated analog of Upstart. init.d contains the last startup script options for systems that don't have Upstart capabilities.

forever

forever is a module that allows us to start Node.js apps/servers as daemons and keeps them running *forever*. Yes, that's right. If the node process dies for some reason, it brings it right back up!

forever is a very neat utility because it's an NPM module (very easy to install almost anywhere) and it's very easy to use without any extra language. A simple use case is as follows:

```
$ sudo npm install forever -g
$ forever server.js
```

If you're starting from another location, prefix the file name with the absolute path, e.g., $ forever /var/. A more complex forever example looks like this:

```
$ forever start -l forever.log -o output.log -e error.log server.js
```

To stop the process, type:

```
$ forever stop server.js
```

To look up all the programs run by forever, type:

```
$ forever list
```

To list all available forever commands, type:

```
$ forever --help
```

■ **Warning** The app won't start on server reboots without extra setup/utilities.

Upstart Scripts

"Upstart is an event-based replacement for the /sbin/init daemon that handles starting of tasks and services during boot..."—the Upstart web site (http://upstart.ubuntu.com). The latest CentOS (6.2+), as well as Ubuntu and Debian OSs, come with Upstart. If Upstart is missing, try typing sudo yum install upstart to install it on CentOS, and try sudo app get install upstart for Ubuntu.

A very basic Upstart script—to illustrate its structure—starts with metadata:

```
author      "Azat"
description "practicalnode"
setuid      "nodeuser"
```

We then start the application on startup after the file system and network:

```
start on (local-filesystems and net-device-up IFACE=eth0)
```

We stop the app on server shutdown:

```
stop on shutdown
```

We instruct Upstart to restart the program when it crashes:

```
respawn
```

We log events to /var/log/upstart/webapp.log:

```
console log
```

We include environment variables:

```
env NODE_ENV=production
```

Command and file to execute:

```
exec /usr/bin/node /var/practicalnode/webapp.js
```

A more useful example from a file webapp.conf in /etc/init follows:

```
cd /etc/init
sudo vi webapp.conf
```

The simplistic content of an Upstart script is as follows:

```
#!upstart
description "webapp.js"
author       "Azat"
env PROGRAM_NAME="node"
env FULL_PATH="/home/httpd/buto-middleman/public"
env FILE_NAME="forever.js"
env NODE_PATH="/usr/local/bin/node"
env USERNAME="springloops"

start on runlevel [2345]
stop on shutdown
respawn
```

This part of the script is responsible for launching the application webapp.js (similar to our local $ node webapp.js command, only with absolute paths). The output is recorded into the webapp.log file:

```
script
    export HOME="/root"

echo $$ > /var/run/webapp.pid
exec /usr/local/bin/node /root/webapp.js >> /var/log/webapp.log 2>&1

end script
```

The following piece is not as important, but it provides us with the date in the log file:

```
pre-
start script
    # Date format same as (new Date()).toISOString() for consistency
    echo "[`date -u +%Y-%m-%dT%T.%3NZ`] (sys) Starting" >> /var/log/webapp.log
end script
```

The following tells us what to do when we're stopping the process:

```
pre-stop script
    rm /var/run/webapp.pid
    echo "[`date -u +%Y-%m-%dT%T.%3NZ`] (sys) Stopping" >> /var/log/webapp.log
end script
```

To start/stop the app, use:

```
/sbin/start myapp
/sbin/stop myapp
```

To determine the app's status, type:

```
/sbin/status myapp
```

■ **Tip** With Upstart, the Node.js app restarts on an app crash and on server reboots.

The previous example was inspired by Deploy Nodejs app in Centos 6.2 (http://bit.ly/1qwIeTJ). For more information on Upstart, see How to Write CentOS Initialization Scripts with Upstart (http://bit.ly/1pNFlxT) and Upstart Cookbook (http://upstart.ubuntu.com/cookbook/upstart_cookbook.pdf).

init.d

If Upstart is unavailable, you can create an init.d script. init.d, which is a technology available on most Linux OSs. Usually, development operations engineers resort to init.d when Upstart is not available and when they need something more robust than forever. Without going into too much detail, Upstart is a newer alternative to init.d scripts. We put init.d scripts into the /etc/ folder.

For example, the following init.d script for CentOS starts, stops, and restarts the node process / file home/nodejs/sample/app.js:

```
#!/bin/sh

#
# chkconfig: 35 99 99
# description: Node.js /home/nodejs/sample/app.js
#

. /etc/rc.d/init.d/functions

USER="nodejs"

DAEMON="/home/nodejs/.nvm/v0.4.10/bin/node"
ROOT_DIR="/home/nodejs/sample"

SERVER="$ROOT_DIR/app.js"
LOG_FILE="$ROOT_DIR/app.js.log"
```

```
LOCK_FILE="/var/lock/subsys/node-server"

do_start()
{
        if [ ! -f "$LOCK_FILE" ] ; then
                echo -n $"Starting $SERVER: "
                runuser -l "$USER" -c "$DAEMON $SERVER >> $LOG_FILE &" && echo_success || echo_failure
                RETVAL=$?
                echo
                [ $RETVAL -eq 0 ] && touch $LOCK_FILE
        else
                echo "$SERVER is locked."
                RETVAL=1
        fi
}
do_stop()
{
        echo -n $"Stopping $SERVER: "
        pid=`ps -aefw | grep "$DAEMON $SERVER" | grep -v " grep " | awk '{print $2}'`
        kill -9 $pid > /dev/null 2>&1 && echo_success || echo_failure
        RETVAL=$?
        echo
        [ $RETVAL -eq 0 ] && rm -f $LOCK_FILE
}

case "$1" in
        start)
                do_start
                ;;
        stop)
                do_stop
                ;;
        restart)
                do_stop
                do_start
                ;;
        *)
                echo "Usage: $0 {start|stop|restart}"
                RETVAL=1
esac

exit $RETVAL
```

The init.d script above was borrowed from this GitHub gist (https://gist.github.com/nariyu/1211413). For more info on init.d, see this detailed tutorial (http://bit.ly/1lDkRGi).

Serving Static Resources Properly with Nginx

Although, it's fairly easy to serve static files from Node.js applications, and we can use sendFile or Express.js static middleware, it's a big no-no for systems that require high performance. In other words, this step is optional but recommended.

The best option is to use Nginx (http://nginx.org), Amazon S3 (http://aws.amazon.com/s3) or CDNs, e.g., Akamai (http://www.akamai.com) or CloudFlare (https://www.cloudflare.com), for the purpose for which they were specifically designed, i.e., serving static content, and let Node.js apps handle interactive and networking tasks only. This tactic decreases the load on Node.js processes and improves the efficiency of your system.

Nginx is a popular choice among development operations engineers. It's an HTTP and reverse-proxy server. To install Nginx on a CentOS system (v6.4+), type:

```
sudo yum install nginx
```

As a side note, for Ubuntu, you can use the apt packaging tool: sudo apt-get install nginx. For more information about apt, refer to the docs (https://help.ubuntu.com/12.04/serverguide/apt-get.html).

But, let's continue with our CentOS example. We need to open the /etc/nginx/conf.d/virtual.conf file for editing, e.g., using a VIM (Vi Improved) editor:

```
sudo vim /etc/nginx/conf.d/virtual.conf
```

Then, we must add this configuration:

```
server {
    location / {
        proxy_pass http://localhost:3000;
    }

    location /static/ {
        root /var/www/webapplog/public;
    }
}
```

The first location block acts as a proxy server and redirects all requests that are not /static/* to the Node.js app, which listens on port 3000. Static files are served from the /var/www/webapplog/public folder.

If your project uses Express.js or a framework that's built on top of it, don't forget to set the trust proxy to true by adding the following line to your server configuration:

```
app.set('trust proxy', true);
```

This little configuration enables Express.js to display true client IPs provided by proxy instead of proxy IPs. The IP address is taken from the X-Forwarded-For HTTP header of requests (see next code snippet).

A more complex example with HTTP headers in the proxy-server directive, and file extensions for static resources, follows:

```
server {
    listen 0.0.0.0:80;
    server_name webapplog.com;
    access_log /var/log/nginx/webapp.log;
```

```
    location ~* ^.+\.(jpg|jpeg|gif|png|ico|css|zip|tgz|gz|rar|bz2|pdf|txt|tar|wav|bmp|rtf|js|flv|swf
|html|htm)$ {
        root    /var/www/webapplog/public;
    }

    location / {
        proxy_set_header X-Real-IP $remote_addr;
        proxy_set_header HOST $http_host;
        proxy_set_header X-NginX-Proxy true;

        proxy_pass http://127.0.0.1:3000;
        proxy_redirect off;
    }
```

■ **Note**   Replace 3000 with the Node.js app's port number, webapplog.com with our domain name, and webapp.log with your log's file name.

Alternatively, we can use upstream try_files (http://wiki.nginx.org/httpCoreModule#try_files). Then, start Nginx as a service:

```
sudo service nginx start
```

After Nginx is up and running, launch your node app with forever or Upstart on the port number you specified in the proxy-server configurations.

To stop and restart Nginx, use:

```
sudo service nginx stop
sudo service nginx start
```

So far, we've used Nginx to serve static content while redirecting nonstatic requests to Node.js apps. We can take it a step further and let Nginx serve error pages and use multiple Node.js processes. For example, if we want to serve the 404 page from the 404.html file, which is located in the /var/www/webapplog/public folder, we can add the following line inside the server directive:

```
error_page 404 /404.html;
location   /404.html {
    internal;
    root /var/www/webapplog/public;
}
```

If there is a need to run multiple Node.js processes behind Nginx, we can set up location rules inside the server in exactly the same way we used location for dividing static and nonstatic content. However, in this case, both destinations are handled by Node.js apps. For example, we have a Node.js web app that is running on 3000, serving some HTML pages, and its URL path is /, whereas the Node.js API app is running on 3001, serving JSON responses, and its URL path is /api:

```
server {
  listen 8080;
  server_name webapplog.com;
```

```
location / {
  proxy_pass http://localhost:3000;
  proxy_set_header Host $host;
}
location /api {
  proxy_pass http://localhost:3001;
  rewrite ^/api(.*) /$1 break;
  proxy_set_header Host $host;
}
}
```

In this way, we have the following trafficking:

- The / requests go to http://localhost:3000.

- The /api requests go to http://localhost:3001.

Caching with Varnish

The last piece of the production deployment puzzle is setting up caching using Varnish Cache (https://www.varnish-cache.org). This step is optional for Node.js deploys, but, like a Nginx setup, it's also recommended, especially for systems that expect to handle large loads with the minimum resources consumed.

The idea is that Varnish allows us to cache requests and serve them later from the cache without hitting Nginx and/or Node.js servers. This avoids the overhead of processing the same requests over and over again. In other words, the more identical requests the server has coming, the better Varnish's optimization.

Here's a nice Varnish Cache video (http://youtu.be/x7t2Sp174eI). It does a good job at summarizing the tool in just less than three minutes.

Let's use yum again, this time to install Varnish dependencies on CentOS:

```
$ yum install -y gcc make automake autoconf libtool ncurses-devel libxslt groff pcre-devel
pkgconfig libedit libedit-devel
```

Download the latest stable release (as of May 2014):

```
$ wget http://repo.varnish-cache.org/source/varnish-3.0.5.tar.gz
```

and build Varnish Cache with the following:

```
$ tar -xvpzf varnish-3.0.5.tar.gz
$ cd varnish-3.0.5
$ ./autogen.sh
$ ./configure
$ make
$ make check
$ make install
```

For this example, let's make only minimal configuration adjustments. In the file `/etc/sysconfig/varnish`, type:

```
VARNISH_LISTEN_PORT=80
VARNISH_ADMIN_LISTEN_ADDRESS=127.0.0.1
Then, in /etc/varnish/default.vcl, type
backend default {
 .host = "127.0.0.1";
 .port = "8080";
}
```

Restart the services with:

```
$ /etc/init.d/varnish restart
$ /etc/init.d/nginx restart
```

Everything should be working by now. To test it, CURL from your local (or another remote) machine:

```
$ curl -I www.varnish-cache.org
```

If you see "Server: Varnish" this means that requests go through Varnish Cache first, just as we intended.

Summary

In this chapter, we covered deployment using the Git and Heroku command-line interfaces to deploy to PaaS. Then, we worked through examples of installing and building a Node.js environment on AWS EC2, running Node.js apps on AWS with CentOS. After that, we explored examples of forever, Upstart, and init.d to keep our apps running. Last, we installed and configured Nginx to serve static content, including error pages, and split traffic between multiple Node.js processes. Then, we added Varnish Cache to lighten the Node.js apps' loads even more.

■ ■ ■

CHAPTER 12

Publishing Node.js Modules and Contributing to Open Source

One of the key factors that contributed to the rapid growth of the Node.js module ecosystem is its open-source nature and robust packaging systems (with registry). As of April 2013, JavaScript and Node.js had already surpassed any other language/platform in the number of packages contributed per year (source) (http://caines.ca/blog/programming/the-node-js-community-is-quietly-changing-the-face-of-open-source/):

- Python: 1351 packages per year (29,720 packages in 22 years)

- Ruby: 3022 packages per year (54,385 packages in 18 years)

- Node.js: 6742 *packages per year* (26,966 packages in 4 years)

This year's (2014) numbers are even higher, and expectations are that, by mid 2014, Node.js will surpass other platforms, in absolute numbers, with Maven and Rubygems being the top dogs (source) (http://modulecounts.com/). Other factors that attribute to the Node.js popularity include:

- Ability to share code between front-end/browser and server-side (with projects such as browserify (http://browserify.org/) and ender.js) (https://github.com/ender-js/Ender)

- Philosophy of small (in terms of lines of code and functionality) functional modules vs. large, standard/core packages (i.e., granularity)

- Evolving ECMAScript standard and expressive nature, and ease of adoption of the JavaScript language

With this in mind, many Node.js enthusiasts find it rewarding to contribute to the ever-growing open-source community. When doing so, there are a few conventions to follow as well as concepts to understand:

- Recommended folder structure

- Required patterns

- package.json

- Publishing to NPM

- Locking versions

Recommended Folder Structure

Here is an example of a good, structured NPM module:

```
Webapp
  /lib
    webapp.js
  index.js
  package.json
  README.md
```

The index.js file does the initialization whereas lib/webapp.js has all the principal logic. If you're building a command-line tool, add the bin folder:

```
Webapp
  /bin
    webapp-cli.js
  /lib
    webapp.js
  index.js
  package.json
  README.md
```

Also, for the CLI module, add the following to package.json:

```
...
"bin": {
    "webapp": "./bin/webapp-cli.js"
},
...
```

The webapp-cli.js file starts with the line #! /usr/bin/env node, but then has normal Node.js code.

It's a good idea to add unit tests to your external module, which increases confidence and the likelihood of other people using it. Some programmers go as far as not using a module that doesn't have any tests! The added benefit is that tests serve as a poor man's examples and documentation.

TravisCI, which we covered in previous chapters, allows free testing for open-source projects. Its badges, which turn from red to green, depending on the status of tests (failing or passing), became the de facto standard of quality and are often seen on the README pages of the most popular Node.js projects.

Required Patterns

There are a few common patterns for writing external (meant for use by other users, not just within your app) modules:

- module.exports as a function pattern (recommended)
- module.exports as a class pattern (not recommended)
- module.exports as an object pattern
- exports.NAME pattern; which could be an object or a function

Here is an example of the `module.exports` as a function pattern:

```
var _privateAttribute = 'A';
var _privateMethod = function () {...};
module.exports = function(options) {
  //initialize module/object
  object.method = function() {...}
  return object;
}
```

And here is an example of an equivalent with a function declaration:

```
module.exports = webapp;
function webapp (options) {
  //initialize module/object
  object.method = function() {...}
  return object;
}
```

___

■ **Tip** For info about named function expressions vs. function declarations, visit the comprehensive resource, *Named Function Expressions Demystified*. (`http://kangax.github.io/nfe/#named-expr`)

___

The file in which we include the module looks like this:

```
var webapp = require('./lib/webapp.js');
var wa = webapp({...}); // initialization parameters
```

More succinctly, it looks like this:

```
var webapp = require('./lib/webapp.js')({...});
```

The real-life example of this pattern is the Express.js module (source code) (`https://github.com/visionmedia/express/blob/master/lib/express.js#L26`).

The `module.exports` as a class pattern uses the so-called *pseudoclassical instantiating/inheritance pattern* (`http://javascript.info/tutorial/pseudo-classical-pattern`), which can be recognized by the use of `this` and prototype keywords:

```
module.exports = function(options) {
  this._attribute = 'A';
  ...
}
module.exports.prototype._method = function() {
  ...
}
```

Notice the capitalized name and the new operator in the including file:

```
var Webapp = require('./lib/webapp.js');
var wa = new Webapp();
...
```

The example of this `module.exports` as a class pattern is the OAuth module (source code) (https://github.com/ciaranj/node-oauth/blob/master/lib/oauth.js#L9).

The `module.exports` as an object pattern similar to the first pattern (functional), only without the constructor. It may be useful for defining constants, locales, and other settings:

```
module.exports = {
  sockets: 10,
  limit: 200,
  whitelist: [
    'azat.co',
    'webapplog.com',
    'apress.com'
    ]
}
```

The including file treats the object as a normal JavaScript object. For example, we can set `maxSockets` with these calls:

```
var webapp = require('./lib/webapp.js');
var http = require('http');
http.globalAgent.maxSockets = webapp.sockets;
```

■ **Note**   The `require` method can read JSON files directly. The main difference is that JSON standard has mandatory double quotes (") for wrapping property names.

The `exports.NAME` pattern is just a shortcut for `module.exports.NAME` when there's no need for one constructor method. For example, we can have multiple routes defined this way:

```
exports.home = function(req, res, next) {
  res.render('index');
}
exports.profile = function(req, res, next) {
  res.render('profile', req.userInfo);
}
...
```

And we can use it in the including file the following way:

```
var routes = require('./lib/routes.js');
...
app.get('/', routes.home);
app.get('/profile', routes.profile);
...
```

package.json

Another mandatory part of an NPM module is its package.json file. The easiest way to create a new package.json file, if you don't have one yet (most likely you do), is to use $ npm init. The following is an example produced by this command:

```
"name": "webapp",
"version": "0.0.1",
"description": "An example Node.js app",
"main": "index.js",
"devDependencies": {},
"scripts": {
"test": "test"
},
"repository": "",
"keywords": [
"math",
"mathematics",
"simple"
],
"author": "Azat <hi@azat.co>",
"license": "BSD"
}
```

The most important fields are name and version. The others are optional and self explanatory, by name. The full list of supported keys is located at the NPM web site. (https://www.npmjs.org/doc/json.html)

■ **Warning**   package.json must have double quotes around values and property names, unlike native JavaScript object literals.

It's worth noting that package.json and NPM do not limit their use. In other words, you are encouraged to add custom fields and devise new conventions for their cases.

Publishing to NPM

To publish to NPM, we must have an account there. We do this by executing the following:

```
$ npm adduser
```

Then, simply execute from the project folder:

```
$ npm publish
```

Some useful NPM commands are as follows:

- $ npm tag NAME@VERSION TAG: tag a version
- $ npm version SEMVERSION: increment a version to the value of SEMVERSION (semver) (http://semver.org/) and update package.json

- `$ npm version patch`: increment the last number in a version (e.g., 0.0.1 to 0.0.2) and update `package.json`

- `$ npm version minor`: increment a middle version number (e.g., 0.0.1 to 0.1.0 or 0.0.1 to 1.0.0) and update `package.json`

- `$ npm unpublish PACKAGE_NAME`: unpublish package from NPM (take optional version with @)

- `$ npm owner ls PACKAGE_NAME`: list owners of this package

- `npm owner add USER PACKAGE_NAME`: add an owner

- `$ npm owner rm USER PACKAGE_NAME`: remove an owner

Locking Versions

The rule of thumb is that when we publish external modules, we don't lock dependencies' versions. However, when we deploy apps, we lock versions in `package.json`. This is a common convention that many projects on NPM follow (i.e., they don't lock the versions). So, as you might guess, this may lead to trouble.

Consider this scenario: We use Express.js that depends on, say, Jade of the latest version (*). Everything works until, unknown to us, Jade is updated with breaking changes. Express.js now uses Jade that breaks our code. No bueno.

The solution: Commit `node_modules`! The following article describes nicely why committing your application's `node_modules` folder (not the one for the external module!) to Git repo is a good idea: *node_modules in git* (`http://www.futurealoof.com/posts/nodemodules-in-git.html`).

Why do this? Because, even if we lock dependency A in our `package.json`, most likely this module A has a wild card * or version range in its `package.json`. Therefore, our app might be exposed to unpleasant surprises when an update to the A module dependency breaks our system.

One significant drawback is that binaries often need to be rebuilt on different targets (e.g., Mac OS X vs. Linux). So, by skipping `$ npm install` and not checking binaries, development operations engineers have to use `$ npm rebuild` on targets.

On the other hand, the same problem might be mitigated by using `$ npm shrinkwrap` (official docs) (`https://www.npmjs.org/doc/cli/npm-shrinkwrap.html`). This command creates `npm-shrinkwrap.json`, which has *every* subdependency listed/locked at the current version. Now, magically, `$ npm install` skips `package.json` and uses `npm-shrinkwrap.json` instead!

When running Shrinkwrap, be careful to have all the project dependencies installed and to have only them installed (run `$ npm install` and `$ npm prune` to be sure). For more information about Shrinkwrap and locking versions with `node_modules`, see the article by core Node.js contributors: "Managing Node.js Dependencies with Shrinkwrap". (`http://blog.nodejs.org/2012/02/27/managing-node-js-dependencies-with-shrinkwrap/`)

Summary

Open-source factors have contributed to the success and widespread use of the Node.js platform. It's relatively easy to publish a module and make a name for yourself (unlike other mature platforms with solid cores). We looked at the recommended patterns and structures, and explored a few commands to get started with publishing modules to NPM.

Practical Node.js Conclusion

Lo and behold, this is the end of the book. There was a study that showed that the majority of programmers read zero books per year (source) (`http://blog.codinghorror.com/programmers-dont-read-books-but-you-should/`). So, pat yourself on the back, because you're on the road to awesomeness when it comes to building Node.js web apps. ☺

Regarding the material covered in *Practical Node.js*, we explored real-world aspects of the Node.js stack. To do this, many things were essential, and by now you should have an awareness of how pieces fit together. For some technologies such as Jade and REST API, our coverage was quite extensive. However, most of the packages are very specific and tailored to our apps' goals, so those topics were given a brief introduction, with references for further learning. Here's a list of topics we covered:

- Node.js and NPM setup and development tools

- Web apps with Express.js

- TDD with Mocha

- Jade and Handlebars

- MongoDB and Mongoskin

- Mongoose MongoDB ORM

- Session, token authentication, and OAuth with Everyauth

- REST APIs with Express and Hapi

- WebSockets with ws, Socket.IO, and DerbyJS

- Best practices for getting apps production ready

- Deployment to Heroku and AWS

- Structuring and publishing NPM modules

Further Reading

If you enjoyed this book, you might like the programming blog about software engineering, startups, Agile development, and Node.js: webapplog.com (`http://webapplog.com`). You can also follow the author of this book on Twitter at @azat_co (`http://twitter.com/azat_co`) for tips and news about Node.js.

Here's the list of other books by the author Azat Mardan:

- *Pro Express.js* (Apress, coming 2014)

- *Rapid Prototyping with JS*: (`http://rpjs.co/`) *Agile JavaScript Development*

- *Express.js Guide*: (`http://expressjsguide.com/`) *The Comprehensive Book on Express.js*

- *JavaScript and Node.js FUNdamentails*: (`http://leanpub.com/jsfun`) *A Collection of Essential Basics*

- *ProgWriter*: (`http://progwriter.com/`) *Complete Guide to Publishing Programming Books*

Errata and Contacts

If you spotted any mistakes (I'm sure you did), please open an issue or even better fix it and make a pull request to the GitHub repository of the book's examples: `https://github.com/azat-co/practicalnode`. For all other updates and contact information, the canonical home of the Practical Node.js book on the Internet is `http://practicalnodebook.com`.

Index

■ U

■ V

■ W, X, Y, Z

Get the eBook for only $10!

Now you can take the weightless companion with you anywhere, anytime. Your purchase of this book entitles you to 3 electronic versions for only $10.

This Apress title will prove so indispensible that you'll want to carry it with you everywhere, which is why we are offering the eBook in 3 formats for only $10 if you have already purchased the print book.

Convenient and fully searchable, the PDF version enables you to easily find and copy code—or perform examples by quickly toggling between instructions and applications. The MOBI format is ideal for your Kindle, while the ePUB can be utilized on a variety of mobile devices.

Go to www.apress.com/promo/tendollars to purchase your companion eBook.